Pueblos, Gods and Spaniards

Books By
John Upton Terrell

PUEBLOS, GODS AND SPANIARDS

APACHE CHRONICLE

AMERICAN INDIAN ALMANAC

THE MAN WHO REDISCOVERED
AMERICA

TRADERS OF THE WESTERN MORNING

JOURNEY INTO DARKNESS

ZEBULON PIKE

ESTEVANICO THE BLACK

FAINT THE TRUMPET SOUNDS

PUEBLO DE LOS CORAZONES

SUNDAY IS THE DAY YOU REST

LAND GRAB

BUNKHOUSE PAPERS

THE NAVAJO

LA SALLE

THE SIX TURNINGS

BLACK ROBE

FURS BY ASTOR

WAR FOR THE COLORADO
RIVER

PLUME ROUGE

ADAM CARGO

THE LITTLE DARK MAN

(Twelve works for young readers not listed)

The Dial Press
New York
1973

JOHN
UPTON
TERRELL

Pueblos,

Gods and

Spaniards

Library of Congress Cataloging in Publication Data

Terrell, John Upton, 1900–

Pueblos, Gods and Spaniards.

Bibliography: p.

1. Pueblo Indians—History.   2. Southwest, New—History—To 1848.   I. Title.

E99.P9T47   970.4'9   73-7793

To My Good Friend
Charles E. Beardsley

CONTENTS

LIST OF MAPS

AUTHOR'S
NOTE

The Indians we call Pueblos are not one people. They belong to four distinct stocks.

While similarities are clearly recognizable in their respective cultures, actually their traditional spiritual beliefs, tenets, ideologies, and religious symbols differ in many respects. Rather than being inherent, the noticeable similarities are more likely to be adaptations of each other's mores. This development is understandable if one remembers that, after all, these peoples have lived in relatively close association for a very long time.

Pueblo is not an Indian name. It is a Spanish word meaning "town," and it came into common usage in early historical times as a convenient general term to designate natives who dwelt in permanent buildings constructed of stone, timber, and adobe. Tribes living in fragile temporary shelters, such as skin tents and brush wickiups, who moved with the seasons in their foraging and hunting and engaged in long excursions of warfare, were identified by individual names.

This work ends with the final years of the seventeenth century, but it would be well, I think, to make some brief remarks here that take the reader forward to the time of my own generation.

No Indians in the region of the United States suffered for a longer period from intrusions by white military, civil, and religious forces than the Pueblos. Soldiers slaughtered them, government officials stole their resources and enslaved them. If priests did not attack them with guns, they employed cruel methods, both mental and physical, to break their resistance to Christianity and to obliterate their ancient ritual. Each of these oppressive elements was calamitous to them, but the most irremediable traumata were inflicted by ecclesiastical decrees enacted by three powers—Spanish, Mexican, and American. For considerably more than four centuries, virtually every facet of their personal lives was grievously affected by these onerous policies.

In the unwritten lexicon of the Pueblos, as in the case of every other Indian people discovered by the Spanish, the words *Christian* and *Christianity* were synonyms for *disaster* and *death*. Symbols vividly illustrated the accuracy of the definitions—the gun, the sword, the lance, and the cross. Over the invaders and their instruments waved the banners of church and state, signifying an amalgamation of forces that were indivisible under the existing Spanish system of government. For the doctrines of the Roman Catholic church were walls and roof enclosing the social, economic, and legal beams of the Spanish monarchal structure.

The Pueblos gained no relief with the lowering of the Spanish national emblem and the raising of the Mexican flag over their country in 1821. Indeed, in some ways conditions became worse.

If the political power of the church had been dissipated somewhat by the successful Mexican revolt against Spain, the change had no immediate salutary effect in the immense northern province of New Mexico. Priests stationed there, far distant from all high church authorities, maintained the tyrannical practices by which they sought to drive the Christian gospel down the throats of involuntary Pueblo parishioners.

The infant regime in Mexico City had neither the military

strength nor the funds to enforce the reforms it so en-
thusiastically promulgated. Moreover, the constant struggling for power and favors between politicians kept its own
house in a state bordering on complete chaos. The result
was that in such a remote colony as New Mexico, with
which communications frequently were disrupted by
Apache warfare, almost no control of the activities of
church and civil officials was possible. Enjoying such license, they, too, contributed to the prevalent lawlessness
and disorder by engaging in bitter clashes to gain suzerainty
over the helpless Pueblos.

The army of the United States, acting in accord with the
political doctrine of Manifest Destiny proclaimed in Washington, occupied New Mexico in 1846 and inaugurated
American constitutional government. The First Amend-
ment decreed that "Congress shall make no law respecting
the establishment of religion, or prohibiting the free exer-
cise thereof. . . ." This guarantee of religious freedom, however, was not applicable to Indians. Ironically, by the same
token, it was detrimental to their welfare.

Indians were not legally identified as citizens of the
United States. They were classed as foreigners. The Constitution delegated to the legislative branch of the government the power "To regulate commerce with foreign nations and among the several states, and with the Indian
tribes." Here the words *foreign nations* and *Indian tribes*
appear in a single sentence. To the Congress, it seemed
apparent that the framers of the Constitution intended that
Indian tribes were to be dealt with in the same manner as
other countries, that is, through treaties.

Pursuing this curious course of reasoning, the legislators
and other federal officers associated the guarantee of religious freedom (which could not be applied by statute to
foreign nations) with the decision that Indian reservations

were free country, the same as the rest of the United States (which they could not be unless they were made political subdivisions of the national territory). This could not be done, of course, without granting to savages the privileges inherent in full citizenship, including suffrage, an unthinkable state of affairs.

At last Congress itself committed a gross violation of a fundamental Bill of Rights provision—the separation of church and state—in the guise of a "peace policy." The announced objective was to civilize and Christianize the backward red infidels. This goal was to be achieved by "the assignment of religious and education work (among the Indians) to the various religious denominations on a regional basis."

The unconstitutional congressional action (eventually it would be abrogated) left only two basic differences between the official American religious policy and the official policy which Spain had initiated more than three centuries earlier: (1) instead of only one denomination, the United States government authorized numerous affiliates of the Protestant church, as well as the Catholic church, to impose their beliefs on captive people, and (2) the American missionary-educators were not empowered, as were the Spanish, to call upon the military to force recalcitrant Indians at gunpoint to attend religious services. American politicians did not care whether Indians went to church or remained in their hovels on Sunday.

To many Indian peoples, warfare could be a way of life, and banditry could be a form of economy. Each could complement the other. Often they could be inseparable, each a vital part of the other. Often they could be so thoroughly blended as to be indistinguishable. And, with a single exception, into each could be compounded the same basic ingredients inherent in all mankind: greed, jealousy, and desire.

The single exception was religion. In the way of Indian thinking, it could not be a cause for armed conflict. Unlike white men, the Indian did not engage in religious crusades. The Indian did not slaughter large numbers of enemies in the name of a holy spirit. Unlike white men, an Indian tribe did not invade, attack and destroy, or even condemn, other Indians whose persuasions and convictions and ritual contrasted with those it harbored and performed. And unlike white men, Indians made no attempt to force white men to accept and adhere to their beliefs.

No American Indians are more influenced by supernatural beings or deities than the Pueblos. They devote more of their time to spiritual worship and religious ceremony than to any other aspect of their way of life. Unlike white society, which tends to turn religion on and off as needs demand or moods please, a Pueblo is seldom, if ever, detached from it, day or night. It affects very nearly everything he does, everything he thinks, and every decision he makes.*

According to Driver, most prayers of the Pueblos "are magic formulas which must be recited verbatim to bring the desired result. They are not spontaneous outpourings of the troubled heart, but carefully memorized, emotionally mild requests asking for an orderly life, pleasant days, and protection from violence. Their religious dances likewise must be done exactly as prescribed by the gods themselves in order to carry enough appeal to the supernatural to be sure of bringing results to man. Practically all religious authority is vested in the four major and eight minor priesthoods, and all public religious ceremonies are conducted by one or the other of these groups. Almost all ceremonial activity is for the benefit of the entire pueblo, and even ceremonies to

---

*One is obliged to write of the Pueblos in both the present and the past tense, for they still live in their ancient homelands.

cure a sick person often have rain-making or fertility features built in."

Buildings intended solely for public religious services were never constructed by the Pueblos. Spanish missionaries, supported by soldiers, forced them to labor at building churches without compensation or reward of any type. Protestors were severely punished. The early Catholic houses of worship in the Rio Grande towns were destroyed in the Pueblo rebellion of 1680. New churches were built after the Spanish regained power about the beginning of the eighteenth century, the missionaries and civil and military authorities again forcing captive Pueblos to do the work.

The only native sacred chamber was (and is) the kiva. Usually the greater part of it was below ground surface, and members of the priesthood, counselors, and others entitled to use it entered through a small aperture in the roof and descended to the floor by a ladder. The early kivas of the Rio Grande pueblos were circular, but in the western villages of the Zuni and Hopi, they were rectangular. Wooden pillars and cross-beams supported roofs made of poles and osiers covered with adobe mortar. Thin sandstone slabs covered earthen floors. Smooth rock and adobe walls were sometimes decorated with symbolic paintings of animals. Adobe benches capped with flagstones were the only seats. In the center of the floor was a shallow firepit. Smoke escaped through the roof hatchway. At one side of the kiva was a stone or cottonwood slab containing a small hole. This was the opening to *sipapu,* * the underworld, and it symbolized the place of origin and the final resting place of the earth people. Underwood states that the hole usually was closed with a stone on which dancers stamped loudly,

---

*Spelling of the word differs in various Pueblo languages.

so that the dead below might hear, but that on the "awesome occasion . . . when the dead took part in the initiation ceremony for young male tribal members, it was left open."

Small pueblos may have only one kiva, but large towns may have half a dozen or more. In Old Oraibi, for example, there were thirteen, and thirty-three were noted in the Hopi villages after the beginning of the American period.

The kiva, which was almost exclusively a male province, was not used only for religious ceremonies. It might be likened in some respects to a town forum. Leaders gathered in it to discuss political, criminal, social, and military problems. It was a fraternal chamber in which representatives of moities, clans, and countless societies held business meetings, conducted ceremonies, entertained each other with stories, or passed a pleasant hour or two chatting. Women were permitted to enter a kiva only to clean or to take food to their husbands and sons. Some tribes permitted women to be spectators at certain ceremonies, but on these special occasions they were present by command and not as the result of personal choice.

While ritual, ceremonies, fetishes, symbols, supernaturals, deities, dances, spiritual beliefs, katchinas,* and all other religious forms and conceptions vary, sometimes to a great extent, among the Pueblo peoples, one origin myth is common to all of them. It concerns their emergence from *sipapu,* the world beneath the surface of the earth.

The religion of the Pueblos is a system of imitative and sympathetic magic aimed ritually at fulfillment of the requirements for life and living. They have no conception of a hereafter, such as the Christian heaven and hell. In their theology, states Underwood, "the abode of the dead was a blessed place and the dead themselves bringers of blessings.

---

*Katsinas in the Rio Grande pueblos.

Thus they were buried just outside the pueblo . . . Babies were placed under the hearth in the hope of a rebirth. The funeral ceremony allayed not the fear of the survivors but their grief.

"The gorgeously costumed katchinas are the ancestral dead who come to dance in the plaza, bringing promise of rain and fertility. These spirits themselves do not come; they did so once but the result of each visit was that someone went away with them, that is, someone died. Now the spirits are represented by reverent maskers who temporarily have the katchinas' power.

"The dead themselves they do not forget. Prayer sticks are planted for them at certain times as they are for various gods and spirits. Bits of food are placed in the fire for them at meals . . ."

The Pueblos see themselves as being inextricably woven into the natural scheme of the entire universe. They are not simply pieces of bone and flesh, not simply possessors of certain faculties. They are those things, but they are also of the sands, the winds, the stars, the plants and grasses, the thunder, lightning, rain, the sun and the moon, and the seasons—everything that is born and lives and dies in the eternal cycle of life.

No Pueblo needed to seek a vision. Consolation and help in any exigency was available in every village from various societies, from priests and medicine men, as well as from an extensive pharmacopoeia. The welfare of an individual was indivisible from the welfare of the entire pueblo.

Both the Spanish and the American governments attempted to halt their "barbaric, pagan ritual." Spanish priests destroyed katchina masks and costumes and other Pueblo religious articles, flogged the dancers, put them in stocks, or imprisoned them. As Bahti states, the American Bureau of Indian Affairs "made a number of attempts to suppress native religion with a series of departmental regulations . . . This anti-Indian movement culminated in a set of regulations known as the Code of Religious Offenses which was used as late as the 1920's in an attempt to crush Pueblo religion."

The Pueblo dances and other ceremonies were termed "half-animal, sadistic, obscene" by the Indian Bureau, and a campaign was launched to turn public opinion against them. One United States senator went so far as to declare the Pueblo religious practices un-American, and to charge that they were inspired by Communist agents. Bahti aptly remarks: "It is ironic that the very people who took inordinate pride in the fact that their immigrant ancestors came to this country to escape religious persecution tolerated such a move."

The administration of President Franklin D. Roosevelt did not tolerate it. In 1934, Commissioner of Indian Affairs John Collier brought the persecution to an abrupt halt with a directive which said: "No interference with Indian religious life or ceremonial expression will hereafter be tolerated. The cultural liberty of Indians is in all respects to be considered equal to that of any non-Indian group."

Neither the Spanish nor the Americans, however, had been able to achieve their goals. They did not destroy Pueblo ritual; the Pueblos simply continued their ceremonies in secret. They did not succeed in making Christians out of the Pueblos, for, as Eggan states, the Pueblos "have managed to retain their cultural independence in the face of almost overwhelming political and religious pressures. . . .They became nominal Catholics, but they took their own religion underground and have maintained it to the present day, guarding their ceremonies and their inner life against the outside world."

As the result of Collier's directive, many of the Pueblo

religious dances, with the spirit representatives costumed and masked, were held again in the pueblo plazas. One can, if one is fortunate and can learn when they will take place, see them, and they are still incomparably dramatic, beautiful, and inspiring.

These passages regarding religion are not intended to be an antireligious diatribe. They are cold history, and taken together they constitute background scenery that is indispensable if the drama of the Pueblos is to be properly presented. They reflect on a subject to which many historians, regrettably, have paid little attention. Indeed, some have deliberately excluded it from their works, as if it were irrelevant in an account treating with the subjugation of Indians. I believe it is a vital part of the history of the conflict between red and white people, and that omission of it would preclude a comprehensive understanding of that history.

The characteristics and capabilities of the Pueblos cannot be gauged by glimpses of a few squaws vending mediocre souvenirs at roadside and street stands. Cursory observations, wherever made, do not even suggest that the Pueblos are predominantly a people of superior intellect, perspicacious, imaginative, and possessing indestructible self-faith and remarkable stamina. One must know them well to appreciate that the symphonic functioning of their inherent qualities made it possible for them to survive.

Long before any white man set foot in their country, the Pueblos were unquestionably the finest artisans of all American Indians. They were unexcelled as engineers, constructing large and efficient irrigation works to bring water to their fields. They were superb architects, designing and building communal apartment houses with as many as five levels and containing several hundred rooms. They were expert tanners and incomparable weavers and potters, producing a great variety of garments, shawls, blankets, and utensils. They manufactured large quantities of jewelry— strings of beads, rings, necklaces, broaches, pendants—skillfully making use of shells, turquoise, coral, feathers, chalcedony, steatite and argillite. They fashioned articles bearing intricate designs and carvings of turtles, frogs, snakes, and birds, and they made mosaics with bases encrusted with pyrites held in place by a durable adhesive. One group of Arizona Indians, who although not technically classified as Pueblos, dwelt in permanent villages and were greatly influenced by Pueblo culture, made what were probably the first etchings in the world—on shells.

The Pueblos, especially those living in northern New Mexico, were shrewd and enterprising traders, and their intertribal commerce extended for long distances over the prehistoric trade trails that ran between California and the southern Great Plains, and between Mexico, Zuni, and the upper Rio Grande. Their products have been discovered by archaeologists in the Midwest, Texas, the Dakotas, and on the Pacific coast.

Neither the spiritual beliefs nor the traditional way of life of the Pueblos has been completely obliterated. Some of them still live in buildings that were old when the first Spanish invader appeared. The drums beat and the dancers move and the chorus chants and the clowns carry on their antics and the shamans perform their ritual much as they did centuries before the time of Columbus.

The Pueblos of today represent the longest continual Indian parade in recorded American history, a parade that began in the third decade of the sixteenth century, a parade that is still passing.

John Upton Terrell

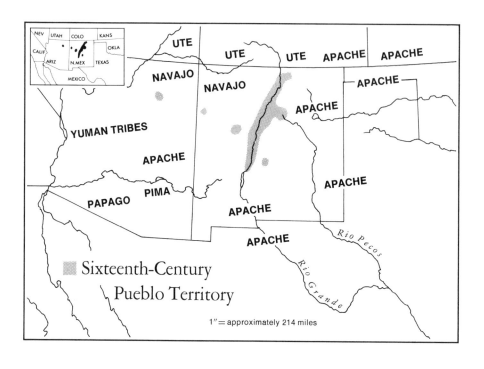

Sixteenth-Century Pueblo Territory

1″ = approximately 214 miles

PART ONE

*The Vaults
of Time*

1529

The roots of recorded events sometimes can be traced back to ancient fables. The fables sired wild, turbulent, exciting visions and beliefs that were impervious to any force of reason.

At the end of the prehistoric period in the Southwest of the United States, the various peoples who would be called Pueblos were far removed from the scenes of these conceptions, but they were not detached from the fetal results. They were inescapably linked to them by the illimitable umbilical cord of Fate.

In the sixteenth century, the legend of the Seven Cities had been harbored in the minds of Spanish adventurers for seven hundred years. It said that after the Moors from Africa had invaded the Iberian Peninsula, oppressed Christians led by seven bishops had sailed westward into the mysterious Ocean Sea. The fugitives had discovered an incredibly beautiful island which they had named Antilia. Each of the bishops had founded a city. The island had been developed into a utopian commonwealth, was fabulously rich in gold and jewels, and was abundantly supplied with rare foods and fine wines.

Although countless searches had been made by daring navigators for the Island of the Seven Cities, it had never been found. Still, nearly four decades after the first voyage of Columbus, when much of the Western Hemisphere already had been explored, few persons—and least of all those with an insatiable desire for wealth—were willing to believe that the tale was a myth. Certainly there was no good reason to forget it, for no one had proved it false, and remembering it sustained an inspiring dream.

The dream suddenly was given an aura of reality by an Indian's story. His name was Tejo, and he was a slave of Nuno Beltran de Guzman, who, in 1527, had become governor of the Mexican province of Panuco and president of the Audencia, the administrative and judicial board that governed the colony. The two posts gave Guzman extreme powers, and he wielded them with wanton disregard for either the benefit of New Spain or the welfare of the subjects he ruled. He inflicted unspeakable cruelties on the natives, hanging and torturing them to death for no more of an infraction than failing to sweep streets before him in villages through which he and his heavily armed escort occasionally passed. He sold hundreds of healthy young men and women into slavery in the West Indies, and he forced all residents of his jurisdiction to pay such excessive tribute to him that they existed in poverty, on the verge of starvation. His tenure had been of short duration when high church officials began registering protests against his barbarities with the Spanish king.

Guzman was reprimanded and told to govern his province with justice and in accordance with colonial statutes, but the warning had less than the desired effect. If he was obliged to curb his brutality and illegal activities to some degree in Panuco, he was not precluded from looking farther afield for opportunities to gratify his avarice.

Now, only two years after Guzman had ascended to his high office, the lowly Tejo came upon the stage to play a role that would gain for him a permanent place in the history of the New World.

It seems doubtful that Tejo had heard the legend of the Seven Cities of Antilia. However, he must have been a personal servant of the governor in order to be able to speak directly with him, and he must have been aware of the trend of Guzman's thinking. Whatever the case, the story he related apparently caused Guzman's cold blood to grow hot with excitement.

How old Tejo was at the time is not known, but that he was a man in middle life is indicated by his statements. He was the son of a trader who had been dead for many years. As a youth he had gone with his father on a number of trading trips into the wilderness. He recalled that one journey had been much longer than the others, and on it he and his father had traveled for more than forty days to the north. At last, after crossing high mountains and desert regions, they had reached a fine country in which there were many people and some large cities. Among the articles they had carried as trade goods were the plumes of tropical birds and shells which had come from the South Sea (Gulf of California). In exchange for these, they had received woven garments, turquoises and other stones even more colorful, and ornaments of precious metals. Tejo avowed that he could remember seeing streets filled with silver workers and other craftsmen. The large cities in this rich land were *seven in number.*

That was all Guzman needed to hear to spur him into action. Who could produce evidence to show that a great sea, into which the seven bishops had sailed, did not lie north of Mexico? Who could say that the magic kingdom in which they had built their cities was not an island but the shore of that northern sea? With all the geographical darkness that still existed in the New World, what justification was there for believing that the Seven Cities were not to be found? Indeed, what reason was there to believe than an ignorant Indian slave had not seen them?

When Guzman started from central Mexico, he rode at

the head of an immense expedition. In the long column that crawled westward through the great valleys and over the rugged ranges were four hundred Spanish soldiers, several thousand Indian servants, burden bearers, and livestock herders, and a number of wealthy gentlemen who had eagerly accepted the governor's invitation to participate in the conquest—at their own expense, of course.

Tejo had been accorded the rank of guide, but it soon became apparent that any knowledge of the country that he may have possessed as a youth had eluded him. He insisted, however, that before turning toward the mysterious north it was necessary to cross Mexico to the South Sea. Guzman had no other choice than to accept the instructions.

The trail they followed passed through some of the highest mountains and roughest terrain in Mexico. Furious and disappointed at the slowness and hardships of the march, Guzman gave vent to fiendish cruelties, killing without reason or mercy Indians they encountered, destroying their food supplies and burning their villages. Fall was well advanced when the large company descended the Pacific slope in the province of Culiacan.

Probably fortunately for him Tejo died.

And there a courier from Mexico City reached Guzman with bad news. His greatest personal and political enemy, Don Hernan Cortes, had returned from a trip to Spain with a new high title and lucrative awards that made him one of the most powerful men in Mexico. There was no doubt in Guzman's mind that a series of new charges, inspired by a vengeful Cortes, would be brought against him.

Pedro de Castaneda, an early colonist in Culiacan, would write that after Guzman and his treasure hunters broke through to the Pacific "they tried to cross the country, but found the difficulties very great, because the mountain chains which are near that sea are so rough that it was impossible, after great labor, to find a passageway in that region. His whole army had to stay in the district of Culiacan for so long on this account that some rich men who were with him, who had possessions in Mexico [City], changed their minds, and every day became more anxious to return." It should be noted, however, that some of Guzman's more intrepid adventurers, bent on taking slaves, ranged several hundred miles to the north, penetrating country never before entered by Europeans.

1531

Late in the year 1531, totally discouraged, Guzman abandoned his quest and turned homeward.*

Perhaps it was true that Tejo had gone with his father to trade with Pueblos in the present states of Arizona and New Mexico. At least, it is indisputable that he knew of their existence; he knew something of their culture and economy, and he knew that they lived in large, permanent multistoried buildings. This, of course, was common knowledge among peoples of northwestern Mexico, such as the Opata and the Pima Bajo, as well as among peoples of the Rio Grande in northeastern Mexico, such as the Jumano, Cholome, and Manso. Trade between these and other tribes of Mexico and the Pueblos living in the American Southwest had been carried on for centuries, perhaps long before the beginning of the Christian era.

*For his cruelties and violations of provincial laws, he would be deposed, arrested, and confined in jail. An appeal to Spain failed, and he was banished to Torrejon de Velasco, where he died in poverty in 1544.

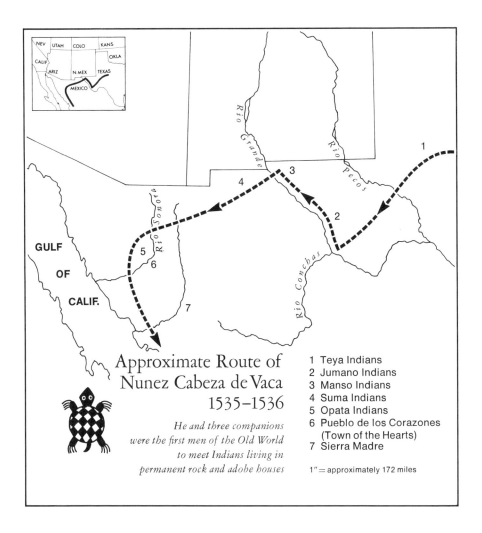

Approximate Route of
Nunez Cabeza de Vaca
1535–1536

*He and three companions
were the first men of the Old World
to meet Indians living in
permanent rock and adobe houses*

1 Teya Indians
2 Jumano Indians
3 Manso Indians
4 Suma Indians
5 Opata Indians
6 Pueblo de los Corazones
  (Town of the Hearts)
7 Sierra Madre

1″ = approximately 172 miles

1535

In the last month of this year, three Spaniards and a Negro Moor, followed by a throng of Texas Indians, came out of the east into the Rio Grande. They were the first Europeans to reach the perimeter of the land that, more than three centuries later, would be the Southwest of the United States.

The white men, all former officers of the Spanish army, were Alvar Nunez Cabeza de Vaca, Andres Dorantes de Carranca, and Alonso del Castillo Maldonado. The black man, a slave owned by Dorantes, was called Estevanico by the others, and if he had any other names, they have not been preserved in history.

Exactly where they struck the great river flowing from the north is uncertain, but Nunez Cabeza de Vaca's own account and other early documents indicate that they first gazed on it near the mouth of the Rio Conchos, which empties out of Chihuahua.

More than seven years earlier, in the spring of 1528, Panfilo de Narvaez, newly appointed governor of Florida, had set out from the vicinity of Tampa Bay with an expedition of three hundred soldiers, adventurers, and priests to find the treasure he believed awaited discovery in the unexplored jungles of his vast jurisdiction. In northern Florida, a number of the men had been slain in fights with Indians, and others had died of malnutrition, dysentery, and fever. In a desperate struggle to save themselves, the remaining members of the company, most of whom were dangerously weakened, wounded, or ill, had constructed five makeshift barges and had sailed westward along the northern coast of the Gulf of Mexico. Totally ignorant of the geography of the region, they mistakenly believed the closest place of salvation to be Panuco, a slaving port in Mexico.

The boats had been destroyed in a November storm at various places on the Texas coast below Galveston. Almost six years after this disaster, Nunez Cabeza de Vaca, Dorantes, Castillo, and Estevanico were the only men of the company still living. They were agreed that their best chance of escaping from the coastal Indians holding them captive was to strike out westward, and pray that they would be able to reach some Spanish settlement on the South Sea

(Pacific). Late in September, 1534, they had managed to slip away from their captors. It had taken them more than a year to cross Texas.

For three weeks they traveled up the Rio Grande, until they were only a short distance below El Paso del Norte. The people along the river were the first they had encountered who dwelt in permanent structures constructed of rock and adobe. In the numerous villages along the route, the buildings were only one story in height, but they were clustered together to form irregular compounds. These were relatively small towns, but in many respects similar to thousands of pueblos that had existed for centuries throughout the Southwest.

If the four strangers had gone less than two hundred miles farther up the river, they would have been the first explorers to see any of the immense pueblos that rose tier upon tier around plazas and contained hundreds of rooms.

But they were told of these large settlements by Indians on the Rio Grande, and these people told them, as well, that the inhabitants of the big towns cultivated large fields of maize, and possessed many valuable things, such as beautiful adornments of bright stones, fine soft white buckskins, and robes and garments woven of fibers.

The people the four men met as they traveled up the Rio Grande were the Shuman, although they also may have encountered some Cholome, who lived west of the river in northern Mexico close to the present international border. Both of these tribes were Apache, subdivisions of the enormous Athabascan linguistic family.

The Shuman were divided into two main groups. The western division, known as the Suma, lived south of El Paso and westward from the Rio Grande to the Rio Casas

Grandes. The eastern division, more commonly called Jumano, ranged far eastward and northward from the Rio Grande, and they, in particular, can be identified by Nunez Cabeza de Vaca's statements.

Although they lived in permanent houses along the river, the Jumano cannot be classed as sedentary Indians. They spent a large part of their time hunting buffalo on the Llano Estacado, the great plains of eastern New Mexico and western Texas through which the Rio Pecos passes. While wandering over this sea of grass, they lived in brush and skin shelters, and exhibited the traits of typical Plains Indians.

Because of their periodic buffalo hunts, on which they traveled as much as two hundred miles from their Rio Grande dwellings to the plains along the Rio Pecos, Nunez Cabeza de Vaca called them the Cow Nation. One passage in his own *Relacion* of the epic journey vividly illustrates a Jumano practice characteristic of Plains people.

"How curious and diversified are the contrivances and ingenuity of the human family," he wrote. "Not having discovered the use of pipkins, to boil meat they would eat, they fill the half of a large calabash [gourd] with water, and throw on the fire many stones of such as are most convenient and readily take the heat. When hot, they are taken up with tongs of sticks and dropped into the calabash until the water in it boils from the fervor of the stones. Then whatever is to be cooked is put in, and until it is done they continue taking out cooled stones and throwing in hot ones. Thus they boil their food."

He did not know, of course, that this manner of cooking, so peculiar in his eyes, was common among nonsedentary Plains Indians who could not transport heavy, breakable utensils from place to place. If the Rio Grande Indians did not use pipkins—clay or stone cooking pots—it was not because they did not know of them.

By the end of the sixteenth century, most of the Jumano had left the area in which Nunez Cabeza de Vaca met them. Some were living near the Salinas in eastern New Mexico. A few years later, there were Jumano on the Texas plains east of the Pecos. As late as the middle of the nineteenth century, they were mentioned in connection with the Kiowa, and some were in the Mexican state of Nuevo Leon. It is believed that the western division of the Shuman, the Suma, were destroyed in intertribal warfare.

1536

*we ever held it certain that going towards the sunset
we must find what we desired. Thus we took our
way . . .*

—Nunez Cabeza de Vaca

They left the Rio Grande soon after the beginning of the year. With Shuman guiding them, Nunez Cabeza de Vaca, Dorantes, Castillo, and Estevanico followed a desert trail that twisted southeastward from the site of the village of San Agustin, about thirty miles south of Juarez. After a gruelling journey of more than thirty days, they saw ahead a gigantic range of mountains. They had come in sight of the Sierra Madre.

Sometime in late February, they reached the domain of the Opata, a beautiful and bountiful country on the Pacific slope of the mountains. Here again they found people living in permanent dwellings, and here once more they heard of the fabulous pueblos far to the north and of the trade conducted with them.

In every village they were hospitably received and entertained. At one banquet, the hearts of six hundred deer were served, and Nunez Cabeza de Vaca named the place Pueblo de los Corazones. He would write of the Opata:

"Some houses are of earth, the rest all of cane mats . . . we marched through more than a hundred leagues of country, and continually found settled domiciles, with plenty of maize and beans . . . flour and pumpkins . . . and cotton shawls better than those of New Spain, many beads and certain corals found on the South Sea, and fine turquoises that come from the north. Indeed they gave us everything they had. To me they gave five emeralds [probably malachites] made into arrow heads, which they use at their singing and dancing. They appeared to be very precious. I asked whence they got these; and they said the stones were brought from some lofty mountains that stand toward the north, where were populous towns and very large houses, and that they were purchased with plumes and the feathers of parrots."

As they went southward, the first Europeans to cross North America north of central Mexico, they were hailed as heroes. In Culiacan they were guests of Melchior Diaz, lieutenant governor of the province and a veteran frontiersman, whom Nunez Cabeza de Vaca called "honest, honorable, and compassionate." In every settlement along the road to Mexico City, fiestas were held in their honor.

They entered Mexico City on July 24, approximately eight years and three months after landing in far-off Florida. In the capital they were borne along the avenues as the residents wildly cheered and waved flags. They were, recorded Nunez Cabeza de Vaca, "very handsomely treated" by the viceroy, Don Antonio de Mendoza, and the Marquis de Valle, the famous Don Hernan Cortes.

There is no record to indicate that the four men told Viceroy Mendoza anything but the truth about their experiences or about what they had learned on their long journey. They had heard of some large pueblos which purportedly existed far to the north, but they had not seen them. Nunez Cabeza de Vaca himself would note that when repeating stories told them by Indians, they had reminded Mendoza that the tales had been told to them in the sign language, which they might have misinterpreted.

Of course, with their own eyes they had seen some things of more than passing interest. They had met people who dwelt in permanent rock and adobe houses. They had traveled through fertile valleys in which maize and beans and squash and other wholesome foods were grown in large quantities. They had passed over enormous grass ranges that would support great herds of domestic animals. They had seen cotton textiles of excellent quality and workmanship, turquoises, and finely tanned buckskins and buffalo robes, which the Indians said were obtained in trade with people who lived in large houses, many stories high, a long distance north of the route over which they had traveled. They had noted signs which they assumed indicated the presence of valuable metals, perhaps gold, silver, copper, and antimony. However, they had obtained nothing more valuable than some scoria of iron, small bits of mica, a little galena, a few turquoises, and five green arrowheads which might have been manufactured from precious stones. Unfortunately, the arrowheads had been lost.

It was not what Nunez Cabeza de Vaca and his companions reported but what people wanted to believe they had reported that caused turmoil in Mexico City. Like a wild prairie fire driven by high wind, the story spread that they had found the Seven Cities of Antilia, and it grew better with each telling.

Restored to such youthful vigor, the hoary legend rapidly produced a multivalent band of robust and unruly offspring. The four men had been granted long audiences with Mendoza, hadn't they? Would he have spent so much time with them if they had not held his ears with exciting news? Moreover, any number of noblemen—the Marquis de Valle, for example—and high officials had been present at the conferences. They had let it get out that the four men told of fording streams with beds of gold, of seeing Indian children playing with diamonds, pearls, emeralds, and rubies as large as hen eggs, of meeting people who dined on dishes of silver, of passsing a mountain which contained so many jewels that one dared not gaze at it in the sunlight for fear of being blinded. The only reason the men had not brought back an inconceivable fortune was that they had not possessed any means of transporting it. But the treasures were there, and the viceroy was planning a great expedition to get them and to conquer the rich land, all to the glory of king and country. A toast to the king, to the viceroy, to the four discoverers, and blessed be the Savior for guiding them to another Mexico, another Peru!

Viceroy Mendoza was by nature a cautious man. While it was very pleasant to think of opening new lands which possibly contained fortunes, he had no intention of plunging into an expensive conquest without more evidence than he possessed that it was warranted. As things stood, on the basis of what the four men had told him, he could be certain of very little about the unknown lands that purportedly extended a great distance to the north.

He considered the matter for two months. Then he suggested that Nunez Cabeza de Vaca lead a small exploring party to determine the locations and sizes of the cities in the north. Nunez Cabeza de Vaca respectfully declined. He had had all he wanted of wandering in the wilderness. Much more appealing was the thought of going home and reuniting with his wife.

Mendoza gave his attention to other problems.

The Bering Strait is a shallow, narrow passage between North America and Asia. Where it separates the two great land masses by only fifty-six miles, it is broken by islands. The widest expanse of open sea is approximately twenty-five miles, and on a clear day people on one side can distinguish features of the opposite coast. If the water level of the strait were to fall about one hundred and twenty feet, it would not exist—it would be a land bridge connecting the continents.

That a land bridge did connect Alaska and Siberia for a very long time during the Pleistocene Ice Age has been indisputably proven by scientific evidence. This was the road over which passed the first human beings to dwell in the Western Hemisphere . . . the Mongoloids we call Indians.

Never was all of northern North America covered by ice at one time. As climatological metamorphoses occurred, glaciers advanced and retreated, reaching deep into the continent and withdrawing, scarring the earth and changing its contours. There were, as well, periods which geologists call interstadials, when ice would not have confronted man with impassable barriers. Moreover, during the Ice Age, sea levels were much lower than they were after it ended, because a large part of the world's water was locked in the great glaciers. Thus, immense areas of the sea bottom were exposed. The Bering Strait was one area from which water disappeared.

There were no mass migrations over the Bering Strait land bridge. Being totally dependent on hunting and the gathering of wild vegetal foods for their existence, the immigrants were prevented from traveling together in large numbers for long distances. They moved in relatively small bands, probably shifting at one time no farther than necessary to obtain needed sustenance. This does not mean, however, that constant shifting was always mandatory. Obviously, some wanderers were the nuclei of permanent populations in regions in which dependable and adequate quantities of food, fuel, and skins could be obtained. When these populations increased to an extent where demands exceeded readily available supplies, segments of them moved on into the unknown. There was plenty of room.

The wanderers who crossed from Siberia to the New World originally came from various parts of the Old World. Many of them carried blood strains and showed characteristics of Mediterranean, European, and African, as well as Asiatic, peoples. They spoke many tongues, displayed many cultural variations, and held many spiritual beliefs. All suffered the rigors and endured the exigencies of an extremely primitive life. However, those with a common bond, such as consanguinity, language, or other affinities, persisted in their efforts to remain united as much as possible. This is indicated by the existence of widely separated islands of people derived from one stock. Some Indians in the Southwest, for example, belong to stocks still inhabiting territories in Alaska and northern Canada.

If it cannot be scientifically proven when or why these islands were established—they existed for thousands of years before any European set foot on North American soil —certain postulations are justified. The diminishing of animals in an area was only one cause for the division of people with inherited relationships. The migrations from Siberia continued for an unknown number of millennia, probably a constant rivulet that may have diminished to a trickle at times but which never entirely stopped flowing.

Meanwhile, as Amsden remarks, lineal descendants of those who had already made the crossing "would be pushing along in their turn; not deliberately, not continually, but as the season favored and the lure of virgin territory beckoned them on. Hunting folk drift easily, like the animals they hunt. So in the fullness of time all North America would get a sprinkling of human inhabitants . . . creeping as ink creeps through the blotter . . ." To which should be appended, I think, mention of some factors which acted as magnets, drawing them onward: the farther south they went the more temperate the climate became, the more hunting improved, and the greater the profuseness and the diversity of plants.

When the Mongoloid ancestors of the Pueblos first reached North America, and when the Pueblos themselves arrived in their homelands of the Southwest, are questions for which there can be no definitive answers. It is not possible to devise a chronological table indicating even approximately when a specific Indian people began their long migration to this continent, how long they wandered, or which route they followed to reach the locality in which they were first discovered by Europeans. Anthropologists have made strides in their struggles to solve such mysteries, but their findings remain largely in the realm of supposition. For instance, the last major glacial period was at its height upwards of twenty-five thousand years ago, but it has been established beyond any doubt that Indians were living in numerous parts of the United States area for at least twelve millennia, and in some places for fifteen, before that time. This is no more true of any geographical section than of the Southwest, where ample evidence of man's presence at such early periods has been found. The conclusion that man came to America from Asia at least forty thousand, and perhaps fifty thousand, years ago, therefore, is strongly supported.

1537

Nunez Cabeza de Vaca, having spent the winter working on his famous *Relacion,* sailed for Spain in the spring. Castillo had elected to remain in Mexico and marry a well-to-do widow. Dorantes had gone to Veracruz and was waiting to embark for Cadiz when he received a message from Viceroy Mendoza asking him to return to Mexico City for a conference. Obediently, he went back.

With regard to Estevanico, accounts of the day differ. During the long journey across the continent, he had enjoyed the freedom and respect of a colleague. These advantages and honors, so freely bestowed and so well deserved, were lost to him when he reached Mexico City and became subject to the rigid codes of its officialdom and its society. There he was automatically returned to his former status as a slave.

Some documents relate that Dorantes voluntarily presented Mendoza with what at the time was his most valuable chattel, Estevanico the Black. Other chronicles, no less creditable, intimate that there was more involved in the transaction than a mere gesture of friendship, and they point out that Mendoza was not only fully aware of Estevanico's ability as an explorer and wilderness ambassador, but understood, as well, the value of the training he had received as a companion of the great Nunez Cabeza de Vaca. Moreover, Mendoza had stated that in the event an investigation of the north should be undertaken, Estevanico would be "most useful for the purpose, he being an intelligent person." Under such circumstances, therefore, it would not have been strange if the viceroy had asked

Dorantes to place Estevanico in his service. Dorantes would not have been in a position to refuse such a request.

Whatever the case, when Dorantes got back to Mexico City from Veracruz, Mendoza proposed that he undertake the northern exploration. Estevanico, forty or forty-five mounted Spaniards, and the required number of camp tenders, herdsmen, and servants would be assigned to accompany him. Reluctantly Dorantes agreed to accept the mission.

Rapidly the company was organized and was prepared to start when the unhappy Dorantes mustered enough courage to announce that he had changed his mind and did not care to go. There was more reason for his decision than a desire to avoid wilderness hardships. He had abandoned all thoughts of going home, for, like Castillo, he had become enamored of a widow of property, and his proposal of marriage had been accepted by her.

Thoroughly exasperated, Mendoza lamented to the king that he had "spent a great deal of silver for the expedition . . . From all the preparations I have made there are left to me only a Negro who came with Dorantes, some slaves whom I have purchased, and some Indians, natives of the [northern] country, whom I have assembled."

Although Estevanico remained the man most qualified to lead the investigation, Mendoza was precluded from using him in such a capacity. A Negro slave, regardless of his ability, trustworthiness, and experience among the Indians, could not be placed in command of an exploring party. If natives would loyally serve him, Spanish soldiers or civilians would resent his authority, and not only might refuse to obey him in the wilderness but might well dispose of him with a timely shot in the back.

Moreover, Estevanico was a Moor by birth and not a Christian. It may have been this consideration, perhaps more than anything else, which set Mendoza on the course that would ultimately lead him to a solution of the problem. Numerous padres had been intrepid explorers and skillful diplomats to the Indians. They willingly and eagerly went into the unknown armed only with messages of hope and the word of God, whereas soldiers and greedy adventurers carried deadly weapons and were not averse to using them. If he could find a friar with the required courage and zeal, he could proceed with the conservative plan he had in mind.

Fate decreed that such a man should appear in Mexico City at precisely the right moment. He was Fray Marcos de Niza. For more than seven years, submitting to a craving for adventure and sightseeing, he had gallivanted throughout various parts of both North and South America. He had registered strong protests with Bishop Zumarraga of Mexico City about the atrocities inflicted on natives by the conquerors of Peru and Ecuador, and the bishop had asked him to come to the Mexican capital and prepare written reports for submission to authorities in Spain.

Fray Marcos had complied promptly with the bishop's request. He was presented to Mendoza, who, being a humane person, was as shocked and distressed by his accounts as Zumarraga. Ensuing conversations convinced the viceroy that the peripatetic missionary was admirably suited to serve as the chief emissary of the government on the northern venture. Obviously a religious with great courage, Fray Marcos had spent several years among wilderness Indians, was physically strong, and brimming with ardor and optimism. The bishop and other high church officials shared Mendoza's opinion, adding that besides being "reliable, of approved virtue, and fine religious zeal," the friar was "skilled in cosmography and in the arts of the sea, as well as in theology."

Although there was no doubt in his own mind as to the practicality of the action he wished to take, in view of the failure of his previous attempts to launch the project, Mendoza chose to remove from his own shoulders the burden of making a final decision. He wrote to the Spanish sovereign for permission—actually unnecessary under the powers of his high office—to send Fray Marcos and Estevanico on a scouting expedition beyond the limits of known territory in the north.

As replies to letters from Mexico City, even official communications, could not be expected to arrive from Spain in less than a year, Mendoza once more put aside the matter of the northern investigation. He could be patient as well as circumspect.

As late as 1926, most scientists favored the belief that Indians had inhabited the Southwest no earlier than a very few millennia—perhaps only three or four at the most—before the beginning of the Christian Era. In this year, however, near the little town of Folsom, New Mexico, paleontologists came upon spearheads embedded between the rib bones of several immense Pleistocene bison belonging to a species known to have been long extinct. Made of flint, the Folsom spearpoints were grooved and had been shaped by flaking. Within a short time, projectiles of the same type were recovered under similar conditions in other widely separated sites. Various means of dating them dispelled all doubts that Folsom hunters had ranged the southwestern plains and deserts no less than eleven thousand and perhaps as much as twenty thousand years ago.

Another new schedule was soon added to the anthropological timetable.

The Sandia Mountains, near Albuquerque, are in the heart of the Pueblo country. Archaeologists and geologists uncovered artifacts incontrovertibly proving that a cave of this range had been occupied by Indians before the final advance of the Ice Age glaciers, which took place upwards of 23,000 B.C. Among the bones of such Pleistocene animals as camels, mammoths, and mastodons were flaked spear points of a kind previously unknown, as well as a number of stone and bone implements. Their antiquity was established by the determinable ages of the geological strata covering them.

The Sandia is the earliest Pueblo country culture about which we have knowledge substantiated by material evidence that is universally acceptable to scientists. Yet by no means is it the oldest.

In what is termed a Pre–Projectile Point stage, people lived in the Southwest who had not learned to make knives and spearheads from materials that could be thinned, sharpened, and shaped by flaking. Their tools and weapons were formed by natural erosive pressures, or were splintered bones and whole or split stones. These crude artifacts have been unearthed at numerous sites from Texas to Southern California. Ages claimed for them range from 29,000 to 38,000 years. A scholarly though not always mild controversy revolves about them, however. The circumstances and conditions under which they were found, and various other factors, including the antiquity ascribed to many of them, have prompted questions that remain unanswered to the satisfaction of the scientists propounding them.

One fact at least is indisputable: the Indians who used the crude stone tools and weapons inhabited the Southwest in the Pre–Projectile Point stage.

It would be unwise to assume, moreover, that irrefutable evidence showing they were there earlier than 40,000 B.C. will not be found. Amazing new methods of dating, products of the atomic age that involve the measurement of radioactive carbon and the use of chemicals and gases, have been developed. Each year more secrets that for so long have been locked in dust are being revealed.

1538

In August a nobleman, only twenty-eight years of age, was appointed by Mendoza to be governor of the new west coast province of Nueva Galicia, which contained some of the settlements founded by the deposed Guzman. He was Don Francisco Vasquez de Coronado.

About the same time that approval of the proposed northern exploration was received from Charles V, Fray Marcos and a companion, Fray Onarato, had been wandering in western regions for several months, and when they returned to Mexico City in September, Mendoza instructed them to prepare for the journey. Estevanico would go with them as their guide.

As Coronado was ready to leave for his new post, the viceroy requested him to take the trio and their servants under his protection as far as Culiacan. It was not an obligation unwelcome to the young governor. He was enthusiastic about the project and would have liked to participate in it, for his own dreams of conquest were no less fervid than those of any other conquistador in New Spain.

Through pleasant fall days, a procession of soldiers, gentlemen adventurers, Indian slaves, and herds of sheep, cattle, and horses crawled over the high rocky road that ran out of the Valley of Mexico to Guadalajara and on to the distant Pacific. Accompanying the column was a group whose appearance was in sharp contrast with the splendor and ostentation of Coronado and his escort. Beside the strapping, ebony Estevanico paddled the two friars, Marcos and Onarato, clad in dull robes of Zaragosa cloth. Behind them were a score of half-naked Indians charged with caring for their personal bundles and the few articles of equipment they would take with them beyond the outposts of civilization.

The written instructions Mendoza had given to Fray Marcos were long and detailed. In view of the unforeseen events that would occur, some of them would prove to be especially significant.

"You shall make clear to the Indians," he told the missionary, "that I am sending you in the name of his Majesty to tell them that the Spaniards shall treat them well, to let them know that he regrets the abuses and harm they have suffered, and that from now on they shall be well treated and those who may mistreat them shall be punished.

"Likewise, you are to assure them that no more slaves shall be taken from among them and that they are not to be taken away from their lands: on the contrary, they shall be left alone as free people, without suffering any harm. Tell them that they should not be afraid, but acknowledge God, our Lord, Who is in Heaven, and the emperor, as he has been placed on earth by His hand to rule and govern it."

These passages would please the king, who had issued similar proclamations, and undoubtedly Mendoza had written them with that thought in mind. Other instructions were more practical than politic.

Regarding Estevanico, Mendoza commanded that he must obey Fray Marcos "as he would obey me in person," and should he fail to carry out all orders given him, Estevanico "will be at fault and incur the penalties falling on those who disobey the persons empowered by his Majesty to command them." These were strong words for such a commonplace issue. Slaves were not in the habit of being disobedient, and seldom a threat containing a reference to the king was needed to hold them in line. Possibly Mendoza realized that Estevanico was not only intelligent but strong-willed and daring, and unlike most slaves, was not fearful of asserting himself. If that is so, he was right.

Mendoza was very specific in telling Fray Marcos what to look for: "You shall be very careful to observe the number of people that there are . . . and whether they are scattered or living together. Note also the nature, the fertility and climate of the land; the trees, plants and domestic and wild animals there may be; the character of the country, whether it is broken or flat; the rivers, whether they are large or small; the stones and metals which there are; and of all things that be sent or brought, send or bring samples of them in order that his majesty may be informed of everything."

It was not only His Majesty whom Mendoza wished to inform. He was sticking his own neck out on what might prove to be an unfortunate undertaking, and he told Fray Marcos: "Send back reports with the utmost secrecy so that appropriate steps may be taken without disturbing anything, because in the pacification of what is discovered the services of our Lord and the welfare of our natives shall be taken into consideration." Serving the Lord and protecting the natives were handy reasons for secrecy, until the value of any discoveries, such as gold mines and mountains of jewels, could be firmly secured for the royal government and would not fall into the hands of unscrupulous adventurers.

Obviously Mendoza had not rejected the popular belief that at each end of North America was a narrow isthmus between two oceans, for he admonished Fray Marcos to "endeavor always to learn if there is any information about the seacoast, both the North and South Seas, for it may be that the land narrows and that a sea inlet reaches the interior of the land . . . leave letters buried at the headlands, at the foot of some tree outstanding for its size, telling of what you think should be known. Mark the tree with a cross where the letters are left, so that they may be found. Likewise, at the mouths of rivers and suitable harbors, on prominent trees near the water, make the same sign, a cross, and leave letters . . . if I send ships they will be advised to look for this sign." Thus it is known that Mendoza already was considering sending a sea expedition to solve the northern mystery, a plan that eventually would result in the first exploration of the Colorado River, the first *entrada* into Alta California, and the discovery that Baja California was a peninsula and not an island.

Compostela was reached in December, and, as the year ended, Coronado, his company, and his soldiers and retinue, and the two friars, Estevanico, and their Indians were moving along the jungle trail toward Culiacan.

The pueblos occupied at the time of the Spanish *entrada* to the Southwest did not represent a very recent architectural development. Quite to the contrary, very old ruins widely distributed in the Pueblo country certified that these Indians had lived for innumerable generations in towns that contained structures with several levels facing on terraces, public plazas, underground ceremonial chambers (kivas), and intersecting passageways. Their remote forebears, moreover, although possessing less expertise, had employed the same type of construction, using rocks, poles, and adobe mortar in various combinations to fashion storage cists and pithouses.

The storage cist was in common use long before the advent of the dwelling that was created by roofing a pit in the earth. In contrast to nomadic hunters who existed primarily on the meat, bone marrow, and other by-products obtained from Pleistocene animals, some contemporary inhabitants of the Southwest followed a more sedentary way of life. They dwelt in permanent stream-side camps, in large and small caves and in depressions in canyon walls that afforded some protection. That they were hunters is demonstrated by the bones of animals that have been found at the sites of their abodes. The presence in abundance of metates, or milling stones, however, is proof that they also derived a very large part of their sustenance from native foods, such as edible plants, seeds, fruits, tubers, and nuts. These perishable commodities could be harvested, of course, only at certain times of the year. The Indians cut, pounded, and ground them into shreds, pulp, and meal, and they also sought to preserve quantities not immediately needed.

Metates and small pits that obviously were used for storage have been found, for example, in association with stone implements of the Cochise culture, which is known to have been in existence at least thirteen millennia before the time of Christ. The artifacts belong to the earliest state of the culture, called by archaeologists the Sulphur Spring period, which ended approximately ten thousand years ago. Nothing of comparable antiquity that may be related to housing has been unearthed.

Important cultural developments came to the Southwest from Mexico, but it seems unlikely that the pithouse was one of them. Scientists favor the theory that it reached there by slow diffusion from either California or far northern regions. Another possibility should not be omitted, however. Storage cists were pits dug in the floors of caves and other places thought suitable for the purpose. Besides being lined with flat stones and mud, the pits were covered with interlaced fibers, sticks, and rocks to protect their valuable contents from precipitation, heat, and thieving animals. No great acumen would have been required to realize that if the walls of storage vaults were expanded, they also would provide shelter.

It seems probable that the pithouse was in widespread use in the Southwest, and in areas peripheral to it, two thousand years before the beginning of the Christian Era. This is speculation, but it may be stated with certainty that pithouses were built during the San Pedro period of the Cochise culture, which endured from 3000 to 500 B.C.

But if it cannot be determined when the pithouse reached the Southwest or whence it came, its development and distribution can be delineated with considerable accuracy.

Various types evolved during the centuries of its existence. In the beginning, most pits probably had a circular form, but later they were quadrangular, rectangular, triangular, and even L-shaped. Roof shapes also differed, but whether flat, convex, or conical, they were constructed of poles on which were placed layers of brush and grass, and adobe mud was used as a sealant. All contained a round or square hole which served as a hatch through which smoke from cooking or heating fires escaped. Access to the house was by way of steps or a ramp in an enclosed entranceway. It was the custom of some people to cook outside in favorable weather. Some pithouses were lined with flat rocks and plastered with adobe. Storage cists were constructed in the walls as well as floors.

In some of the older ruins, pits that once were houses have been damaged to such an extent by erosion and other natural forces that their original dimensions cannot be gauged with any exactness. In other sites, however, it has been ascertained that floor spaces ranged from one hundred to nine hundred square feet. Some of the larger houses were divided by partitions.

Early pithouses were invariably unconnected units, and

normally were occupied by only one family. Often they stood within a few feet of each other, but location was not decided on the basis of convenience or individual preference. Perils, either potential or actual, were no fewer when people adopted pithouses than when they had lived in caves or open camps. The closer together they were the greater was their capability to protect both themselves and the valuable stores of food on which they depended during the adversities that intermittently occurred.

In time, ragged grouping was superseded by more orderly community plans. These might require that all structures, regardless of their size, be built in straight or curved rows, in circles or rectangles or squares. But whatever the prescribed design, they continued to be detached from each other.

Eventually the advantages of common walls were recognized. The houses were joined, and the result was a kind of compound. This was the large *pueblo* in embryo.

1539

Fray Marcos, his friend [Fray Onarato], the Negro [Estevanico], and other slaves and Indians whom I had given them departed, after twelve days devoted to their preparations.

—Coronado writing to Viceroy Mendoza

Friday, March 7, was the day they left Culiacan on the adventure that not only would be of transcending historical importance, but would involve a chase both extraordinary and humorous, and would end in tragedy.

During the winter, native scouts had been sent north to

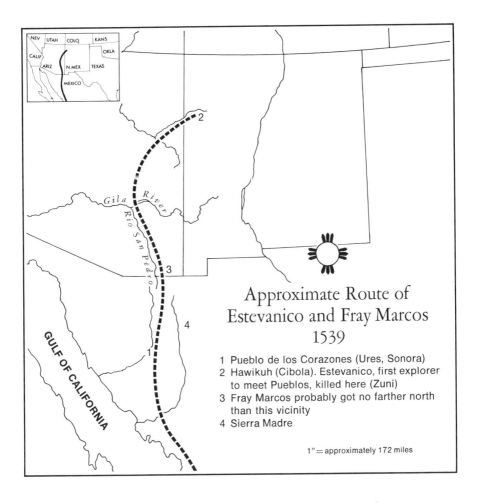

Approximate Route of
Estevanico and Fray Marcos
1539

1 Pueblo de los Corazones (Ures, Sonora)
2 Hawikuh (Cibola). Estevanico, first explorer
  to meet Pueblos, killed here (Zuni)
3 Fray Marcos probably got no farther north
  than this vicinity
4 Sierra Madre

1″ = approximately 172 miles

inform the Indians of the forthcoming expedition and to observe conditions. They had reported that the tribes were peaceful and crops were bountiful, and that the visitors would be hospitably received and assisted. A number of Indians from Petatlan and El Cuchillo had returned to Culiacan with the scouts to welcome the friendly black man whom they had seen three years earlier.

Almost from the beginning, the journey was beset with troubles. Besides the physical hardships, Fray Onarato was ill, and Estevanico was a constant source of annoyance to Fray Marcos. After a wait of three days in Petatlan to allow Fray Onarato to rest, it became apparent that he would be unable to continue. Sadly Fray Marcos ordered that he be carried back by litter to Culiacan, a distance of some sixty leagues.*

Despite Mendoza's warning, Estevanico had no intention of obeying anyone. He fully understood that once they were in the wilderness, beyond the reach of the military, Fray Marcos would be largely, if not entirely, dependent upon him. If he was not commander in name, he was in fact, and he relished the thought of being in such an influential position. He had been over the trail as far as Pueblo de los Corazones. He was the man the Indians knew and liked and trusted. Now, instead of being overshadowed by the great Nunez Cabeza de Vaca, he was a power, a man from the sky, a god in his own right. Undoubtedly his audiences with Mendoza had inflated his ego. He could ask, what other slave had ever been given such consideration and called *intelligent* by a viceroy?

Estevanico had acquired considerable personal baggage, garments, ornaments, a tent, comfortable bedding, and other articles he felt a man of his high station properly should possess. Among his most prized possessions was his *servicio de mesa,* consisting of four large green pottery dinner plates. On them he was ceremoniously served each meal, and he permitted no one else to use them. He dressed in whatever manner happened to strike his fancy. On occasion his powerful legs and arms were decorated with clusters of bright feathers; strings of little bells tinkled merrily on his ankles; plumes accentuated his height; and turquoises and pieces of coral strung on thongs dripped over his big chest. Someone, perhaps Coronado or another officer, had presented him with two greyhounds, and the noble animals

*The Spanish judicial league was the equivalent of 2.634 English miles. Fray Onarato would recover and resume his religious duties in Compostela.

trotted beside him. Several Indian girls whom he found especially pleasing and had persuaded to become his companions straggled along in his wake.

In one of his packs was a sacred medicine rattle made from a gourd. It was one of the several acquired by Nunez Cabeza de Vaca somewhere in Texas. Aware of the universal belief of Indians that medicine rattles were infused by supernatural forces, it had been Nunez Cabeza de Vaca's custom to send one or more ahead with messengers when approaching a tribe not previously encountered. Medicine rattles varied greatly, but unless they were transported between peoples separated by vast distances, their origins could be identified by the materials used in them, by their size, by the designs and symbols painted or carved on them, or by some other type of ornamentation. In the case of Estevanico, he might well have benefited if he had left his rattle in Mexico.

Indians are popularly pictured as being always solemn, stoical, and expressionless. Nothing could be more ridiculous. They love fun, clever pantomime, revelry, and storytelling; indeed, they appreciate entertainment of almost any kind. They laugh uproariously at practical jokes, and like nothing better than to sing and dance, either in serious religious ceremonies or simply for pleasure. Estevanico's gay manner and his willingness to join them in any ritual or social festivity were appreciated, and his forceful and dominating personality evoked their admiration and drew them to him.

It is well to understand these things about one of the most famous explorers of North America. In his *Relacion,* Nunez Cabeza de Vaca makes it clear that Estevanico had been invaluable as a trailbreaker and ambassador to the Indians, "was in constant conversation [with them]; he informed himself about the ways we wished to take, of the towns there were, and the matters we desired to know." Estevanico had been welcomed, respected, and genuinely liked by almost all Indians the four men met. There had been occasions, however, when the Moor's brashness with Indian women had brought objections, and Nunez Cabeza de Vaca had been obliged to be stern with him. It had been Nunez Cabeza de Vaca's belief that the role of "men from the sun" was better played with reserve and detachment. Too much familiarity and sociability, he thought, would tend to lower him and his companions to the level of ordinary men in the eyes of the Indians. He had counseled them to remain aloof, but not cold and disdainful, and never to be patronizing or purposefully amiable.

Although Estevanico had not fully shared this attitude, as had Dorantes and Castillo, he had adopted it most of the time. He recognized that Nunez Cabeza de Vaca's capacity for leadership was far greater than his own or that of the others. Moreover, he wanted to continue to live as much as any of them.

Now, on the wilderness trail north from Petatlan, there was no Nunez Cabeza de Vaca. Now there was only a devout, sober-faced friar with inflexible and narrow morality to command him, or try to, and he did not propose to be restrained by strictness he thought extreme.

For a time, Fray Marcos had held the hope that his guide would grow weary of carousing and heathenish activities, but at last he had become convinced that that was not to happen. Estevanico ignored his remonstrances, engaged in paganish medicine ceremonies, made the sign of the cross over sick persons, danced and sang with Indians through the night, and drank their vile stimulants. Nor would Estevanico obey his demands that he refuse the turquoises and corals and countless other gifts bestowed on him by the natives. In fact, Estevanico had no hesitancy in asking for any article that struck his eye, and in Fray Marcos's opinion, he was amassing more riches than any slave properly should possess.

Easter was near when they reached Vacapa, and Fray Marcos elected to spend the Holy Days in the little Indian settlement.* There he made the mistakes that resulted in disaster for his mission.

He decided that while he gave himself to his devotions, some advantage might be gained if he let the irrepressible Moor go ahead. At least he would not be embarrassed during the Easter period, and discord would be temporarily halted. If Estevanico got into serious trouble, it might teach him a lesson if he were obliged to get out of it by himself the best way he could.

Estevanico was agreeable to the plan. Fray Marcos would write that he instructed him to advance no more than fifty or sixty leagues, and that he "arranged with him that should he learn of some inhabited or rich country—something really important—he should not go any farther but return in person or send me Indians bearing the following sign: If it were something moderate, he should send me a white cross a span in size; if it were of greater importance, he should send me one two spans in size; and if it were something better and greater than New Spain, he should send me a large cross."

Estevanico had been gone only four days when Indians appeared in Vacapa with a cross the size of a man. They also brought the astonished friar a message: Estevanico had reached people who knew of great cities in the north. Indeed, one of the messengers himself had visited them. "This person," Fray Marcos reported, "told me of so many marvels of the land that I postponed believing them until

*In the present state of Sinaloa.

after seeing them or having further verification. He told me that it was thirty days' travel from the place where Esteban was to the first city in the land, which is called Cibola. He said that in the first province there are seven very large cities, all under one ruler, with large houses of stone and lime, all joined in an orderly manner, and the ruler's house is four stories high. The doors have many decorations of turquoises, of which there is a great abundance, and the people are very well clothed. There are other provinces farther on, each one of which he claims to be much more important than these seven cities. I rendered thanks to our Lord.''

In view of Fray Marcos's ability to dramatize his experiences, and his penchant for fabrication—characteristics that would be fully revealed in the near future—one justifiably may wonder how much the messenger actually told him or how much of the message he understood. That does not really matter. His use of the word *Cibola,* however, is a factor of great importance, for it is not known to have appeared previously in a Spanish document. Now the cities believed for so long to exist somewhere in the New World had a new name, the Seven Cities of Cibola.

As for the information about the pueblos purportedly contained in the message, if it was news to Fray Marcos, it was not to anyone else participating in the expedition. Certainly all the Indians possessed such knowledge, and descriptions of the large pueblos had been heard by Estevanico several times, first on the Rio Grande and then in the Valle de Sonora, at Pueblo de los Corazones, and in other Indian settlements. He was fully apprised that trade was carried on between these pueblos and Indians in Mexico.

Fray Marcos left Vacapa two days after Easter in a state of high excitement, for only forty-eight hours after receiv-

any article that struck his eye, and in Fray Marcos's opinion, he was amassing more riches than any slave properly should possess.

Easter was near when they reached Vacapa, and Fray Marcos elected to spend the Holy Days in the little Indian settlement.* There he made the mistakes that resulted in disaster for his mission.

He decided that while he gave himself to his devotions, some advantage might be gained if he let the irrepressible Moor go ahead. At least he would not be embarrassed during the Easter period, and discord would be temporarily halted. If Estevanico got into serious trouble, it might teach him a lesson if he were obliged to get out of it by himself the best way he could.

Estevanico was agreeable to the plan. Fray Marcos would write that he instructed him to advance no more than fifty or sixty leagues, and that he "arranged with him that should he learn of some inhabited or rich country—something really important—he should not go any farther but return in person or send me Indians bearing the following sign: If it were something moderate, he should send me a white cross a span in size; if it were of greater importance, he should send me one two spans in size; and if it were something better and greater than New Spain, he should send me a large cross."

Estevanico had been gone only four days when Indians appeared in Vacapa with a cross the size of a man. They also brought the astonished friar a message: Estevanico had reached people who knew of great cities in the north. Indeed, one of the messengers himself had visited them. "This person," Fray Marcos reported, "told me of so many marvels of the land that I postponed believing them until

*In the present state of Sinaloa.

after seeing them or having further verification. He told me that it was thirty days' travel from the place where Esteban was to the first city in the land, which is called Cibola. He said that in the first province there are seven very large cities, all under one ruler, with large houses of stone and lime, all joined in an orderly manner, and the ruler's house is four stories high. The doors have many decorations of turquoises, of which there is a great abundance, and the people are very well clothed. There are other provinces farther on, each one of which he claims to be much more important than these seven cities. I rendered thanks to our Lord.''

In view of Fray Marcos's ability to dramatize his experiences, and his penchant for fabrication—characteristics that would be fully revealed in the near future—one justifiably may wonder how much the messenger actually told him or how much of the message he understood. That does not really matter. His use of the word *Cibola,* however, is a factor of great importance, for it is not known to have appeared previously in a Spanish document. Now the cities believed for so long to exist somewhere in the New World had a new name, the Seven Cities of Cibola.

As for the information about the pueblos purportedly contained in the message, if it was news to Fray Marcos, it was not to anyone else participating in the expedition. Certainly all the Indians possessed such knowledge, and descriptions of the large pueblos had been heard by Estevanico several times, first on the Rio Grande and then in the Valle de Sonora, at Pueblo de los Corazones, and in other Indian settlements. He was fully apprised that trade was carried on between these pueblos and Indians in Mexico.

Fray Marcos left Vacapa two days after Easter in a state of high excitement, for only forty-eight hours after receiving the first cross, another, also the size of a man, had arrived. Allegedly the message accompanying it consisted of only one word: "Hurry."

Day after day in April and May, Fray Marcos pushed on in a vain attempt to overtake Estevanico. Day after day, in every village through which he passed or in which he paused to rest, he received the same discouraging word that the rascally Moor was only a short distance ahead. Messengers continually arrived to tell him that Estevanico would wait for him in a certain place, but whenever he reached a specified rendezvous, the result was the same: Estevanico was gone.

Pedro de Castaneda would recount that Estevanico had kept well ahead of the friar because he "thought that he could get all the reputation and honor himself, and that if alone he should discover those settlements with such famous high houses, he would be considered bold and courageous." There can be no doubt that Estevanico was desirous of achieving fame as well as wealth, but he was not entirely disloyal to his commander. Fray Marcos had no reason to complain that his guide was not doing a good job as an advance man. Estevanico opened the way so that Fray Marcos could travel in complete safety. Although he struggled on with unabated fury, Fray Marcos was obliged to admit that always awaiting him were a friendly reception, plentiful food, and comfortable lodging.

North of Pueblo de los Corazones, on the Rio Sonora, the trail entered country never reached before by any foreigner, white or black. Now passing over it with Estevanico was a wild and beautiful procession of several score of Indians from Mexico, all wearing their finest garments and most valuable adornments. Beside him, ready to carry out his commands, was Bartolome, a native of Petatlan, and his chief interpreter and aide.

After emerging from the Mexican mountains, the ancient trade trail they were following twisted on through a vast *despoblado,* a desolate region in which few people lived. With each stride Estevanico wrote history in the dust, and late in May he unlocked for the world the southwestern gateway of the future United States.*

Leaving Sonora, the trail ran down the San Pedro River in Arizona. In the vicinity of Benson, it turned northeast, across Arivaipa Valley, to Eagle Pass, twisting between the Santa Teresa and Pinaleno Mountains. Here was the old Indian ruin called Chichilticale (Red House), and near it the trail once more turned northward. Reaching the Gila River, it went on across a country of high plateaus, crooked valleys, and canyons to the Little Colorado River, near St. Johns. Turning northeasterly again, it crossed Carrizo Creek and reached the Zuni River. Ascending this stream, Estevanico entered New Mexico, and soon thereafter from a rise he saw, beyond a vast sweep of mesas, the walls of the first city of Cibola. The Indians told him it was called Hawikuh.

Several messengers were dispatched to announce his approach. One of them carried the sacred medicine rattle, to which had been attached "some strings of jingle bells, and two feathers, one white and one red."

It is possible that the people of Hawikuh, who were Zuni, had heard that both white and black men existed, but it is certain that they had never seen one of either race. Some knowledge of such peculiar breeds might have reached them from two directions. They might have learned that

*From a great ridge of the Huachuca Mountains, up where the air is thin and sweet with the perfumes of evergreens and flowers, one may see the place where he crossed the present international border in a magnificent panoramic view. The area has been set aside as a memorial—but not to him. It is called Coronado National Monument.

Nunez Cabeza de Vaca and his companions had been among the Shuman on the Rio Grande, and they might have been aware that the same four men had been in Pueblo de los Corazones and other Opata towns. They might have known, moreover, that white men had taken Indian slaves along the western coast of Mexico. Such exciting news would have traveled fast over great distances, most likely carried from tribe to tribe by traders.

Whatever the truth may be, the messengers sent into Hawikuh soon returned badly frightened. The medicine rattle had been presented to the cacique of the pueblo, and when he "took it in his hands and saw the jingle bells, he at once hurled the gourd to the ground with much wrath. He told the messengers to leave immediately, for he knew what sort of people they represented, and they should tell them not to enter the city or he would kill them all."

Upon receiving this report, Estevanico had laughed. The same thing had happened when he was with Nunez Cabeza de Vaca. There was, he declared, nothing to fear, for it had been his experience that Indians who were suspicious and unfriendly at first had always become humble and hospitable. Boldly and confidently he marched on until he stood before the entrance to the pueblo.

There on that early summer day, his trail of discovery abruptly ended. Rapidly a circle of men armed with clubs and bows and arrows closed about him. He was overwhelmed and taken prisoner.

The people with him, said Castaneda, "had followed him from all the settlements he had passed, believing that under his protection they could traverse the whole world without any danger. But as the people in this country [Cibola] were more intelligent than those who followed Estevan, they lodged him in a little hut they had outside their village, and the older men and the governors heard his story and took steps to find out the reason he had come. . . . For three days they made inquiries about him. . . .

"The account which the negro gave them of two white men who were following him,* sent by a great lord, who knew about things in the sky, and how these were coming to instruct them in divine matters, made them think that he must be a spy or a guide from some nations who wished to come and conquer them, because it seemed to them unreasonable to say that the people were white in the country from which he came and that he was sent by them, he being black.

"Besides . . . they thought it was hard of him to ask them for turquoises and women, and so they decided to kill him. They did this, but they did not kill any of those who went with him, although they kept some young fellows [Bartolome was one of them] and let the others, about sixty persons, return freely to their own country."

To prove that Estevanico was not immortal, not a man from the sky, but an ordinary human being, they cut his body into little pieces. Bits of bone, flesh, and skin were dried and distributed among neighboring tribes with a warning to kill any other invaders, black or white, who appeared. His executioners kept his turquoises, his corals, his feathers, his greyhounds, and his green dinner plates. They threw away the medicine rattle.

Fray Marcos would claim that he was only three days' journey from Hawikuh when an Indian runner reached him with word that Estevanico had been slain. There is ample evidence, however, to indicate that he did not get as far north as the international border. Subsequent investigations would reveal the falsities in the account he prepared. His

---

*Castaneda apparently had forgotten that only one priest, Fray Marcos, was following Estevanico, the ill Fray Onarato having been left in Petatlan.

statements regarding his own actions after he had heard of the tragic event obviously were made with the intention of picturing himself as an incomparably courageous explorer and servant of the king. His descriptions of Cibola were not only fabrications but were absurd.

"In view of this wretched news," he said, "I thought I should be lost. I feared not so much to lose my life, as not to be able to return and report on the greatness of the country, where God our Lord can be so well served, His Holy faith exalted and the royal patrimony of His Majesty increased.

"I distributed among the chiefs [with me] all the clothing and articles of trade I carried, and told them not to be afraid but to accompany me, which they did."

Pushing on, he soon met two more Indians who had been with Estevanico. He claimed that they were bloodstained and suffering from severe wounds, and that they "confirmed the unhappy news that Esteban, and all those who were with him, who numbered more than three hundred men, besides many women, had been killed by those of Cibola, and only they had escaped."

This was a terrible situation—only three survivors out of more than three hundred—a major catastrophe!

Still, even in the face of such peril, Fray Marcos refused to turn back, and "I finally persuaded two of the chiefs to accompany me, and with my own Indians and interpreters, I proceeded on my journey until coming in view of Cibola. . . .

"This pueblo has a fine appearance, the best I have seen in these regions. The houses are as they have been described to me by the Indians, all of stone, with terraces and flat roofs, as it seemed to me from a hill where I stood to view it.

"The city is larger than the city of Mexico."

Fray Marcos declared he was "tempted to go to the pueblo, because I knew I was risking only my life, and this I had offered to God the day I began the journey. In the end, realizing my danger, I feared that if I died no information would be obtained regarding this land *which in my opinion is the greatest and best of all that have been discovered.*"

One might wonder if he had forgotten the rich natural resources, the mines from which inconceivable fortunes in precious metals had been taken, and the great cities of the tropical and mountainous countries to the south—the West Indies, Peru, Ecuador, Guatamala, and even Mexico. He had traveled extensively in all of them. Yet, he dared to bestow greater praise on an arid country and on a single old pueblo . . . not a very large one, either.

Assertedly, Fray Marcos obeyed his orders: "I thought it appropriate to name that land the new Kingdom of St. Francis. And so, with the aid of the Indians, I gathered there a pile of stones, and on top of it I erected a small and slender cross, as I had no materials with which to make a larger one." To which it might be added that if he really had been in the high country of western New Mexico, he would have found cottonwoods growing along the streams or where there was seepage water, and he would have found large pinons on the hills and mesas.

He continued: "When I told the chieftains how well impressed I was with Cibola, they told me that it was the smallest of the Seven Cities, and that Totonteac is much larger and better than all the seven, that it has so many houses and people that there is no end to it.

"I declared that I was erecting that cross and landmark as a sign of possession, in the name of Don Antonio de Mendoza, viceroy and governor of New Spain, for the emperor, our Lord . . . I stated that I was taking possession there of all the Seven Cities and of the Kingdoms of Totonteac, Acus, and Marata, but I was not going to visit them, in order that I might return to give a report of what had been done and seen." Thereupon, he started back to Mexico "with more fear than food."

Castaneda, who would see Cibola himself the following year, would record, undoubtedly with greater accuracy, that when Fray Marcos learned of Estevanico's death he gave away everything he possessed, except his holy vestments, gathered up his skirts, and fled "by double marches without seeing any more of the country. . . ."

Fray Marcos was back in Compostela late in June. If he had gotten anywhere near Cibola, in northern New Mexico, as he claimed, then he had by some miracle acquired wings for his sandals. The airline distance between these places is considerably in excess of a thousand miles. The distance by twisting trail over mountains, across deserts, and through tortuous canyons could hardly be less than five hundred miles longer. It was near the middle of May when he purportedly gazed on Hawikuh. To have completed the return journey in approximately five weeks, he would have had to travel about forty miles a day—on foot.

In Compostela, according to Castaneda, Fray Marcos told Coronado "such great things about what the Negro Esteban had discovered and what they had heard from the Indians, and about other things they had heard about the South Sea and islands and other riches, that, without stopping for anything, the governor set off at once for the City of Mexico, taking Friar Marcos with him, to tell the viceroy about it." Coronado "made the things seem more important by not talking about them to anyone except his particular friends, under promise of the greatest secrecy, until after he had reached Mexico and seen Don Antonio de Mendoza." A few remarks were all that were needed to kindle the fire, and "it began to be noised abroad that the Seven Cities for which Nuno de Guzman had searched had already been discovered.''

Not only Mexico City was in a state of feverish excitement. Soon after Fray Marcos and Coronado had conferred with the viceroy, news of the discovery had spread rapidly throughout the West Indies. A distinguished traveler in Havana swore under oath that Fray Marcos had told him Cibola "is a land rich in gold, silver and other wealth, and has great cities . . .'' The fabulous stories, however, were not disseminated only by persons of prominence and position. A Mexico City barber attracted attention to himself and his shop by declaring that while he was shaving Fray Marcos, the padre, being in a chatty mood, had whispered to him through the lather that in Cibola there "were many walled cities guarded by gates. The people were rich, the women even wearing belts made of gold. In the country there were silversmiths, blacksmiths, slaughterhouses, baths, sheep and partridges.''

Mendoza's innate caution once more asserted itself. He had agreed to send a large expedition, by land and by sea, to conquer the northern country. Coronado would be in command. Fray Marcos would lead a contingent of priests. Even if one were to discount to a large degree the glowing report of the friar, the situation was encouraging. The stories that Nunez Cabeza de Vaca had heard from Indians had been substantiated in numerous respects. Although no material evidence had been produced to indicate the extent of the riches that might be gained, there could be no doubt that a vast unclaimed country awaited a conqueror. The prospect of bringing it under the jurisdiction of Spain was inspiring. Nothing could be more pleasant than to think about taking possession of new lands and acquiring treasures for the crown. And it was, after all, his duty to take every opportunity to increase as well as preserve the royal estate.

Still, Mendoza was unable to dislodge a nagging suspicion that much of the information presented as fact by Fray Marcos in reality might have evolved from flights of fancy, or simply from honest mistakes. He decided to make an attempt to find out. The entire winter would be needed to organize, equip, and assemble the Coronado expedition on the Pacific coast. Meanwhile, he would order a preliminary investigation in the hope of obtaining answers to the questions annoying him.

A courier sped westward with an urgent dispatch for Melchior Diaz, now alcalde-mayor of Culiacan. As Mendoza well knew, Diaz was an officer of unassailable integrity, with many years of frontier experience, an established reputation for dealing competently and justly with Indians, and a realist who would not be taken in by tall tales. Diaz, said Mendoza's instructions, was to leave as soon as possible with a small company of horsemen on a reconnaissance to the north and seek to verify the fabulous claims of the missionary.

It was mid-November when Diaz, with forty-five mounted soldiers and Indians, left Culiacan on the trail to Cibola. His journey is historically significant not because it was a daring venture or because of the intelligence he obtained, but because he and his men took the first horses into the immense territory that would comprise the western United States.

Now there were days when the red peoples of northern Sonora and Arizona heard a new kind of thunder, a rhythmic beating on the earth in tempos they had never known, the sound of horses' hooves. Now there were nights when the lights of campfires caught the sleek sides of the wondrous beasts tethered about the mud and mat houses, and there were new sounds in the shadows, the sounds of them munching their fodder and stamping and swishing their tails, and there were the strange smells of their sweat and

their manure. A new way of life had been revealed to the
Indians of the West.

The Pueblo Indians belong to four linguistic stocks:

1—Keresan, a distinct linguistic family.

2—Hopi, a dialectic division of the Shoshonian branch of
the Uto-Aztecan linguistic family.

3—Zunian, a distinct linguistic family.

4—Tanoan, a linguistic family that is part of the Kiowa-
Tanoan stock.

1540

*There were so many men of such high quality among
the Spaniards, that such a noble body was never
collected in the Indies. . . .*

—Pedro de Castaneda

In the beauty and richness of full spring, the army of
Coronado was crawling northward on the coastal road, and
the splendor and pageantry rivaled the glory of the dream.
To the east of the coastal plain, the Sierra Madre lifted its
immensity in tier after tier and peak after peak to the blue
haze of awesome heights, and on the west, the shimmering
Pacific reached away into illimitable distance.

In the procession that stretched out for miles were some
340 white men from many levels of New Spain society, and
several hundred Indian and a few Negro servants, camp
tenders, and herdsmen. Behind the expedition, stirring up
a great dust, were pack trains and the long ragged files of
cattle, sheep, oxen, horses, and mules. Many types of weapons were carried; guns, lances, swords, and knives by the

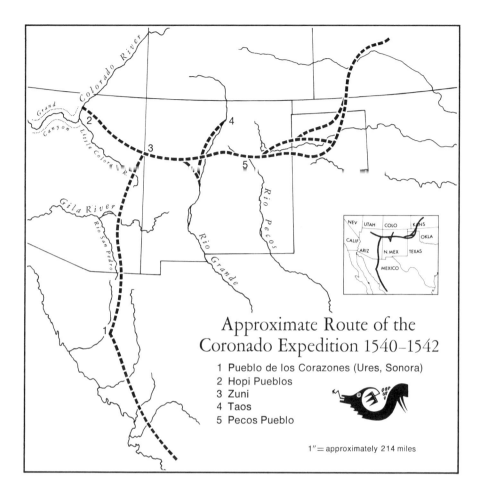

Approximate Route of the
Coronado Expedition 1540–1542

1 Pueblo de los Corazones (Ures, Sonora)
2 Hopi Pueblos
3 Zuni
4 Taos
5 Pecos Pueblo

1″ = approximately 214 miles

Spaniards, and bows and arrows, clubs, spears, and slings by
the Indians.

Not a few of the gentlemen in the force were mere
youths, some in their teens; many were in their twenties,
and comparatively few were older than thirty. If all of them
would have been more at home in a drawing room than on
a rugged wilderness trail, all possessed spirit and optimism
and eagerness for adventure, and all were inspired by a
vision of wealth awaiting them that gave them the courage
and determination to endure whatever hardships were encountered. If the counsels of the small number of men who

had known the ordeals and disappointments inherent in frontier conquests were heard, they were not heeded by the younger dreamers. Some of the soldiers had wives and children with them. The size of the contingent of priests in the column is not a matter of historical record. There may have been eight or ten, but besides Fray Marcos, now the most famous ecclesiastic in New Spain, the names of only five others are known. In sandals and robes, they plodded along with foot soldiers assigned to protect them.

Chiametla had been reached when Melchior Diaz and his men appeared, weary and worn from their northern scout. They gave Coronado a discouraging report. Snow and extreme cold, which they had not been equipped to withstand, had prevented them from reaching Hawikuh. Several men had died from exposure. After spending a fortnight or more in flimsy mat shelters near Chichilticale (Arizona), they had started back. But Diaz had not returned without some reliable information. At every opportunity, he had talked with Indians, some of whom had been to Cibola and some of whom had traveled with Estevanico and Fray Marcos. There was no doubt how Estevanico had met his death, but there was considerable doubt about other things Fray Marcos had reported.

To begin with, Diaz told Coronado, Fray Marcos had said that the trail to Cibola was good and easily traversed, when in fact it was extremely difficult and in numerous areas virtually impassable. Although there were large pueblos, they by no means merited the description of "great cities" which Fray Marcos had bestowed upon them. Nor had Diaz been able to learn anything to support the padre's claim that in Cibola were to be found silver, gold, and jewels. Indeed, not a single Indian with whom he had talked had even implied that the people of Cibola possessed such valuables. The Cibolans had turquoises, although nowhere near as many as Fray Marcos said he saw.

Although Coronado made an effort to keep Diaz's report secret, wrote Castaneda, "the bad news leaked out . . . Friar Marcos, noticing that some were feeling disturbed, cleared away these clouds, promising that what they should see would be good, and that he would place the army in a country where their hands would be filled, and in this way he quieted them . . ."

The army went on, but the spirit and optimism which had previously prevailed were noticeably dampened, if not by Diaz's story, by the increasing ruggedness of the country and the never-ending hardships suffered by both men and animals. After resting a few days in Culiacan, Coronado decided to go ahead of the others with a selected company of cavalry and infantry on a rapid march to Cibola. His reasoning was that in view of Diaz's statements that the road was rough and difficult and that the northern country was sparsely inhabited by Indians, he might save the main army from taking unnecessary risks by ascertaining himself the facts of the situation. The remainder of the force would advance at a necessarily slower pace as far as Pueblo de los Corazones, establish a base camp there, and await orders.

With him Coronado took between 105 and 110 men, about 80 of them cavalry and the others foot soldiers. All had been chosen with care, with special consideration given to their physical condition and known reliability and courage. Also in the vanguard were the priests, none of whom had been willing to stay behind. A large number of Indians and Negroes was taken to handle the pack trains and livestock and serve as camp tenders.

Travel between the Rio Mayo and Pueblo de los Corazones was extremely slow and hazardous. Several servants died and ten or twelve horses had been killed. In a dispatch to Mendoza, Coronado wrote: "We all marched cheerfully along a very difficult way, where it was impossible to travel without making a new road or repairing the one already there. This troubled the soldiers not a little because everything the friar [Marcos] had said was found to be quite the reverse; for among other things he had said and declared was that the way would be plain and good . . . But the truth is that there are mountains which, however well the trail might be repaired, could not be crossed without great danger that the horses would fall over the cliffs. Indeed, it was so bad that many of the animals . . . were lost on this part of the route, because of the roughness of the rocks. The lambs and wethers lost their hoofs along the way, and most of those I had brought from Culiacan I left at the river Yaqui because they were unable to travel."

A quantity of maize was obtained in exchange for trinkets from Indians in the valley of Sonora, and the march across the *despoblado* to the north was begun. On an early summer day, following the trail down the Rio San Pedro which Estevanico had taken a year earlier, Coronado and the vanguard entered Arizona.

For more than three and a half centuries, historians did not question the statements of early Spanish authors that when Coronado reached Hawikuh, the province of Cibola was composed of "Seven Cities." In 1917, the anthropologist Leslie Spier expressed the belief that no more than six Zuni towns had existed in 1540, and wrote: "Even the most ambitious attempts to identify the pueblos do not indicate the seventh . . ." Archaeological investigations, notably those directed by Frederick Webb Hodge, shortly afterward confirmed Spier's opinion.

The six Zuni pueblos of Coronado's time were:

Hawikuh, fifteen miles southwest of the present town of Zuni, with buildings two and three stories high;

K'ianawa (or *Kechipawan*), on a mesa across a small valley from Hawikuh, with buildings three and four stories high;

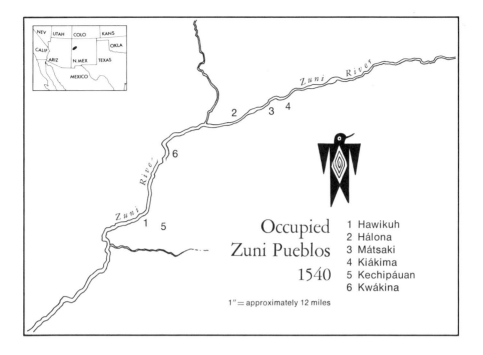

Occupied
Zuni Pueblos
1540

1 Hawikuh
2 Hálona
3 Mátsaki
4 Kiákima
5 Kechipáuan
6 Kwákina

1" = approximately 12 miles

Kwakina, on the Zuni River, four miles below the present Zuni, with buildings three and four stories high;

Halona, on both sides of the Zuni River, on the site of the present Zuni, with buildings three and four stories high;

Matsaki, three miles east of the present Zuni near the northwestern base of Towayalane Mountain, with buildings four and five stories high;

K'iakima, at the southwestern base of Towayalane Mountain, with buildings two and three stories high.

A family of 4 persons usually occupied three rooms. The permanent population of Hawikuh is estimated by archaelogists to have been approximately 700 persons, or 175 average families, occupying some five to six hundred rooms. Applying this scale to all six pueblos—probably two were larger and three were smaller than Hawikuh—it is unlikely that they were occupied by more than 4,000 persons when the Spanish first appeared. An even more conservative estimate is favored by some archaeologists.

The ethnologist Frank H. Cushing, who lived among the

Zuni for several years at the end of the nineteenth century, was the first scientist to maintain that they were descended from two main parental stocks. Subsequent studies by archaeologists have confirmed his thesis. The first stock to migrate to the Zuni River came from somewhere in the north. The second stock can be more clearly identified. It came from the west or southwest, probably from the basin of the lower Colorado River, for its culture resembled that of Yuman people. While these two stocks were undoubtedly the nucleus of the present Zuni tribe, the times of the migrations must remain insoluble mysteries. The western stock may have amalgamated with the northern stock long after the latter had settled in the Zuni territory, and some anthropologists believe this to be the case.

It may be said, however, that Indians who possessed only crude bone and stone implements—the Paleolithic stage—inhabited the general region more than twenty thousand years ago, but whether they or any of their descendants were ancestors of the Zuni is a question that can never be answered. It may be authentically stated, as well, that when the Anasazi culture began to arise in the Southwest, several centuries before the beginning of the Christian Era, the Zuni were, and probably had been for a very long time, a cognate people inhabiting their present location.

After the merger of the two parental stocks, whenever it occurred, there were accretions from other tribes, as well as desertions. The Zuni, therefore, were a composite Pueblo people. The mingling of bloods did not have a deleterious effect, however. Indeed, the Zuni were strong and highly intelligent.

The Zuni call themselves *A'shiwi,* meaning "the flesh," and they call their country *Shi'wona,* "the land that produces flesh." The name *Zuni* was first applied to them by the Spanish explorer Antonio de Espejo in 1583, and has been popularly used ever since. It is a corruption of *Sunyitsi,* a Keresan word of unknown meaning.

In recounting that man emerged through several stages from a dark underworld, the Zuni origin myth is similar to those of other Pueblo peoples. The Zuni religion, however, as Bahti (1971) states, is "probably the most complex of all native religions in the Southwest, and every aspect of Zuni life is completely integrated with their religion . . . Six esoteric cults (in addition to the ancestor cult to which all Zunis belong) form the basis of Zuni ceremonials. These are the cults of the Sun, Rainmakers (this cult is in charge of twelve priesthoods), Koko (or kachinas), Priests of the Koko, War Gods and Beast Gods (representing the animal patrons of twelve related curing societies). Each cult has its own priests, fetishes, rituals and ceremonial calendar. Basic to the religious philosophy of the Zuni is the recognition of man's oneness with the universe and the absolute necessity of maintaining this harmony through the correct execution of prescribed rituals."

Some comprehension of the complex Zuni religious philosophy may be gained from Cushing (1896), who wrote that they "suppose the sun, moon, and stars, the sky, earth, and sea, in all their phenomena and elements; and all inanimate objects, as well as plants, animals, and men, to belong to one great system of all-conscious and interrelated life, in which the degrees of relationship seem to be determined largely, if not wholly, by the degrees of resemblance . . . In this system of life the starting point is man . . . In just so far as an organism, actual or imaginary, resembles his, it is believed to be related to him and correspondingly mortal; in just so far as it is mysterious, is it considered removed from him, further advanced, powerful and immortal. It thus happens that the animals, because alike mortal and endowed with similar physical functions and organs, are considered more nearly related to the gods than is man, because more mysterious, and characterized by specific instincts and powers which man does not of himself possess. Again, the elements and phenomena of nature, because more mysterious, powerful and immortal, seem more clearly related to the animals than are the higher gods, because their manifestations often resemble the operations of the former."

In consequence of this philosophy, and through the confusion of the subjective with the objective, stated Cushing, "any element or phenomenon in nature, which is believed to possess a personal existence, is endowed with a personality analogous to that of the animal whose operations most resemble its manifestation.

"For instance, lightning is often given the form of a serpent, with or without an arrow-pointed tongue, because its course through the sky is serpentine, its stroke instantaneous and destructive; yet it is named Wi-lo-lo-a-ne, a word derived not from the name of the serpent itself, but that of its most obvious trait, its gliding, zigzag motion.

"For this reason, the serpent is supposed to be more nearly related to lightning than to man; more nearly related to man than is lightning, because mortal and less mysterious."

The Spanish, steeped in the biblical myths, were unqualifiedly intolerant of the first Indian mythology they encountered in the southwest. Three hundred years later, the Americans would react in the same manner. As Bahti aptly remarks, "Superstition is the other man's religion." To which may be appended the truism that after more than four centuries of conflict, no reconciliation of Christian and Zuni religious philosophy has occurred. The bells of Christian churches peal in the Zuni country, and the ringing is countered by the drums and medicine rattles and the chanting of the ancient ceremonials. And so it is as it always was and perhaps always will be.

1 5 4 0 *(cont.)*

> ... *when they saw the first village, which was Cibola, such were the curses that some hurled at Friar Marcos that I pray God may protect him from them. It is a little, crowded village, looking as if it had been crumpled all up together.*

—Pedro de Castaneda

Exhausted, hungry, and dirty, Coronado and his men gazed on the pueblo of Hawikuh with sinking hearts.

Smoke signals rose from surrounding mesas to the summer sky. Before the front wall, two or three hundred warriors, armed with bows and arrows and clubs and wearing leather shields, stood in battle formation. What the Spaniards did not know was that the Zuni had been warned of the approaching invaders several days before, and had made preparations to repulse them. The women, children, and the aged had been sent to safety in the mountains. Men had come from other Zuni pueblos to aid in the defense of Hawikuh, and as many able fighters were secreted in the pueblo as were gathered before it.

Coronado, wearing his best armor and a gilded helmet with a crest of plumes, was an imposing figure as he sat on his horse, disbelief and disappointment reflected in his handsome face, and observed the situation. His men were weakened from the ordeals of the long march, without sustenance, and in no condition to fight, yet advance he must, whatever the consequences, for there was no alternative.

He ordered Captain Garcia Lopez Cardenas to approach the pueblo with a small escort, which included two priests, and assure the defenders that he came in peace. As Cardenas moved forward, the Zuni warriors sprinkled sacred cornmeal in a line and warned him not to cross it. An interpreter—presumably a Mexican Indian—delivered Coronado's message, and Cardenas and the others embellished it with pantomime, laying down their weapons and making other signs that they had no wish to engage in hostilities. The answer came in the form of arrows. A notary and one of the priests were struck, but not seriously hurt.

Coronado, accompanied by a few soldiers, joined Cardenas and made another effort himself to conciliate the Cibolans by offering them gifts. Wild shouts, menacing gestures, and more arrows made it plain that his overtures were futile.

"I did not wish them attacked," Coronado would write Viceroy Mendoza, "and although my men were begging me for permission, I enjoined them from doing so . . . On the other hand, when the Indians saw we did not move they took greater courage, and grew so bold that they came almost to the heels of our horses to shoot their arrows . . . On this account I saw the time for hesitation had passed . . ."

He gave the order to charge, and the entire vanguard dashed forward, firing their guns, but, as Coronado would state, "there was little to do, for the Indians suddenly took to flight, some running toward the city . . . and others toward the plain, or wherever chance led them. Some of them were killed, and others might have been slain if I had allowed them to be pursued. But I saw that in this there would be little advantage . . ." The number of Zuni killed in the skirmish is variously recorded as ten, twelve, and twenty.

The objective now was the walled pueblo. The only entrance was narrow and crooked, and could be easily defended from within. The Zuni were crowded along the first terrace. As the Spaniards, both horsemen and infantry, rushed forward, arrows and stones showered on them in such great number that they were forced to withdraw out of range.

Coronado decided that an attack on foot would provide a better chance of gaining the entrance, and he and most of the horsemen dismounted. Crossbowmen and harquebusiers were sent ahead to drive the Zuni from the terrace, and the remainder of the force dashed toward the gateway. Arrows and stones rained down on the attackers. The lower wall was reached, but, according to Coronado, "the crossbowmen soon broke the strings of their crossbows, and the musketeers could accomplish nothing because they had arrived so weak they could scarcely stand on their feet." Some scaling ladders apparently were secured, but the men did not have the strength to climb them.

Coronado, recognized by the Zuni as the commander, became a main target. Twice he was knocked flat by stones. Castaneda said that he would have been killed had not Captains Cardenas and Hernando de Alvarado heroically thrown themselves over him, "receiving the blows of the stones, which were not few." The captains carried their leader to safety. For an hour or more he lay unconscious, and the battle had ended when he revived. He had suffered several wounds in the face, an arrow had pierced one foot, and his body had been badly bruised by stones.

Returning to the fray after rescuing Coronado, Cardenas led a successful assault on the entrance, and the Spaniards entered the pueblo. The Zuni pleaded for mercy and asked permission to abandon Hawikuh. Cardenas told them they were welcome to remain as long as they were peaceful. They chose to leave.

Hawikuh was well supplied with food, and the starving

Spaniards gorged themselves. One of them would state, "There we found something we prized more than gold and silver . . . plentiful maize and beans, turkeys . . . and salt better and whiter than I have ever seen . . ." The salt came from the famous Zuni saline, a few miles from Hawikuh.

As he rested and recovered from his wounds, Coronado was not idle. He sent messengers to the Zuni, who had concealed themselves in the adjacent mesas and mountains, to tell them that if they returned to Hawikuh—to which, incidentally, he had given the name Granada, the viceroy's birthplace—they would be well treated. He requested that his presence be made known to all other pueblos, and announced that he was eager to consult with Indian chieftains about the country.

In response to the summons, a delegation of Zuni headmen soon appeared. Coronado held long conferences with them, and one of the important things he learned, said Castaneda, was about "a province with seven villages of the same sort as theirs, although somewhat different . . . This province is called Tusayan. It is twenty-five leagues from Cibola. The Villages are high and the people are warlike."

Coronado was being told of the Hopi and their pueblos on high mesas in northern Arizona. Within a week after the capture of Hawikuh, he had dispatched Captain Pedro de Tovar and a small contingent to visit them.

The Zuni ambassadors pledged obedience to the Spanish king, and expressed a desire to become Christians. They took their departure after promising that peace would prevail, and that the residents of Hawikuh would return. But within a few days, Coronado was informed that the Zuni pueblos were almost completely deserted and that the people had taken refuge in remote country. He made a short reconnaissance. Another effort to induce the Zuni to return to their homes was successful. They came down from the hills, with the old and the young, women and children, and Coronado felt that he had, indeed, progressed in his attempt to make Christians of them. The priests were busy and delighted.

The first reliable description of Pueblo Indians ever written was contained in the long letter Coronado wrote to Viceroy Mendoza under the date of August 3. It clearly reflects his profound disappointment, and he made no attempt to conceal facts, nor to proffer false hope to Mendoza, whom he fully understood would be as disappointed as he.

Speaking of Fray Marcos's report on Cibola, Coronado bluntly told Mendoza: "To make a long story short, I can assure you he has not told the truth in a single thing he has said, for everything is the opposite of what he related except the name of the cities and the large stone houses."

Of the Zuni: "the people of these towns are fairly large and seem to me to be quite intelligent . . . most of them are entirely naked except for the covering required for decency. They have colored fabrics like the one I am sending you. They do not raise cotton, because the country is extremely cold, but they wear mantas . . . and it is true that some cotton thread was found in their houses. They wear the hair on their heads like the Mexicans, and are well formed and comely. I think they have many turquoises, but removed them with all the rest of their goods except the maize."

Of treasure: "Two points of emeralds and some little broken stones, rather poor, which approach the color of garnet, were found in a paper (?) under some stone crystals . . . So far as I can judge, it does not appear to me there is any hope of finding either gold or silver, but I trust in God that if there is any to be had we shall get our share of it, and it shall not escape us through any lack of diligence in the search."

Of the Cibola country and its resources: "We found fowls [turkeys] here . . . very good and larger than those of Mexico . . . There are no [cultivated] fruits or fruit trees . . . Very good grass was found . . . both for pasturage for our horses and for mowing to make hay, of which we have great need, because our horses were so weak and feeble when they arrived.

"The food consists of maize, of which they have a great abundance, beans, and game . . . They make the best tortillas I have ever seen anywhere . . . They have the very best apparatus and method of grinding that were ever seen, and one of these Indian women will grind as much as four of the Mexicans.

"So far as I can find out, these Indians worship water, because they say it makes the maize grow and sustains their life . . .*

"There are many animals here . . ." Although he called some of them by incorrect names, Coronado mentioned bears, mountain lions, porcupines, elk, peccaries, deer, wildcats, and mountain sheep. He spoke of "finely tanned cattle skins," obviously buffalo robes obtained in trade with Indians of the Great Plains.

Coronado wrote his famous letter to Mendoza before the Zuni had permitted their women to leave the refuges in the mesas, and he ruefully remarked: "I am unable to give your Lordship any reliable information about the dress of the women, because the Indians keep them so carefully hidden that I have not seen any except two old ones. They wore two long robes reaching down to their feet, with a girdle, and fastened with some cotton strings. Since the Indians were not willing to let me see the women, I asked them to give me a sample of what they wear to send to you. So they

---

*When and how the Pueblos obtained maize, or corn, is discussed later. See the index.

brought me two mantas . . . painted almost all over." Besides turquoises, skin paintings, and baskets, he sent to Mendoza "two pads such as the women ordinarily wear on their heads when they carry water from the spring, just as they do in Spain. One of these women, with such a pad on her head, will carry a jar of water up a ladder without touching it with her hands." He thought the pictures of animals which had been painted on skins at his request were not very good, and stated: "I have seen other pictures on the walls of the houses with better proportion and much better done."

Coronado's historic letter is interrupted briefly here with invaluable observations by Castaneda, who arrived in Cibola some weeks later with the main army. "These people are very intelligent," he wrote of the Zuni. "They cover their privy parts and all the immodest parts with cloths made like a sort of table napkin, with fringed edges and a tassel at each corner, which they tie over the hips. They wear long robes of feathers and the skins of hares, and cotton blankets. The women wear blankets, which they tie or knot over the left shoulder, leaving the right arm out. These serve to cover the body. They wear a neat well-shaped outer garment of skin. They gather their hair over the two ears, making a frame which looks like an old-fashioned headdress.

"They plant in holes. Maize does not grow high . . . They collect the Pine nuts [pinon nuts] each year, and store them . . . A man does not have more than one wife. There are estufas or hot rooms [kivas] in the villages, which are the places where they gather for consultation.

"They do not have chiefs as in New Spain, but are ruled by a council of the oldest men. They have priests who preach to them, whom they call papas.* The priests go up

*A true Zuni word meaning literally "elder brother."

on the highest roof of the village and preach to the village from there, like public criers, in the morning while the sun is rising, the whole village being silent and sitting in the galleries to listen. They tell them how they are to live, and I believe that they give certain commandments for them to keep, for there is no drunkenness among them nor sodomy nor sacrifices, neither do they eat human flesh nor steal, but they are usually at work. The estufas belong to the whole village. It is a sacrilege for the women to go into the estufas to sleep."

As to the condition of the vanguard, Coronado told Mendoza: "We have great need of provisions, and you should know that among all of us here there is not one pound of raisins, nor any sugar, nor oil, nor wine, except barely a pint saved for saying Mass, for everything has been consumed, some of it having been lost on the way. You may provide us whatever seems best, but if you are planning to send us cattle you should know they will have to spend a year on the road, because they cannot come in any other way nor any quicker." Four shepherds had just arrived, bringing with them "only twenty-four lambs and four wethers; the rest of them having died from the hardship, although they did not travel more than two leagues a day." These were emergency rations, pushed ahead as fast as possible. The surviving sheep had been on the road four months from Culiacan. The remainder of the livestock were still in the valley of Sonora near Pueblo de los Corazones.

A pledge and a lament. Coronado assured Mendoza that even if he had found the greatest treasures in the world in Cibola, he could not have done more "than I have performed in coming here . . . all my companions and myself carrying our provisions on our backs for three hundred leagues, and traveling on foot many days, making our way over hills and rough mountains, not to mention other hardships that I refrain from recounting." He had decided to send men "throughout all the surrounding regions in order to find out if there is anything worthwhile; [and] to suffer every hardship rather than abandon this enterprise; and to serve his Majesty if I can find a way to do so.

"Nor shall I think of ceasing my efforts until death overtakes me, if it serves his Majesty or your Lordship to have it so.

"God knows I wish I had better news, but I must tell you the truth . . . I must inform you of the bad as well as the good."

When Captain Tovar was sent by Coronado to investigate the province of Tusayan, it contained seven main Hopi pueblos. They stood on four high mesas 100 to 110 miles northwest of Zuni (in Arizona). From east to west, they were:

Jeddito Mesa: *Awatobi* and *Kawaiokuh.*

First Mesa: *Walpi.*

Second Mesa: *Shipaulovi, Shongopovi* and *Mishongnovi.*

Third Mesa: *Oraibi.**

Hopi was contracted from *Hopitu,* their own name, which signifies "peaceful ones." They are the only Shoshonian people, as far as is known, who ever adopted a Pueblo culture. Their language connects them with the Shoshoni of Wyoming, the Paiute of Oregon, Nevada, and eastern California, the Ute of western Colorado and Utah, and the Comanche of the Great Plains, who separated from the Shoshoni in the seventeenth century. The Hopi also are remotely related to the Aztecs of Mexico.

---

*Built about A.D. 1150, Oraibi is believed to be the oldest continuously occupied town in the United States. The Keresan pueblo of Acoma may be as old or nearly as old.

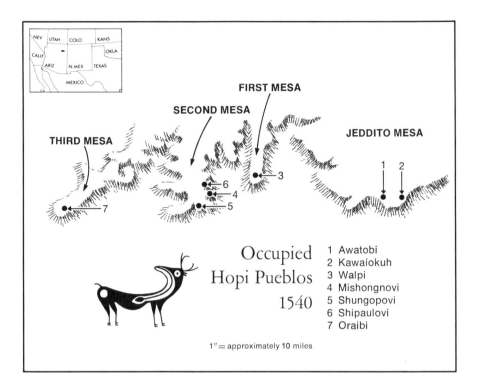

Occupied Hopi Pueblos 1540

1 Awatobi
2 Kawaíokuh
3 Walpi
4 Mishongnovi
5 Shungopovi
6 Shipaulovi
7 Oraibi

1″ = approximately 10 miles

When the Hopi first reached the Southwest cannot be known. Both they and their culture are composites, formed of accretions from widely divergent sources. Obviously the tongue of the Shoshonian family prevailed, but the Hopi dialect contains many archaic words not found in other dialects of the same language, as well as words of Pueblo stocks. It is certain, however, that the Hopi have been in the southwestern region a very long time. Ruins of their ancient villages have been found scattered from the Grand Canyon to the Verde River in the Tonto Basin of Arizona, and from the Flagstaff area to the Rio Grande in northern New Mexico, suggesting that they shifted frequently in prehistoric times. While enemy attacks and drought undoubtedly were responsible for some of these moves, anthropologists believe that towns were abandoned and new ones built as the result of cleavages between phratries, each of which adhered, and still does, to its own customs, dances, and other ceremonials. There were many phratries among the Hopi at the beginning of the historical period, each composed of several clans, and most of them still exist.

The Hopi origin myth tells of their emergence from a series of superimposed underworlds to the earth's surface. Each village has its own version of the myth, and legends connected with it may vary with each clan. They are, however, basically similar. One version, as explained by Nequatewa, states that in the underworld home of all men, the powerful upper class of human beings stole women from the lower-class men, and made life very difficult for these hard-working people. At last the troubled men assembled in the kiva and called on the birds to help them find a way to escape.

Canary and even the Eagle failed, but little Shrike found a passageway and returned to tell of a world without people, but where there were many animals and birds and bright sunshine. At last Chipmunk made a plant grow up through the opening that Shrike had discovered, and all the good people climbed up it to the surface world of sunshine. One-horned priests stayed at the foot of the plant to prevent evil ones from climbing to the surface world, and ever since, the one-horned people have been Hopi guardians. But one evil woman managed to climb the plant, and she killed a little girl. The good people were about to kill her, but she saved herself by taking them to the opening of the underworld. Looking down, the good people could see the little girl playing happily, and they were pleased, and after that the spirits of the dead returned to the underworld.

Some comprehension of the Hopi's belief in the supernatural may be gained from the knowledge that their pantheon includes between thirty and forty deities. Bahti states that the deities range in importance from culture heroes to major gods, and that there are "often considerable differences in the functions and appearances of these deities among the various Hopi villages. The myths relating to the gods . . . may differ greatly from one mesa to the next."

Scholars do not agree on the number of principal Hopi deities, much less on the spelling of their names. For example, Stephen names seven and Bahti lists eleven. This is excusable, for it is doubtful if one Hopi priest would agree with another on either the number or the spellings. It seems safe to say, however, that Sotuqnangu, god of the sky, is the most important deity, for he is believed to have created the earth, and he controls the heavens, lightning, and the clouds, and sends rain to make plants grow. Masauu is the god of death, a fertility god of man and animals, is associated with fire, and is the god who causes all metamorphosis. The god Muingwa lives in the interior of the earth and is the guardian of life. His female counterpart is Sand Altar Woman, who is associated with childbirth.

Kachinas, says Bahti, are "symbolic representations, in human form, of the spirits of plants, animals, birds, places or ancestors. Since it is only the spirit that is depicted, there is no attempt at realism in the portrayals." The Hopi have about thirty chief kachinas who take part in the most important annual ceremonies, but there are several hundred others who may appear at various times.

Kachina cults exist in each village. They might be likened to a number of Protestant churches in an American town of today, for, as Driver writes, "they shared much in common but at the same time had separate sets of officers and assembled in separate sacred structures . . . kivas.

"Boys are usually initiated into the Kachina Cults at ten or twelve years of age. Up to that time they, along with the women and girls, are supposed to believe that the masked dancers are indeed supernatural visitors from the village of the spirits. . . . The boys are severely whipped by the kachina spirit-impersonating priests to impress them with the gravity of the occasion, to inspire awe of the supernatural, and remove sickness and contamination from their persons. Then they are told that they are the ones who will wear the masked costumes in the future, thus making it clear that the dancers are human beings in disguise.

"In addition to the Kachina Cults, which embraced all the mature males, there were men's societies restricted to only a part of the mature males, sodalities restricted to only a part of the mature women in most of the villages, and also restricted sodalities with both men and women members.

"Perhaps the most distinctive characteristic of Pueblo sodalities is their dedication to the welfare of the entire society of which they are a part, rather than the selfish interests of the members."

The Hopi were outstanding weavers and artisans. Hopi textiles, made from a native cotton which they cultivated, were unexcelled and were in great demand throughout the prehistoric Southwest and northern Mexico. Some of their early pottery is considered to be among the finest ceramics ever manufactured by Indians. They were expert at dying and embroidering blankets, belts, kilts, and sashes. They were (and are) competent agriculturalists, growing maize, beans, pumpkins, onions, chili, and sunflowers. They were skilled hunters, traveling to the great forest of the Grand Canyon region to kill deer, antelope, elk, and other big game. They hunted with bows and arrows, but they were also clever at catching animals in pitfalls or driving them into concealed corrals. They had flocks of domesticated turkeys. Rabbits were killed in communal drives by boomerangs, and birds were caught in snares.

The affluence of the Hopi and the great variety and high value of their manufactured products attracted raiders as well as peaceful traders from far and near. They were forced to maintain strong and extensive defenses. They lived up to the name "peaceful ones" as much as possible, but they were brave and fierce fighters against invaders.

The Hopi were, and are, monogamists, and a marital scandal was a rarity. If a man and woman were unhappy together, resolving the problem was easily accomplished. The wife simply put her husband's belongings outside the door. That was all she needed to do to send him back to his mother's house. Both were free to marry again. Law and order were maintained in the Hopi pueblos more by intelligent reasoning than by force. Murder was unknown, thefts seldom occurred, and liars were condemned and ostracized.

1540 *(cont.)*

In midsummer, these activities were taking place:

1. Captain Pedro de Tovar was on his way to the Hopi towns.

2. Trusted dispatch bearers were en route to Mexico with Coronado's reports to the viceroy. With them were Fray Marcos and the famed frontiersman Captain Melchior Diaz.

3. Informed that many pueblos lay to the east, Coronado had sent Indian emissaries to them to summon their headmen to a conference with him.

Some documents state that Fray Marcos had become ill and thought it best to return to Mexico City for treatment; Castaneda, however, declared bluntly that the celebrated priest went back "because he did not think it was safe for him to stay in Cibola, seeing that his report had turned out to be entirely false, because the kingdoms that he had told about had not been found, nor the populous cities, nor the wealth of gold, nor the precious stones which he had reported, nor the fine clothes, nor other things that had been proclaimed from the pulpits."

Diaz had been given two assignments. He was to organize a base camp in the Valle de Sonora, select a complement to maintain it, and then start the main army on its way to join Coronado in Cibola. Those tasks accomplished, he was to set out with a small contingent of soldiers and Opata to find the ships which had been sent up the Gulf of California under Hernando de Alarcon with supplies for the Coronado expedition.*

*The story of Alarcon and Diaz, while thrilling in itself, is not an essential part of Pueblo history, and will be recounted only briefly here. In 1539 Francisco de Ulloa had sailed up the Sea of Cortez (Gulf of California) until he encountered impassable shoals across the mouth of a great river that was not known to exist. The river was the Rio Colorado. Ulloa had turned back.

When he reached the same vicinity with three vessels laden with supplies for Coronado, in August 1540, Alarcon fought his way through the dangerous shoals and against the raging current of the Colorado in small boats. It was his hope that the river came out of Cibola. He and his sailors were the first white men to ascend the Colorado from its mouth. They went upstream until they had passed the present site of Yuma, Arizona. From Indians they learned that Cibola lay several hundred miles to the east, beyond deserts through which travel was extremely difficult. The Yuman Indians knew that Estevanico had been killed at Hawikuh, and that Coronado had sacked the pueblo. Alarcon pleaded with them to guide him to Cibola, but they refused, giving as a reason their conviction that they would be endangering their own lives by taking more invaders to the Zuni. In September, Alarcon turned back downstream, on the way blazing a tree and leaving letters in a jar at its foot to tell whomever might follow him that he had been there and had made every effort to complete his mission. Then he sailed back to Mexico.

With twenty-five Spaniards and a number of Opata guides, Diaz left the Valle de Sonora in September. The trail they followed crossed a region never before entered by white men and containing some of the most terrible deserts in the world. The Colorado was reached near its confluence with the Gila. Traveling downstream, Diaz found Alarcon's letters. Although profoundly disappointed, Diaz did not turn back at once to inform Coronado that the supply ships had returned. He chose to explore more of the country, and he crossed the Colorado and rode some distance westward. Thus, he and his men were the first Europeans to traverse any part of the land that would one day be the state of California.

A short distance south of the present international border, Diaz was gravely

Late in July, Captain Tovar, with seventeen mounted men, three or four foot soldiers, Fray Juan Padilla, several Zuni guides, and a pack train, came in sight of the Hopi pueblos. According to Castaneda, "they entered the country so quietly that nobody observed them . . . the people do not leave the villages except to go to their farms, especially at this time, when they had heard that Cibola had been captured by very fierce people, who traveled on animals that ate people."

The speed with which the news of the Spaniards' invasion of Cibola was carried on foot across the barren wastes and mountains of the Southwest was nothing less than remarkable. Probably in no more than a fortnight, every pueblo in New Mexico, the Yuman people on the Colorado, four hundred miles to the West, and the Apache of the Llano Estacado, an equal distance to the east, had been informed that the Zuni had fallen.

Don Pedro and his men approached the Hopi towns cautiously "after nightfall and were able to conceal themselves under the edge of the village, where they heard the natives talking in their houses," said Castaneda. "But in the morning they were discovered and drew up in regular order, while the natives came out to meet them, with bows, and shields, and wooden clubs . . . The interpreter was given a chance to speak to them and give them due warning, for they were very intelligent . . ."

Don Pedro's demand that the Hopi capitulate and swear allegiance to God and the king brought shouts of defiance. Indians ran forward and drew lines with sacred cornmeal,

---

wounded in a freakish accident. For three weeks his loyal men carried him on a litter in a desperate attempt to reach San Geronimo, Sonora, where Coronado's base camp had been established, "in time for him to be confessed, for a priest was stationed there." They lost the race. Somewhere along the desert trail in southern Arizona, Diaz died and was buried. His grave has never been found.

warning the Spaniards not to cross them. While the yelling and the argument continued, some of the soldiers acted as if they intended to cross the lines of cornmeal, and "one of the natives lost control of himself and struck a horse a blow on the cheek of the bridle with his club." Fray Padilla, who had been an army officer before becoming a priest, became impatient, and called out to the captain: "To tell the truth, I do not know why we came here."

Captain Tovar gave the order to charge, and his horsemen sprang forward "so suddenly that they ran down many Indians." The battle lasted only a few minutes. The Hopi retreated in disorder, and the Spaniards reassembled, preparing to attack the town; but an assault was unnecessary. Headmen came out bearing gifts of cotton cloth, dressed skins, a few turquoises, and maize, announcing that "they wanted to be friends." Indian messengers were sent to the other pueblos, and before the day had ended, "all the natives had assembled" and had promised obedience.

In this way were the second Pueblo people ever seen by white men easily conquered. No Spaniard was injured in the brief fight, and probably no more than two or three Hopi were wounded.

In his talks with Hopi headmen, Tovar was given information of great importance. He was told that not far to the west was a big river, "and that downstream several days were some very tall people with very large bodies." He would have liked to continue on to the river, but his orders instructed him to go no farther than the Hopi towns, and being an obedient soldier he started back.

He reached Cibola about the middle of August. After hearing his report of the existence of a great river in the west, Coronado immediately made plans to find it. This might be the river that Ulloa had discovered in 1539, and the river that was the destination of Alarcon's supply ships.

Within a few days after Tovar's return, another small expedition of twenty-five men, led by Garcia Lopez de Cardenas, was on the way to Tusayan with orders to locate the "river of the giants," and find out where it went.

The Hopi willingly offered to guide Cardenas. After traveling for some hundred miles on a twisting trail that ran a little north of west from the Hopi towns, they came to an unbelievably deep and immense gorge.

They were the first white men to gaze into the awesome colored depths of the Grand Canyon. Castaneda wrote of the event: "They spent three days on this bank looking for a passage down to the river, which looked from above as if the water was six feet across, although the Indians said it was half a league wide. It was impossible to descend. . . . Captain Melgosa and one Juan Galeras and another companion, who were the three lightest and most agile men, made an attempt to go down at the least difficult place, and went down until those who were above were unable to keep sight of them. They returned about four o'clock in the afternoon, not having succeeded in reaching the bottom . . . because what seemed to be easy from above was not so, but instead very hard and difficult. They said they had been down about a third of the way and that the river seemed very large from the place which they reached. . . ."

The Hopi guides informed the Spaniards that it would be impossible for them to follow the river along the canyon brink, as there was no water for great distances, and they had no means of carrying enough to supply both men and horses. When the Hopi made such a journey, "they take with them women loaded with water in gourds, and bury the gourds of water along the way, to use when they return, and besides this, they travel [on foot] in one day over what it took the Spaniards two days to accomplish [on horses]."

Captain Cardenas took his little company back to Cibola,

and the remote Hopi towns "remained peaceful, since they were never visited again, nor was any attempt made to find other peoples in that direction."

No gold had been found, indeed nothing of value, in either Cibola or Tusayan, but an event occurred which gave Coronado new hope that treasure could be discovered—to the east.

In the Four Corners area—parts of Colorado, New Mexico, Utah, and Arizona—several centuries before the beginning of the Christian Era, perhaps as many as fifteen or twenty, the most influential Indian culture ever known in the Southwest began to arise. Although it deteriorated rapidly after the arrival of the white man, in numerous phases it still exists. Archaeologists have given it the overall name Anasazi, a word of the Athapascan language meaning "the old ones," but it probably had reached its zenith before the Athapascan Navajo and Apache had established themselves in the southwestern region following their long migrations from Alaska and northern Canada.

From its indefinite beginning on extremely primitive levels, the Anasazi culture progressed continuously through a sequence of stages to become the most highly developed of all prehistoric civilizations north of Mexico. It is the culture from which evolved the great communal dwellings we call cliff houses. It is the culture that produced industrial and horticultural skills, arts and crafts, as well as a rigid, complicated religious ceremonialism, that have few, if any, rivals in any other aboriginal society in the region of the United States.

It is the culture of the Pueblos.

The earliest people of the Anasazi culture are called Basket Makers, and for good reason. A few years before the beginning of this century, ninety bodies were discovered in a southern Utah cave. With them were a great many finely woven baskets. Subsequent excavations in other adjoining areas, especially in the high arid country through which the San Juan River passes, produced similar baskets in profusion. Scientists soon determined that the people of the baskets were predecessors of the cliff-house builders who had dwelt in the same region. In order to provide the older residents with a distinct identity, they were given the name Basket Makers. With the passage of a few more years, a series of connected stages of the Anasazi culture had been recognized, and given the following designation:

Basket Maker: ? to A.D. 500.

Modified Basket Maker: A.D. 500 to 700.

Pueblo I: A.D. 700 to 900.

Pueblo II: A.D. 900 to 1050.

Pueblo III: A.D. 1050 to 1300.

Pueblo IV: A.D. 1300 to 1700.

Pueblo V: A.D. 1700 to ?.

While no beginning date can be given for the Basket Makers, simply because it is not known from whence they came or when they emerged from the Paleolithic stage, no terminal date can be given to Pueblo V for the simple reason that it has not ended. Elements reflecting the ancient Anasazi culture—rituals, beliefs, customs, and to some extent even arts and crafts—still survive. It may be suggested, however, that it probably will not be long before they are completely obliterated by the increasing pressures of atomic age culture.

The Basket Makers did not have the bow and arrow. They hunted and defended themselves with atlatls (spear-throwers) and clubs. They dwelt in pithouses constructed in caves and in the open. They gathered native vegetal foods and stored them in baskets. Some of the baskets were so finely woven that food could be cooked in them. "The problems which these ancient people faced stagger the imagination of modern man," says the eminent anthropologist Wormington. "They had no metal, no pottery, no cotton or wool, no draught animals. [They had dogs.] Really all they did have was their own ingenuity to wrest the necessities of life from a none too favorable environment. It is remarkable how, by utilizing wood, bone, stone, plant fibers, and even their own hair, they not only produced all that they needed to survive, but also provided a base from which arose the high culture which culminated in the great communal dwellings of later times."

They buried their dead in flexed positions, wrapping the corpses in fur or woven fiber blankets or deerskins. Apparently they believed in a "later life," for in each grave they placed a new and unused pair of sandals. Other grave offerings included personal possessions of the deceased, baskets, ornaments, stone knives, clothing, food, and even cradles —all articles that might aid the departed in the journey to the hereafter. Fortunately, they chose to inter their dead in caves where moisture did not reach them. Because of this protection and the dry air of the Southwest, many of the bodies became thoroughly desiccated, and were mummified with the dehydrated flesh still on the bones and the hair looking much as it did in life. These favorable burial conditions also preserved the mortuary artifacts through the centuries.

The Basket Makers were primarily hunters and gatherers. They had no pottery, but they did have maize and pumpkins, the seeds of which they planted in holes in the ground made with a stick, their only farming implement. These factors—the absence of ceramics and the presence of a limited agriculture—reflect significantly on the development of Pueblo culture.

Maize is a relative of wild plants that flourish in Central

America and the most tropical region of South America. Scientists believe it was first domesticated in southern Mexico. When this domestication was achieved, however, can only be gauged by the discovery in southern Puebla, Mexico, of maize that was grown nearly seven thousand years ago. The most ancient maize ever found, it is both a pop corn and pod corn, for each kernel is enclosed in a separate pod.

In 1949, botanists Mangelsdorf, Reeves, and Smith reported that in the previous year, deep in Bat Cave, New Mexico, they had discovered maize which laboratory analysis showed to be at least six thousand years old. It, also, was both a pop corn and a pod corn, but its ears were not enclosed in husks. Shortly afterward, on higher levels of the same cave, they found a much newer type with larger cobs and kernels and a husk similar to modern species. Here was evidence of long crossbreeding to improve yield.

The early Bat Cave corn is the oldest thus far discovered in the Southwest. How soon after it had reached New Mexico from tropical Mexico it was acquired by the Basket Makers is, of course, not known. There seems to be no doubt, however, that they were planting it a very long time before the beginning of the Christian Era. Other finds indicate that probably between 600 and 500 B.C. another variety of maize reached the Basket Maker country, and botanists believe that it came from the middle-west or southeastern regions of the United States. When it was crossed with the Mexican types, a corn with greater drought-resistant capabilities resulted. The hybrid was particularly adaptable to the arid southwestern area, and crop production was increased.

Notable cultural changes occurred in the period called Modified Basket Maker. The people began to build pit-houses with contiguous rooms, either in straight lines or in the shape of a crescent. They now had beans to supplement their vegetable diet, and flocks of domesticated turkeys. The bow and arrow had supplanted the spear-thrower. The most important development of all, however, was that they had acquired the ability to manufacture crude pottery.

Ceramics, like maize and other agricultural foods, reached the Southwest by diffusion from South America and Mexico. It arrived as a fully developed craft, probably no less than six or seven thousand years old. Twenty-five hundred years ago, the people of the San Pedro period of the Cochise culture, living in southeastern Arizona and southwestern New Mexico, had obtained pottery from Mexican Indians, but perhaps more than a century had passed before they became adept at making it.

Some archaeologists believe that it was from these people that the Basket Makers received their first knowledge of pottery, but other scientists favor the view that it came to the Basket Makers from the people of the Mogollon culture, which grew out of the Cochise culture.

As might be expected, the earliest Basket Maker pottery was constructed in basket molds and was dried in the sun. Not much time had elapsed, however, before it was molded freehand, and the technique of firing had been learned. Skill in pottery making steadily developed until the Pueblos had become the outstanding ceramists of the Indian world.

In the Pueblo I and Pueblo II periods of the Anasazi culture, significant changes in architecture and construction methods occurred. Villages became more compact; walls were constructed of stones laid horizontally, and were more massive. In Pueblo I, pithouses were used for storage and ceremonial purposes. In Pueblo II, separate underground kivas had come into use.

The great cliff houses and immense multistoried buildings built on mesa tops belong to Pueblo III. This is called the classic period or golden age of the Anasazi culture, during which it reached the zenith of its development.

While many of the immense dwellings demonstrated the remarkable ability of the classic period Pueblos to erect multistoried apartment houses, Pueblo Bonito was outstanding for its size, beauty, and architectural skill. *It was the largest building ever built in the area of the United States before structural steel made possible the construction of skyscrapers.*

Standing in the shadow of the towering north wall of Chaco Canyon in northwestern New Mexico, Pueblo Bonito was semielliptical in form, rose five stories, and contained eight hundred rooms and thirty kivas. Its length was approximately 670 feet, and its width 315 feet.

According to the eminent archaeologist Edgar L. Hewitt, Pueblo Bonito was constructed of dark brown sandstone, and in it was every type of masonry known to Pueblo architecture. Each of the kivas was a circular room built within a square or rectangular structure, and in some cases the interior of the kiva was of fine table masonry, alternated with bands of large blocks, giving an ornamental finish. The timber was exceptionally heavy—logs forty feet in length and eighteen inches in diameter were used. The doorways varied from twenty-four by thirty-six to thirty by fifty inches; the lintels were straight, smooth poles about three inches in diameter; windows varied from six by twelve to twelve by sixteen inches. The rooms were mostly rectangular, but there were many of irregular form, semicircular, trapezoidal, elliptical and even triangular.

About the beginning of the fourteenth century, or shortly thereafter, the cliff houses and big communities were abandoned. They stood silent and crumbling in the winds that swept through the great canyons they overlooked. The Pueblos who had lived in them for two or three centuries moved southward and eastward, resuming their traditional way of life in new towns—some of them also very large, to be sure —in places where there were living streams and where cultivable land was available. They constructed the pueblos in which the first Spanish treasure hunters found them.

No one can say definitely what caused the great exodus, but certain postulations, not entirely without scientific substantiation, may be advanced. I see no reason to amend what I wrote in 1971 after long research on the subject:

"Before the Pueblos built the big cliff houses and towns, they had lived in relatively small independent villages, each perhaps containing no more than several score persons, and each probably in most cases dominated by a social organization, all members of which were related by blood or marriage. There are several theories as to why they saw advantages in amalgamating and building large urban type communities: easier defense, pooling of agricultural labor, development of irrigation systems, manufacture of improved types of utensils and tools by the application of various skills possessed by some individuals and not by others.

"It is improbable that any single force brought the end of this amazing human experiment. Attack by raiders was the least of the pressures which caused the abandonment. There were no Indian adversaries in the Southwest strong enough to sack and destroy the easily defended big towns. Small bands of raiders, perhaps Ute, Navajo and Apache, unquestionably made incursions, pilfering corn and ornaments and carrying off unguarded women and children. That such raids took place against the small pueblos in this period cannot be disputed. The ruins of isolated villages show that they were destroyed by fire, and in some of them arrowheads have been found in skeletons, both male and female, indicating that these victims died defending their homes.

"This was not the case, however, in the great cliff dwellings and the large mesa-top pueblos. Yet it seems illogical to think that people would construct these strong buildings halfway up immense precipices, necessitating the toting of water and provisions up a series of ladders, if not to safeguard themselves. The fear of invaders must have had some influence on their actions, but the fact remains that the cliff buildings and the big urban pueblos were not overthrown and destroyed by attackers, and the inhabitants were not involved in large-scale warfare. Some burned rooms have been found in them, but doubtless these fires were accidental. In a few places charred bones and mashed skulls have been discovered, but it would be unreasonable to assume that violent rows, especially between members of different clans or religious cults, as well as with obstreperous visitors, had not occurred with tragic results.

"The main causes of the Pueblo departures from the big towns appear to be two in number—drought and internal dissension.

"The science of dendrochronology (dating wood by growth rings) provides support for the first. It has shown that a severe drought persisted in the region of the Anasazi Civilization from A.D. 1276 to 1299. Faced with repeated crop failures, the absence of game, and inadequate water, the only alternative for the people of the stricken land would have been to leave for places with more dependable water supplies. Under such circumstances members of cults, clans and phratries would have made an attempt to remain together. Therefore, the composite groups that were united within the 'great houses' once more would have been separated.

"The science of ethnology provides support for the second most likely cause of the extensive shifting. As stated, the people who built the large towns came from many small pueblos, each with its own social mores and religious rites. While the basic material aspects of their culture, and even they themselves in a physical sense, were adjusted to existence in the closer confinement of the big communities, they refused to abandon their respective social and religious practices.

"Martin, Quimby and Collier, I think, have presented a most reasonable explanation of the conflict which evolved. Four towns, for example, each containing fifty people related to each other, gathered together and built a big cliff house. The four groups helped each other in various ways, but each group insisted on maintaining its social and ceremonial structures, which were well adapted to a small town but not to a large one. Therefore, customs, marriage regulations, methods of reckoning blood descent, political and governmental regulations, and a variety of complex ceremonies prevented the development of a strong central administration to act for all of them. Actually, the big town consisted of four independent towns, each functioning differently from the others. The result was that the big town was constantly disturbed by internal feuds. Amicable relationships between cults and clans were impossible. Big Town was a sociological disaster. Finally it collapsed. The various groups moved out, and Big Town was left to the ghosts.

"Unfavorable weather undoubtedly had a discouraging effect on them, but had they not been determined to abandon the big towns they could have returned to them after the drought had ended. It would seem that in temperament, attitude and character the people of 1300 were no different than people of today—getting along with each other was one of the biggest problems they faced."

Noting that some archaeologists have expressed the opinion that the abandonment of the great houses can be traced

entirely to the disastrous drought of 1276–1299, Wormington remarks: "If all the communities had been abandoned
at the same time, this would be a logical assumption. Actually, the time of the abandonment of all the main centers
does not fall between these two dates. Some were deserted
prior to the beginning of the great drought and a few
continued to be occupied after the dry period had begun."

Another theory, offered by Hack, suggests that a really
severe drought was not necessary to upset the economy of
the big town farmers. They depended chiefly on flood-
water farming in valley bottoms. During periods when rain-
fall is deficient, although insufficient to warrant use of the
term drought, arroyos are cut into the flood plains, the
water table is lowered, and flood-water fields become useless. Under such conditions the cliff-house farmers would of
necessity move to other locations where flood-waters were
more dependable.

No one knows, of course, but while drought and internal
dissension appear to be the main causes of the abandonment, some historians suggest that fears, engendered by
religious beliefs, were responsible. They may be correct,
although I do not agree with them. Even among the extremely religious and highly superstitious Pueblos the demands of the stomach and an abhorrence of violent conflict
were dominant. The richness of their culture could never
have been achieved, much less maintained, without bountiful food, a superfluity of material possessions, and a high
degree of social harmony. A great culture arises out of
continually increasing prosperity, not out of turmoil. Physical adversities and religious discord may have a pernicious
effect on it, and even result in drastic transitions, but "fear
that the gods are angry" would not be a sufficient reason for
walking away from a way of life, indeed a civilization, that
was the magnificent achievement of centuries of slow and

difficult progress. The culture of the Pueblos, moreover, was not destroyed when the great cliff houses were abandoned. They shifted, but they continued to live much as they had in the past, wherever they went.

The dominance of the Anasazi culture and the extent of its diffusion are illustrated by archaeological discoveries of its characteristics and influences as far distant from the area of its origin as western Texas, southern Nevada, central Utah and Colorado, southwestern Kansas, and deep into the Mexican states of Chihuahua and Sonora.

1540 *(cont.)*

> . . . *some Indians came to Cibola from a village which was seventy leagues east of this province, called Cicuye.*

—Pedro de Castaneda

Cicuye was the great pueblo to which the Spanish would give the name Pecos, because of its location on that river, and which would become famous as the scene of many dramatic events in the history of the Southwest. Its inhabitants belonged to the Jemez group of the Kiowa-Tanoan linguistic family.

In a delegation from Pecos were two headmen. Probably because he was unable to pronounce the names they gave, Coronado dubbed one Bigotes ("Whiskers") and the other Cacique ("Governor"). The appearance of Cacique is not known, but Bigotes, who wore a long moustache, was described as being a "tall, well-built young fellow, with a fine figure." Apparently the ranking ambassador, Bigotes told Coronado that he and his companions "had come in response to the notice which had been given, to offer themselves as friends, and that if he wanted to *go through* their country they would consider the strange and bold Spaniards as their friends."

Coronado politely thanked the visitors for their invitation and the gifts of tanned hides they had brought him. In return, he presented them with some glass dishes, beads, and little tinkling bells, "which they prized highly, because these were things they had never seen." Perhaps they had never seen the copper cascabels that were products of Mexico, but it is doubtful if there was an Indian in the Southwest who did not know of the little tinkling bells with which Estevanico had adorned both himself and the fateful medicine gourd.

Social amenities completed, Coronado got down to the subject uppermost in the minds of every man of his company—gold, silver, and precious jewels. The Pecos emissaries knew nothing of such things, but they could assure him that their own province, and all the country lying between it and Cibola, was rich in many other ways. There were innumerable pueblos, a great many people, fields of maize and other foods, turquoise mines, and, most important of all, just east of Pecos a short distance were the Great Plains over which vast herds of cows ranged. When Coronado asked for a description of the cows, one of the delegates drew a picture of a shaggy buffalo on a skin. He was promptly given the nickname, Vaquito ("The Calf").

Towns, people, cornfields, cows, and perhaps a few turquoises—nothing of value. Yet, Coronado's indestructible hope would not permit him to conclude that the eastern country was not worth investigating. He would have liked to have gone himself, but the expedition was already widely scattered. Cardenas was searching for the "great river of the west." Melchior Diaz was looking for the supply ships of Alarcon in the Gulf of California. The main army was on its way from the Valle de Sonora with the herds of livestock.

Perhaps dispatches were en route to him from Viceroy Mendoza. He decided that, at least for the time being, it would be wise for him to remain in Cibola. Meanwhile, he would send Captain Hernando de Alvarado and a few men to explore the east, see the cows, and make known to all people of the region that they were now subjects of the Spanish empire and must swear obedience to His Majesty and to God. Alvarado, of course, would also keep a sharp eye out for treasure; it had to exist somewhere in the vast territory, and it had to be found.

On August 29, Alvarado, in high spirits, started on his great journey of discovery. With him were sixteen mounted soldiers, four crossbowmen on foot, Father Juan Padilla, who had gone with Tovar to the Hopi, a pack train, and several Indian vaqueros. Bigotes and Cacique willingly offered to serve as guides, and promised that they would provide the Spaniards with the supplies needed on their trip from Pecos to the range of the cows.

Alvarado and his little company would travel some seven hundred miles through territory never before traversed by white men. They would pass, going and returning, through the heart of the Pueblo country. How many pueblos they actually visited or how many they saw is not a matter of record, but Alvarado would state that the Indian provinces along his route contained "eighty of the kind I have described." The walled, tiered towns stood closely together along the Rio Grande and its tributaries. They passed numerous ruins of large cities, obviously long abandoned, but in some of which walls thirty and forty feet in height were still standing. They would mention them in their accounts, knowing nothing, of course, of the great achievements of the Pueblos in the golden age of their civilization, the age that had come to a mysterious and almost abrupt end more than two centuries earlier.

Acoma, some seventy miles by the trail they took east

from Cibola, utterly astounded them. Standing on the summit of a mesa that rose in sheer walls nearly four hundred feet from the surrounding plain, the Sky City contained more than "two hundred houses and the same number of fighting men," indicating a population of considerably more than a thousand.*

Alvarado thought Acoma "one of the strongest ever seen," but one of his companions called it "the greatest stronghold ever seen in the world," and added that although the inhabitants "came down to meet us peacefully, they might have spared themselves the trouble and remained on their rock, for we would not have been able to disturb them in the least." The houses were "three and four stories high. The people . . . have abundant supplies of maize, beans and turkeys . . .."

Castaneda, who would visit Acoma a few months later, wrote a more valuable and detailed description than its discoverers. Because of its location on the steep-walled mesa, "it was a very good musket that could throw a ball as high. There was only one entrance by a stairway built by hand, which began at the top of a slope which is around the foot of the rock. There was a broad stairway for about two hundred steps, then a stretch of about one hundred narrower steps, and at the top they had to go up about three times as high as a man by means of holcs in the rock, in which they put the points of their feet, holding on at the same time by their hands. There was a wall of large and small stones at the top, which they could roll down without showing themselves, so that no army could possibly be strong enough to capture the village."

*Although the Spaniards thought the people of Acoma to be "the same type as those of Cibola," they were in fact Keresans, belonging to a distinct linguistic family. Acoma was the farthest west Keresan pueblo, and the first of this family ever seen by Europeans.

Alvarado "repented climbing to the top" because the "ascent was so difficult." After an inspection and an exchange of gifts, he and his men descended the stairs, mounted their horses, and rode on into the unknown reaches of Tierra Nueva. After three days' travel, covering some twenty leagues, they reached a river to which they gave the name Nuestra Senora. It was the Rio Grande.

The Keres origin myth is basically similar to those of other Pueblo peoples in that it tells of their emergence from the underworld. Traditions regarding their life after reaching the surface world, however, are unique, for they include tales of at least seven long migrations, and not all of these tales are without some archaeological verification.

There is growing acceptance of their claim that one of the places they stopped during their wanderings was the canyon of the Rito de los Frijoles. In this deep gorge of the Pajarito Plateau, in north central New Mexico, stood some of the finest and largest communal dwellings and cliff houses in the Southwest. One of them, Tyuonyi, contained more than four hundred rooms. It was built in a circle to a height of three stories. Another building, appropriately called Long House, stretched for almost eight hundred feet in a continuous block of rooms along the base of a sheer cliff one hundred and fifty feet high. It, too, had three stories, but many of its rooms, several of its kivas, and some of its storage chambers were caves in the cliff.

The great ruins of Rito de los Frijoles belong to the classic period of the Anasazi culture, which began in A.D. 1050, but some Keres must have lived in them long after A.D. 1300, by which time most of the immense southwestern cliff dwellings had been abandoned. In a cave of the canyon is a smooth wall, some fifty feet in length, obviously used as a "canvas" by several generations of artists. Many drawings executed in a variety of reds and blacks adorn this surface. In time, no more space remained, but not to be denied an opportunity to display their talent where they knew it would be preserved, the last artists superimposed their work on the pictographs of their predecessors. One of the "newest" paintings depicts a Spanish conquistador on horseback, and another is a sketch of a mission church, complete with cross.

The Keres, states Bahti, believe that the deity Thought Woman created all things by thinking them into existence, and she is responsible for the world as it appears. The earth is the center of the universe, and all planets function in accord to make the earth livable. Bahti continues: "The Sun is referred to as Father . . . The earth itself is referred to as Mother . . . At birth each person receives a soul and a guardian spirit . . . At the time of death both the soul and the guardian leave the body but remain in the house of the deceased for four days before making the journey to Shipap, the entrance to the Underworld . . . Depending on the virtue of the individual the soul is assigned to one of the four Underworlds. Those qualified to enter the innermost world become Shiwana (rainmakers) and return to the village in the form of clouds."

More than two centuries before the beginning of the historical period (1539), the Keres began to divide into groups and to build pueblos in the Rio Grande watershed, most of them on or adjacent to the main river. They were living in these when the first Spaniards arrived. How many of the Keres pueblos Alvarado and his soldiers visited or saw cannot be determined, but their route would have taken them close to most of them.*

---

*The difficulty of identifying and locating pueblos occupied in the early years of the historical period is great. Explorers and priests applied different names to the same pueblo. The problem is further complicated by such statements as "We came to a town at the mouth of a creek which we called San Pedro," and "Three

The following Keres pueblos are known to have been occupied in the sixteenth century. Keres people had lived in some of them for two hundred and fifty years or longer, and some of them are still inhabited today.

*Acoma,** about sixty miles west of the Rio Grande in Valencia County.

Buena Vista, near Santo Domingo.

Castil Blanco, across the Rio Grande from Castildabid.

Castildabid, a short distance above San Felipe, on the Rio Grande.

*Cochiti,** on the Rio Grande twenty-three miles southwest of Santa Fe.

Guaxitlan, in the Jemez Valley near Zia.

La Barranca, near Santo Domingo.

La Guarda, near Zia.

La Rinconada, near Zia.

Quirex, on the Rio Grande above Bernalillo.

San Felipe (Number One),* on the Rio Grande twelve miles above Bernalillo.

*Santa Ana,** on Rio Jemez eight miles north of Bernalillo.

*Santo Domingo,** seventeen miles above Bernalillo on the Rio Grande.

---

leagues further on we came to a town which we called Blanco." As archaeologists have discovered, three or four pueblos might have stood "near the mouth of the creek," and two or three pueblos might have existed within three leagues "further on." Distances traveled were guesswork. Indeed, some explorers did not trouble to record distances between pueblos. Descriptions were vague, perhaps entirely omitted. Moreover, pueblos inhabited during the sixteenth century may have been in ruins long before investigations by expert scientists were undertaken.

The Laboratory of Anthropology in Santa Fe has catalogued more than eight thousand archaeological sites in New Mexico. Hundreds of others are located in Arizona and various areas peripheral to the Pueblo country.

Any list of pueblos "discovered" by a certain explorer is bound to be inaccurate to some extent—and justifiably so.

*Still inhabited. The Keres pueblo of *Laguna,* on the Rio San Jose in Valencia County, still inhabited, was not built until late in the seventeenth century.

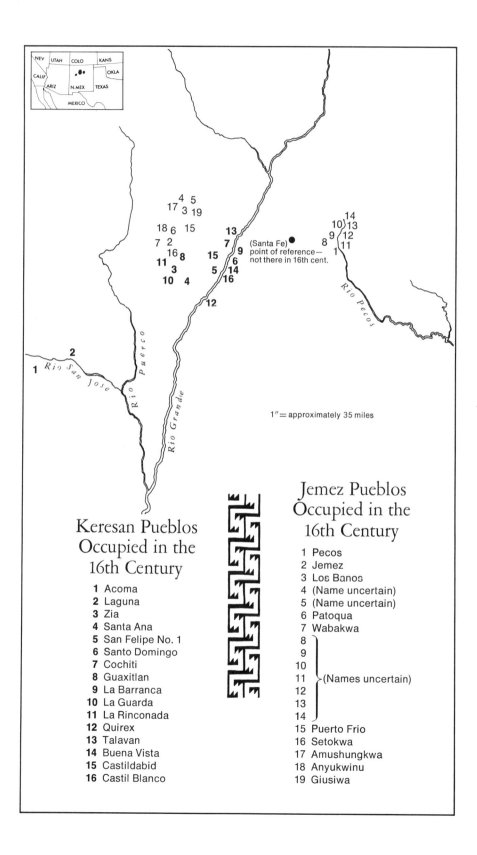

(Santa Fe) ●
point of reference—
not there in 16th cent.

Rio Pecos

Rio Puerco

Rio Grande

Rio San Jose

1″ = approximately 35 miles

Keresan Pueblos Occupied in the 16th Century

1 Acoma
2 Laguna
3 Zia
4 Santa Ana
5 San Felipe No. 1
6 Santo Domingo
7 Cochiti
8 Guaxitlan
9 La Barranca
10 La Guarda
11 La Rinconada
12 Quirex
13 Talavan
14 Buena Vista
15 Castildabid
16 Castil Blanco

Jemez Pueblos Occupied in the 16th Century

1 Pecos
2 Jemez
3 Los Banos
4 (Name uncertain)
5 (Name uncertain)
6 Patoqua
7 Wabakwa
8 ⎫
9 │
10 │
11 ⎬ (Names uncertain)
12 │
13 │
14 ⎭
15 Puerto Frio
16 Setokwa
17 Amushungkwa
18 Anyukwinu
19 Giusiwa

Talavan, near Cochiti.

*Zia,** on Rio Jemez about sixteen miles northwest of Bernalillo.

Keres ceremonials are incomparably spectacular and colorful. White persons are permitted to see some of the seasonal dances, such as the corn dance and some of the animal dances. Katsina ceremonies, however, are closely guarded. An entire pueblo may be closed to visitors, either Anglos, Hispanos, or Indians from other tribes, while they are taking place. Often the katsina rites are conducted in secluded places outside the pueblo. The Keres katsina masks are as cleverly executed and as colorful as those of the Hopi and Zuni. Thirty to fifty elaborate and ingeniously made masks may be used by a katsina cult in a single Keresan pueblo.

A cult in which supernaturals are represented by masks and costumes exists among all Pueblo peoples. Only the cults of the western Pueblos, the Zuni and Hopi, are more complex than those of the Keres. Some western Pueblos admit visitors to kachina ceremonials held in the open plazas. The concern of the Keres and other eastern Pueblos, as Dozier states, "to protect and guard the identity of the cult and its rites is obviously a carryover from the past. Spanish attempts to suppress Pueblo Indian religion focused on the masked rites and the repressive acts of United States government officials in Pueblo ceremonial rites . . . also singled out Katsina activities. The Western Pueblos, because of distance and isolation from Spanish and Anglo population centers, did not experience the full brunt of the repressive measures. It is understandable, therefore, that the Rio Grande Pueblos are more cautious in guarding ceremonial activities, particularly the esoteric rites of the Katsina cult than the Pueblos to the west."

*Still inhabited.

Thousands of persons pass the Keres pueblos on a free-way each year. Those who take the time to stop in them may have the privilege of watching a magnificent public dance and hearing the beautiful singing of a male chorus, but few understand that after centuries of repression the katsina cults still exist in secret and are strong and meaningful to the singers and dancers.

1540 *(cont.)*

Alvarado turned up the Rio Grande in the vicinity of the pueblo of Isleta. Now the time of recorded history had begun for the last of the four Pueblo stocks living in the Southwest—the Tanoans. The people of Isleta belonged to the Tiwa, the largest dialectical group of the Tanoan linguistic family, whose thirty-eight or forty pueblos were scattered over a large part of northern New Mexico.

After Alvarado, traveling up the right bank of the Rio Grande, had passed the site where Albuquerque would stand a century and a half later, more Tiwa settlements were soon encountered. The Spaniards camped near the present community of Bernalillo, and Bigotes was sent with a cross to inform the Pueblos that Alvarado had come among them in peace and in the name of God and the Spanish king. A score of men were surrounded by thousands of Indians, but, obviously, the people of the towns, which the Spaniards called the province of Tiguex, were fully apprised of the powers of the marvelous beasts they rode, and the deadliness of the miraculous weapons they carried that made thunder and belched lightning and smoke. They uttered no threats of resistance, and the only precaution they took was to confine the women and children within the protective, stout walls of the pueblos. Bigotes returned to inform Alvarado that he would be graciously received, and that he and his men would be provided with whatever supplies they might need.

The following day the people of twelve towns, all wearing holiday regalia and their most prized valuables, arrived in a long procession to pay their respects to Alvarado, and he would record: "They marched around our tent, playing a flute, and with an old man for spokesman. In this manner they came inside the tent and presented me with food, cotton cloth and skins . . ."

Alvarado made a trip of inspection. Here is a part of his account, the first ever written about the most populous area of the Pueblo country and the Rio Grande Valley: "This river . . . flows through a broad valley planted with fields of maize and dotted with cottonwood groves. There are twelve pueblos [in Tiguex], whose houses are built of mud and are two storeys high. The natives seem to be good people, more devoted to agriculture than to war." (He would change that opinion before many weeks had passed, when the Tiwa demonstrated that they were courageous and dangerous fighters.) "They have a food supply of maize, beans, melons, and turkeys in great abundance. They clothe themselves in cotton, the skins of cattle, and coats made of turkey feathers, and they wear their hair short . . . the old men are the ones who have the most authority among them. We thought these elders must be wizards, because they said they could ascend to heaven, and other things of that sort." Once more it is apparent that the Tiwa —and probably all other Pueblos who had not yet seen Spaniards—had been briefed by messengers from Zuni and possibly Hopi about the all-powerful Christian God and the significance of the cross. Alvarado's next statement substantiates this conviction. Wherever Fray Padilla erected a cross —many of them very large—the Pueblos "offered their powders and feathers, even the cotton garments they wore. They showed such eagerness that some of them climbed on the backs of others to reach the arms of the crosses to decorate them with plumes and roses. They brought ladders, and while some held them others climbed up to tie the strings in order to fasten the roses with the feathers." This enthusiastic reverence, however, would soon be supplanted by cold indifference, if not violent rejection of the Christian symbols.

Alvarado gave the first description of the Rio Grande Pueblos, but Castaneda wrote a better one when he came along shortly afterward. "In general," he said, "these villages all have the same habits and customs, although some have some things in particular which the others have not.

"They all work together to build the villages, the women being engaged in making the mixture and the walls, while the men bring the wood [timbers] and put it in place. They have no lime, but they make a mixture of ashes, coals, and dirt which is almost as good as mortar, for when the house is to have four stories, they do not make the walls more than half a yard thick. They gather a great pile of twigs of thyme [sagebrush] and sedge grass and set it afire, and when it is half coals and ashes they throw a quantity of dirt and water on it and mix it all together. They make round balls of this, which they use instead of stones after they are dry, fixing them with the same mixture, which comes to be like a stiff clay."

No better description of the intimate life of the people of the Rio Grande at the time the Spaniards first saw them was written than that in Castaneda's invaluable narrative: "Before they are married the young men serve the whole village in general, and fetch the wood that is needed for use, putting it in a pile in the courtyard . . . from which the women take it to carry to their houses.

"The young men live in the estufas, which are in the yards of the village. They are underground, square or round, with pine pillars. Some were seen with twelve pillars and with four in the centre as large as two could stretch around ... The floor was made of large smooth stones, like the baths which they have in Europe. They have a hearth made like the binnacle or compass box of a ship, in which they burn a handful of thyme at a time to keep up the heat, and they can stay in there just as in a bath. The top [of the kiva] was on a level with the ground. Some that were seen were large enough for a game of ball."

Castaneda was a thorough investigator. "When any man wishes to marry," he learned, "it has to be arranged by those who govern. The man has to spin and weave a blanket and place it before the woman, who covers herself with it and becomes his wife. The houses belong to the women, the estufas to the men. If a man repudiates his woman, he has to go to the estufa . . . The women bring up the children and prepare the food.

"The country is so fertile that they do not have to break up the ground the year round, but only have to sow the seed, which is presently covered by the fall of snow, and the ears come up under the snow. In one year they gather enough for seven. A very large number of cranes and wild geese and crows and starlings live on what is sown, and for all this, when they come to sow for another year, the fields are covered with corn which they have not been able to finish gathering."

Castaneda painted a rare picture of Pueblo women:

"They keep the separate houses where they prepare the food for eating and where they grind the meal, very clean. There is a separate room where they have a trough with three stones fixed in stiff clay. Three women go in here, each one having a stone, with which one of them breaks the corn, the next grinds it, and the third grinds it again. They take off their shoes, do up their hair, shake their clothes, and cover their heads before they enter the door. A man sits at the door playing on a fife while they grind, moving the stones to the music and singing together. They grind a large quantity at one time, because they make all their bread of meal soaked in warm water, like wafers. They gather a great quantity of brushwood and dry it to use for cooking all through the year. There are no fruits good to eat in the country, except the pine nuts."

Castaneda found out "several things" from an Indian who had been a captive for a year. One of his questions was "why the young women went entirely naked, however cold it might be? . . . and he told me that the virgins had to go about this way until they took a husband, and that they covered themselves after they had known man."

A peculiar fact stirred Castaneda's interest. Speaking of "cocks with great hanging chins [turkey cocks]," he noted: "When dead, these keep for sixty days, and longer in winter, without losing their feathers or opening, and without any bad smell, and the same is true of dead men. The people . . . had Francisco de Ovando [a Spanish soldier] in Tiguex for forty days, after he was dead, and when the village was captured, he was found among their dead, whole and without any other wound except the one which killed him, white as snow, without any bad smell."

By signs, Alvarado was informed that more pueblos would be found along the river for more than fifty leagues. He sent a dispatch to Coronado in which he urged him to make the bountifully supplied towns of Tiguex Province winter headquarters for the entire expedition. Fray Padilla concurred in the declaration that it was far superior to Cibola, where Coronado had tentatively decided to remain until spring.

Alvarado estimated that there were some eighty pueblos on or adjacent to the Rio Grande north of Isleta. He must have seen many of them as he continued to travel up the river. Between the towns of Tiguex and the most northern Tiwa pueblos in New Mexico, Picuris and Taos, were the settlements of the Tewa group of the Tanoan linguistic family, such historically famous pueblos as San Ildefonso, Tesuque, Santa Clara and San Juan.

Bigotes continued to prove himself an able ambassador. In every town visited, the Spaniards were hospitably received and given presents. At Taos, where the weather was cold, Bigotes induced the elders to offer the visitors lodging inside the pueblo. Alvarado and his men entered, but soon came out and made camp in the open, where they could be close to their precious horses, and where, undoubtedly, there were fewer unfamiliar smells.

From Taos Alvarado set out to see the cows. A few days later, Bigotes led the Spaniards into his home town, the great pueblo of Cicuye (Pecos), on the Pecos River. This celebrated complex stood on the main trail to the Great Plains. Only Taos surpassed it as a trading center. To it with buffalo hides, pemmican, jerky, tallow, and other products came the Plains Apache. To it to obtain these articles came Pueblos with cotton cloth, turquoises, pottery utensils, cosmetics, baskets, blankets, and all manner of ornaments.

The uniqueness of Pecos's architecture is revealed in Castaneda's account: "It is square, situated on a rock, with a large court or yard situated in the middle, containing the estufas [kivas]. The houses are all alike, four stories high. One can go over the top of the whole village without there being a street to hinder. There are corridors going all around it at the first two stories, by which one can go around the whole village. These are like outside balconies, and they are able to protect themselves under these. The houses do not have doors below, but they use ladders, which can be lifted up like a drawbridge. . . . The houses that open on the plain are right back of those that open on the court, and in time of war they go through those behind them. The village is enclosed by a low wall of stone. There is a spring of water inside. . . . The people of this village boast that no one has been able to conquer them." This was not an idle boast. Plains Indians had conquered and pillaged numerous towns, but their assaults on Pecos had been repulsed.

Alvarado saw the cows, "such multitudes of them that I do not know what to compare them with unless it be the fish in the sea," but his trip to the Great Plains was prologue to the greatest frustration of the Coronado expedition.

In Pecos he learned of the slave trade that existed between Pueblos and Great Plains tribes,* and unfortunately he became acquainted with two captive Kansas Indians. One of them, called Turk "because he looked like one," was from "the province of Quivera," and the other, dubbed Ysopete, was a native of "the province of Harahey," which purportedly lay some distance beyond Quivera. When Bigotes decided he was weary after more than forty days of ambassadorial efforts, Alvarado "borrowed" Turk and Ysopete to guide him to the buffalo.

Somewhere along the Canadian River, near the border between Texas and New Mexico, Turk began to play his fateful role. Evidently possessing a talent as a linguist, he had quickly learned a few important Spanish words, such as *oro, plata,* and *metal.* Moreover, he apparently understood that the Spaniards desired these treasures more than anything else. Embellishing his limited Spanish vocabulary

---

*It was carried on until the nineteenth century, some years after the American conquest of the Southwest.

with unmistakable signs, he told Alvarado that instead of going eastward along the Canadian River, the trail that led to the northeast should be followed, for it would take them to Quivera, a fabulous land in which "everything they were looking for was abundant, gold, silver and *metallic* fabrics." Both Bigotes and Cacique were aware of the wealth of Quivera, declared Turk, because when he had been captured he had with him a gold bracelet and they had taken it from him.

Blinded by gold-madness, Alvarado did not suspect that Turk had concocted his story with the hope of getting back to his homeland and escaping captivity. He believed him, and abruptly turned about for Pecos, excited by the prospect of taking the golden bracelet from Bigotes or Cacique. Buffalo could wait.

In Pecos, Bigotes and Cacique stared in astonishment at Alvarado when he demanded the bracelet. Turk, they swore, was lying, and they "denied in all possible ways that they had any such ornament." Disappointed and angered, Alvarado tricked Bigotes and Cacique into his tent and put them in chains, announcing that he would take them back with Turk and Ysopete and let Coronado question them. A brief rough and tumble ensued. Some Pecos warriors, resentful of the treatment accorded their leaders, fired arrows and berated Alvarado for violating the friendship shown him. No one was seriously hurt, however. A few shots from harquebuses stopped the violence.

Then Turk escaped. Alvarado vowed he would not free Bigotes and Cadique until the fugitive was recaptured. When Bigotes promised that if allowed to leave with a few men he would bring Turk back, he was freed. Cacique was held as a hostage. Bigotes kept his word, and Turk was soon retaken.

Again Alvarado pleaded that the bracelet be turned over

to him, but in vain. At last, he gave up, and with Bigotes, Cacique, Turk, and Ysopete in collars and chains, he and his soldiers left Pecos on the road to the Rio Grande. He would let Coronado decide who was the liar.

When he reached Tiguez, Alvarado was surprised to find Captain Cardenas there. Coronado had been greatly cheered by Alvarado's and Fray Padilla's message praising Tiguex, and had sent Cardenas and some men to arrange winter lodgings for the entire expedition. Alvarado decided to wait with his prisoners in Tiguex for Coronado instead of taking them on to Cibola.

It was late fall, snow had fallen on the mountains, and the winds of the high Rio Grande country chilled one's bones. When Cardenas had arrived in Tiguex, says Bolton, he found the Tiwa friendly, "and began to prepare lodgings for the Spaniards outside the pueblos, in order not to cause the natives unnecessary hardship. But when cold weather came on accompanied by snow, his men from the tropics were in distress. So he asked the Indians to vacate one of the twelve pueblos—six on each side of the river—in order that his soldiers might be quartered in it, requesting the displaced natives to find homes for the time being in other towns. The Indians complied without resistance—though not without resentment—vacating the pueblo of Alcanfor.*
... Cardenas and his shivering soldiers moved into the town and began to prepare housing in it for the entire army which, when all assembled, would number some three hundred men, not counting Indian allies and servants."

When the main army reached Cibola, Coronado ordered that it follow him to Tiguex after resting twenty days. He left with some thirty picked troopers for the Rio Grande. The weather was extremely cold, water seemed to have

*On the west bank of the Rio Grande at Bernalillo.

vanished from the land, and both men and animals suffered greatly from thirst for nearly three days until they reached snowy mountains.

For an unknown reason, Coronado did not follow the customary trail to Tiguex. When he reached the Rio San Jose, he turned down it. This course took him to the Rio Grande at a point considerably south of his destination, probably a short distance above the present little town of Bernardo, but this is uncertain. In any case, he came to a group of eight pueblos on the Rio Grande to which the name province of Tutahaco was given. Thus, he and his men were the first Spaniards to reach territory occupied by the Piro group of the Tanoan linguistic family. Learning that more Piro pueblos were to be found farther south along the river and east of it, he assigned Captain Francisco de Ovando and several soldiers to visit them.

Turning up the Rio Grande, he paused in Isleta and several other towns before reaching Alcanfor, where winter quarters had been prepared for him.

Alvarado wasted no time bringing Turk before his commander. The story the prisoner told Coronado electrified him. El Turco's vivid imagination obviously had not been impaired by the uncomfortable iron collar he had worn for a month or more; indeed, if anything, it had greatly improved. He not only told Coronado what he had related about the richness of Quivera to Alvarado on the buffalo plains, but he added touches that brought wild gleams to the eyes of all who heard his tale.

He told them that in Quivera was a great river two leagues wide "in which there were fishes as big as horses, and large numbers of very big canoes, with more than twenty rowers on a side, and that they carried sails, and that their lords sat on the poop under awnings, and on the prow they had a great golden eagle. He said also that the lord of that country took his afternoon nap under a great tree on which were hung a great number of little gold bells, which put him to sleep as they swung in the air. He said also that everyone had their ordinary dishes made of wrought plate, and the jugs and bowls were of gold. Farther inland were even richer kingdoms, called Harahey and Guas."

Coronado demanded the golden bracelet that Turk said he had owned. When Bigotes and Cacique once more stoutly denied that they had ever seen such a thing, they were taken into a plaza of the pueblo and dogs were set upon them. Both were bitten, but they could not be made to confess having the valuable ornament.

Nevertheless, Coronado believed that they and not Turk were liars. He was filled with new hope. If only half of what Turk had said were true, Montezuma's treasure and the gold and silver of the Incas would be mere pocket money by comparison.

As soon as travel was possible in the spring, he would start for Quivera. The old dream had been reborn, glowing with new life in a golden aura.

The Tanoans were artists and craftsmen of note. Especially skillful were the murals on the walls of their kivas. One of the most famous examples of this art medium ever discovered by archaeologists was the paintings at the Tiwa pueblo of Kuaua. Represented in the murals were men in ceremonial costumes, animals, fishes, birds, pottery vessels, corn, gourds, and clouds from which rain was falling. Life forms were depicted with great fidelity. Many colors were used.

In modern times the Navajo had been eulogized for their magnificent sand paintings, but they learned the art from the Tiwa and Tewa groups of the Tanoans. These sand paintings, Driver states, "were part of the sacred altars in

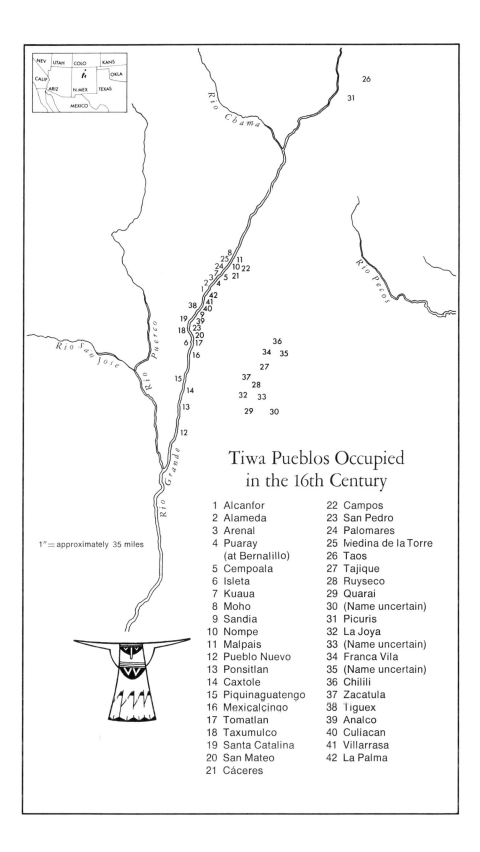

Tiwa Pueblos Occupied in the 16th Century

1"= approximately 35 miles

1 Alcanfor	22 Campos
2 Alameda	23 San Pedro
3 Arenal	24 Palomares
4 Puaray	25 Medina de la Torre
(at Bernalillo)	26 Taos
5 Cempoala	27 Tajique
6 Isleta	28 Ruyseco
7 Kuaua	29 Quarai
8 Moho	30 (Name uncertain)
9 Sandia	31 Picuris
10 Nompe	32 La Joya
11 Malpais	33 (Name uncertain)
12 Pueblo Nuevo	34 Franca Vila
13 Ponsitlan	35 (Name uncertain)
14 Caxtole	36 Chilili
15 Piquinaguatengo	37 Zacatula
16 Mexicalcingo	38 Tiguex
17 Tomatlan	39 Analco
18 Taxumulco	40 Culiacan
19 Santa Catalina	41 Villarrasa
20 San Mateo	42 La Palma
21 Cáceres	

the kivas and were made on the floor in front of the fetishes
and wall paintings associated with the altars. Sand or ochre
of various colors, corn pollen, pulverized flour petals, and
pulverized green leaves were employed as dry pigments in
painting the religious symbols. Handfuls of the dry materials were carefully sprinkled from between the thumb and
forefinger to form the lined and solid figures of the paintings. These figures were conventionalized representations
of the sun, moon, stars, earth, mountain lion, snake, or
kachina; or of something associated with spirits . . . The
purpose of these sand paintings was to influence the spirits
to bring rain, plentiful crops, good health, and other good
things to man.''

As a form of aboriginal art, sand paintings were executed
nowhere else in the world.

The Tanoans were not only expert weavers and potters,
but displayed ingenuity and artistic taste in coloring and
decorating these products. The designs were usually geo-
metrical, but some suggested animals and birds, and
symmetry, contrast, and repetition characterized the oldest
artifacts which have been recovered. Cloth and tapesty
were created in a variety of patterns. Some materials were
dyed before being used, but the designs were painted on
others after the weaving had been completed.

The Tanoan linguistic family comprised four dialectical
groups, Tiwa, Tewa, Jemez, and Piro.*

Tiwa pueblos inhabited in the sixteenth century were:

Alameda, * on the Rio Grande above Albuquerque.

Alcanfor, near Bernalillo.

---

*Coronado's men were the first explorers to reach the Tanoan pueblos, but not
all the names listed were applied by them. Some of the names appear in the
accounts of later priests and adventurers. Pueblos designated by an asterisk are
still occupied. See footnote, page 107.

Analco, on the Rio Grande above San Pedro.

Arenal, two leagues above Alcanfor.

Caceres, on the Rio Grande above Malpais.

Campos, on the Rio Grande above Caceres.

Caxtole, on the east side of the Rio Grande above Ponsitlan.

Cempoala, on the Rio Grande above Puaray.

Chilili, thirty miles southeast of Albuquerque.

Culiacan, on the Rio Grande above Analco.

Franca Vila, east of the Manzano Mountains between Chilili and Quarai.

(Name uncertain), east of Franca Vila.

Isleta,* on the Rio Grande thirteen miles south of Albuquerque.

Kuaua, on the Rio Grande above Bernalillo.

La Joya, on the eastern slope of the Manzano Mountains.

(Name uncertain), east of La Joya.

La Palma, on the Rio Grande above Villarassa.

Malpais, on the Rio Grande above Nompe.

Medina de la Torre, on the Rio Grande above Palomares.

Mexicalcingo, on the Rio Grande opposite Piquinaguatengo.

Moho, on the Rio Grande five leagues north of Arenal.

Nompe, on the Rio Grande above Cempoala.

Palomares, on the Rio Grande opposite Campos.

Picuris,* forty miles north of Santa Fe.

Piquinaguatengo, on the Rio Grande opposite Castole.

Ponsitlan, location uncertain, but probably near the Piro pueblo of El Hosso.

Puaray, at Bernalillo.

Pueblo Nuevo, probably near the Piro pueblo of La Pedrosa.

---

*Still inhabited.

Quari, thirty miles east of the Rio Grande in the Manzano Mountains.

Ruyseco, on the eastern slope of the Manzano Mountains.

(Name uncertain), east of Ruyseco.

Sandia, * on the Rio Grande fourteen miles north of Albuquerque.

San Mateo, on the Rio Grande opposite Santa Catalina.

San Pedro, on the Rio Grande above Santa Catalina.

Santa Catalina, on the Rio Grande above Taxumulco.

Tajique, thirty miles northeast of Belen.

Taos, * on both sides of the Taos River.

Taxumulco, on the Rio Grande opposite Tomatlan.

Tiguex, near Bernalillo on the Rio Grande.

Tomatlan, on the Rio Grande above Mexicalcingo.

Villarassa, on the Rio Grande above Culiacan.

Zacatula, on the eastern slope of the Manzano Mountains.

"The Tewa were living in Sipofene beneath Sandy Place Lake far to the north," writes Ortiz, a social anthropologist born in San Juan pueblo. "The world under the lake was like this one, but it was dark. Supernaturals, men, and animals lived together at this time, and death was unknown. Among the supernaturals were the first mothers of all the Tewa, known as *Blue Corn Woman, near to summer,* or the Summer mother, and *White Corn Maiden, near to ice,* the Winter mother.

"These mothers asked one of the men present to go forth and explore the way by which the people might leave the lake."

The explorer made four trips, one in each direction, but saw nothing but "mist and haze," and reported that the world above was *ochu* (green or unripe). Sent out again, he "came upon an open place and saw all the *tsiwi* (predatory

*Still inhabited.

mammals and carrion-eating birds) gathered there. . . . On seeing the man these animals rushed him, knocked him down, and scratched him badly. Then they spoke, telling him: 'Get up! We are your friends.' His wounds vanished immediately. The animals gave him a bow and arrows and a quiver, dressed him in buckskin, painted his face black, and tied the feathers of the carrion-eaters on his hair. Finally they told him. 'You have been accepted. These things we have given you are what you shall use henceforth. Now you are ready to go.' "

When he returned to the people below, the first explorer of the "Above" went as "Mountain Lion, or Hunt Chief. This is how the first *Made* person came into being."

The Hunt Chief appointed a Summer Chief and a Winter Chief by handing each an ear of white corn. They became the next "Made" persons, and they were to lead the people to the "Above."

Six pairs of brothers called *Towa é* were sent out. Each pair was a different color. The blue, yellow, red, and white pairs reported seeing mountains in each of the cardinal directions. The dark pair saw a large star in the eastern sky. The *all-colored* pair saw a rainbow.

The people started. Summer Chief led the way, but found the surface soft mud. When Winter Chief stepped on it, the ground hardened. And the people began to emerge from the dark underworld. But many became ill, and all returned below, where the original corn mothers and other supernaturals had remained. Summer Chief and Winter Chief agreed that the people were not yet complete, and "something else was needed."

Fear of ghosts, witchcraft, and sorcery is intense in all Pueblo peoples. Each tribe has its own myth telling how these frightening practices were discovered. An excellent example is the Tewa myth.

According to Ortiz, when the people returned to their

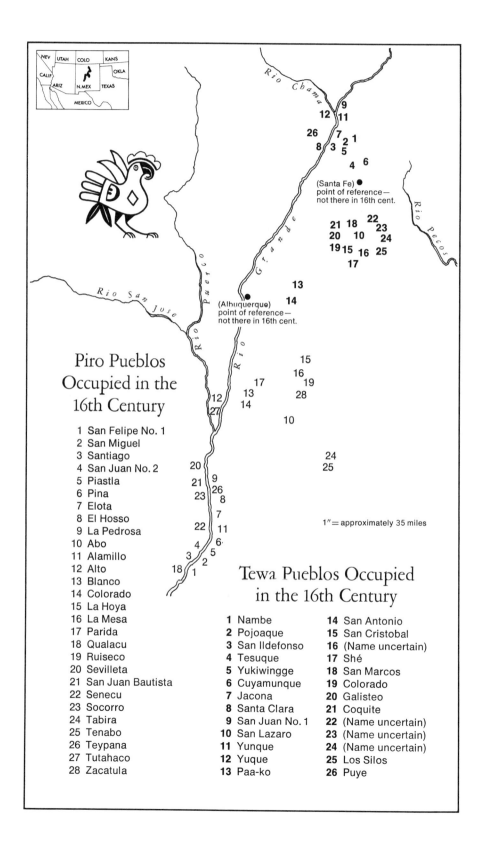

NEV | UTAH | COLO | KANS
CALIF | ARIZ | N.MEX | OKLA
TEXAS
MEXICO

Rio Chama

12 9 11

26 7 1
8 3 2 5

4 6

(Santa Fe) ●
point of reference—
not there in 16th cent.

Rio Pecos

21 18 22 23
20 10 24
19 15 16 25
17

Rio San Jose

Rio Puerco

Rio Grande

13
14

(Albuquerque)
point of reference—
not there in 16th cent.

15
16 19
17 28
13
14
10

12
27

20
21
23 26 8
7
22 11
4 6
3 2 5
18 1

24
25

1″ = approximately 35 miles

Piro Pueblos Occupied in the 16th Century

1 San Felipe No. 1
2 San Miguel
3 Santiago
4 San Juan No. 2
5 Piastla
6 Pina
7 Elota
8 El Hosso
9 La Pedrosa
10 Abo
11 Alamillo
12 Alto
13 Blanco
14 Colorado
15 La Hoya
16 La Mesa
17 Parida
18 Qualacu
19 Ruiseco
20 Sevilleta
21 San Juan Bautista
22 Senecu
23 Socorro
24 Tabira
25 Tenabo
26 Teypana
27 Tutahaco
28 Zacatula

Tewa Pueblos Occupied in the 16th Century

1 Nambe
2 Pojoaque
3 San Ildefonso
4 Tesuque
5 Yukiwingge
6 Cuyamunque
7 Jacona
8 Santa Clara
9 San Juan No. 1
10 San Lazaro
11 Yunque
12 Yuque
13 Paa-ko

14 San Antonio
15 San Cristobal
16 (Name uncertain)
17 Shé
18 San Marcos
19 Colorado
20 Galisteo
21 Coquite
22 (Name uncertain)
23 (Name uncertain)
24 (Name uncertain)
25 Los Silos
26 Puye

home beneath the lake because so many were ill, "Hunt chief opened up Summer chief's corn mother. He discovered that the hollow core was filled with pebbles, ashes, and cactus spines. The Hunt chief replaced these with seeds and declared that one among the people . . . was a witch, for the items discovered in the corn mother were recognized as items of witchcraft. This, then, marked the beginning of witchcraft and other forms of evil. In order to combat these and to make the people well, the Ke (medicine man) was created as the fourth *Made* person."

After being obliged to return to the underworld three more times to resolve serious problems in their characters and cultural structure, the Tewa felt they were complete, and they emerged and moved southward along the Rio Grande. Standing watch on the four mountains of the directions were the Tow é, the four pairs of blue, yellow, red, and white brothers.

Tewa pueblos inhabited in the sixteenth century were:

Colorado, near San Cristobal.

Coquite, near Galisteo.

Cuyamunque, on Tesuque Creek fifteen miles north of Santa Fe.

Galisteo, in the upper Galisteo Basin.

(Name uncertain), near Galisteo.

(Name uncertain), near Galisteo.

(Name uncertain), near Galisteo.

Jacona, on Pojoaque Creek, west of Nambe.

Los Silos, in the Galisteo Basin.

Ohke (see San Juan).

*Nambe,** on the Nambe River sixteen miles north of Santa Fe.

Paa-ko, between Sandia and the San Pedro Mountains.

*Still inhabited.

*Pojoaque,** eighteen miles northwest of Santa Fe.

Puyé, on the Rio Grande, ten miles west of Espanola.

San Antonio, between Sandia and the San Pedro Mountains.

San Cristobal, in the upper Galisteo Basin.

(Name uncertain), near San Cristobal.

San Gabriel (see Yuque).

*San Ildefonso,** on the Rio Grande twenty miles northwest of Santa Fe.

Shé, five miles south of Galisteo.

*Santa Clara,** thirty miles north of Santa Fe on the Rio Grande.

San Marcos, in the Galisteo Basin eighteen miles south of Santa Fe.

*Tesuque,** eight miles north of Santa Fe.

San Juan (Number One) or *Ohke,** on the Rio Grande near the mouth of Rio Chama.

San Lazaro, twelve miles south of Lamy.

Yunque, on the Rio Grande at the mouth of Rio Chama.

Yuque or *San Gabriel,* on the Rio Grande at the mouth of Rio Chama.

Traditions of the Jemez group of the Tanoan family relate that they had their origin far to the north of New Mexico, at a lagoon called Uabunatota—apparently identical with the Sandy Place Lake of the Tewa. From the lagoon they drifted southward slowly over a long period of time, at last making their homes in Guadalupe and San Diego canyons on upper tributaries of the Rio Jemez. Later they moved into the Sandy Valley of the Rio Jemez. It was there that members of the Coronado expedition found them.

Some of the Jemez, however, had continued on eastward and had built a number of pueblos in the upper valley of

*Still inhabited.

the Rio Pecos and the high surrounding mountains. One of these was the famous Pecos Pueblo, which Alvarado and his soldiers were the first white men to see.

The Jemez of the Jemez Valley lived in numerous relatively small towns, instead of congregating in a single large pueblo that could have been more easily defended, as did other Pueblo peoples. Archaeologists attribute this division of the tribe to two factors: (1) cultivable areas in the sandy Jemez Valley were small and at considerable distances from each other, and (2) apparently the Jemez enjoyed amicable relations with their powerful neighbors to the west of them, the predatory Navajo, who periodically raided the towns of most other Pueblo tribes.

Jemez pueblos inhabited in the sixteenth century were:

Amushungkwa, on a mesa west of Jemez Hot Springs.

Anyukwinu, north of Jemez Pueblo.

Giusiwa, near Jemez Hot Springs.

*Jemez,** thirty miles northwest of Bernalillo.

Los Banos, near Jemez Hot Springs.

(Name uncertain), near Los Banos.

(Name uncertain), near Los Banos.

Patoqua, six miles north of Jemez Pueblo.

Pecos, on the Pecos River near the town of the same name. (Castaneda mentions, but does not name, seven other Jemez pueblos in the "snowy mountains" north of Pecos.)

Puerto Frio, in the Jemez Valley.

Setokwa, two miles south of Jemez Pueblo.

Wabakwa, on the mesa north of Jemez Pueblo.

The Piro group of the Tanoan linguistic family was divided into two branches. The pueblos of one division stretched along the Rio Grande from the present com

*Still inhabited.

munity of San Marcial northward to within fifty miles of Albuquerque. These Piro, with abundant water available to them, enjoyed the benefits of a bountiful agriculture. Such was not the case of their relatives, sometimes called Tompiro, who inhabited territory east of the Rio Grande in the vicinity of salt lagoons, or salinas. Theirs was a true desert culture, for they were grouped in an area extending for only twenty-five miles southeast from the Arroyo de Abo, the only perennial stream in the region. Some of the pueblos in this arid reach were entirely dependent on stored rain water.

Long before the arrival of the first Spanish explorers, the Piro suffered greatly from Apache raiders, who swept down on them from both the Llano Estacado on the east and the Gila River country to the west. A number of their pueblos had been abandoned because of this scourge before the beginning of the historical period. Hundreds of them were slain by Spanish soldiers and more pueblos were burned. Within a century after the colonization of New Mexico, almost every Piro pueblo was in ruins, and the few Piro still alive had scattered to other tribes or had moved to a mission near El Paso. There they were soon absorbed by the Mexican population, and their identity forever vanished.

Piro pueblos inhabited in the sixteenth century were:

Abo, twenty miles south of Manzano.

Alamillo, twelve miles north of Socorro.

Alto, six miles south of Belen.

Blanco, east of the Rio Grande on the western rim of Medano, or the great sand flow.

Colorado, adjoining Blanco.

El Hosso, above Elota.

Elota, above Pina.

La Hoya, east of the Manzano Mountains between Chilili and Quarai.

La Mesa, near La Hoya.

La Pedrosa, near El Hosso.

Parida, adjoining Blanco.

Piastla, on the Rio Grande opposite San Juan (Number Two).

Pina, above Piastla.

Qualicu, near San Marcial.

Ruiseco, in the vicinity of La Hoya.

San Juan Bautista, sixteen miles below Sevilleta on the Rio Grande.

San Felipe (Number Two), near San Marcial.

San Juan (Number Two), on the Rio Grande above San Miguel.

San Miguel, two leagues above San Felipe.

Santiago, on the Rio Grande opposite San Miguel.

Senecu, at San Antonio.

Sevilleta, twenty miles above Socorro.

Socorro, at Socorro.

Tabira, twenty-five miles south east of Abo.

Tenabo, near Tabira.

Teypana, near Socorro.

Tutabaco, near the confluence of the Rio Grande and the Rio San Jose.

Zacatula, in the vicinity of La Hoya (may have been Tewa.)

1540 *(cont.)*

Isolated incidents, although troublesome, were like small scattered clouds. Individually they posed no serious threat, but when driven together they became a dark mass presaging dire consequences.

A Spaniard entered a pueblo, discovered an attractive

young woman alone in her home, and forced her to submit to his advances. Her husband and other headmen of the village registered strong protests, but received no satisfaction. The culprit was not punished, not even reprimanded, because he was wealthy, politically influential, and a brother of a high official in Mexico City.

The dog-baiting and other brutalities suffered by Bigotes, Turk, Ysopete, and Cacique, an elderly man, were bitterly resented by the Tiwa.

The hospitality they extended quickly changed to unfriendliness when the Indians came to realize that they would be burdened with several hundred house guests for the entire winter.

Without so much as a polite request, the Spaniards helped themselves to food supplies, and the Pueblos could envision themselves hungering, their turkey flocks gone and their storage bins empty, long before the advent of spring.

The high Rio Grande country lay under a thick mantle of snow, and Coronado sent contingents of shivering soldiers to each pueblo to obtain clothing and robes. "As they were in very great need," said Castaneda, "they did not give the natives a chance to consult about it, but when they came to a village they demanded what they had to give. . ." If the demands of the clothing collectors were not met immediately, they took whatever appeared to be useful, and "these people could do nothing except take off their own cloaks and give them . . . which caused not a little hard feeling."

A soldier in rags was severely beaten when he attempted to take some garments. Four of his attackers were taken by other soldiers before Cardenas, but Cardenas refused to punish them, and cautioned the men to be more courteous and patient in dealing with the natives. It was clothing that was needed, not more trouble.

Tiwa men held long meetings in their kivas. Many of them advocated violent retaliation against the invaders, but for a time calmer leaders were able to prevent it. Not all the angry persons could be controlled, however, and brawls occurred with increasing frequency.

The crisis came one morning when a Mexican who had been guarding the horse herd ran into Alcanfor badly wounded. One of his companion guards had been killed, he said, and a group of Indians had stolen many of the horses and mules. Coronado ordered Cardenas to take eight soldiers, pursue the thieves, and kill them. This was open rebellion that must be quickly put down before it spread. This was an affront by savages to the viceroy of New Spain that could not be tolerated. The people of Tiguex must be made to understand that they were subjects of his Majesty.

The simmering pot had suddenly reached the boiling point. The pueblo of Alameda had been deserted. On the banks of the Rio Grande were twenty-five or thirty dead horses and mules. Indians on the terraces of other pueblos shouted insults and made menacing gestures at Cardenas and his men. The entrance to the pueblo of Arenal, two leagues upstream from the Spanish headquarters in Alcanfor, was barricaded. As the Spaniards rode up to it, they came upon more dead horses, and they "heard a great hullabaloo inside, with horses running around as in a bullring and the natives shooting arrows at them." Cardenas attempted to make himself heard, asking for a council with Pueblo leaders, and shouting that the horse thieves would be forgiven if the rebellion was halted, but "the Indians were all up in arms, and he could do nothing, because they refused to come out in the open, and as the pueblos were strong they could not be harmed." Meanwhile, it was learned that the pueblo of Moho also had been closed by a palisade and the inhabitants were prepared to fight.

Coronado assembled his officers and asked for their opinions. The situation was extremely perilous, for only the vanguard was in Alcanfor, and the main army was not due to arrive for several days. Less than a hundred Spaniards were surrounded by several thousand Indians.

Fray Padilla and Fray Antonio were asked what procedure they advocated, and they replied that while "it was not permissible" for the Spaniards to kill anyone, they would "approve and consider appropriate whatever the general might do." Coronado called for a vote. It was unanimous in favor of an immediate attack, first on Arenal, and when the revolt had been put down there, Moho would be the next target.

Cardenas was given command of the assault. His orders from Corondo were simple: take none of the rebels alive.

Arenal was surrounded by horsemen, so that no one might escape. Then soldiers began their fight to gain the terraces. Throughout the day the battle raged. A score of Spaniards and Mexican Indians had been wounded by arrows before attackers were able to scale the lower walls. "Our men were on top of the houses in great danger," but "they made some good shots with their crossbows and muskets." How many defenders were slain in the assault of the first day is not known.

Throughout the night the soldiers held their positions on top of the pueblo. In the early morning, Cardenas again attempted to persuade the Indians to surrender, but the reply came in the form of war cries, and the attack was renewed. Using logs as battering rams, Spaniards broke through walls and built fires. Smoke filled the pueblo, and the suffocated people were forced to vacate it. Most of them emerged on the highest terraces, "begging for peace."

Spanish officers on the roof, said Castaneda, "answered the Indians with the same signs they were making for peace, which was to make a cross. They then put down their arms and received pardon." The men who had surrendered were herded from the pueblo and held before the big tent Cardenas had erected as his field headquarters.

The atrocity that followed marked the beginning of a bloody struggle that would not end for nearly three centuries. The terrible scenes at Arenal would be duplicated in larger measures in later years, but none, no matter their extent, would be any more barbaric, any more cruel and inhumane.

Cardenas would claim that he knew nothing of the pardon granted by his men on the roof, but assumed the Pueblos had "surrendered of their own accord because they had been conquered." Let Castaneda tell the tragic story: "As Cardenas had been ordered by Coronado not to take them alive, but to make an example of them so that the other natives would fear the Spaniards, he ordered two hundred stakes prepared at once to burn them alive. . . Then when the enemies saw that the Spaniards were binding them and beginning to roast them, about a hundred men who were in the tent began to struggle and defend themselves . . . Our men who were on foot attacked the tent on all sides, so that there was great confusion around it, and then the horsemen chased those who escaped. As the country was level, not a man of them remained alive, unless it was some who remained hidden in the village and escaped that night to spread throughout the country the news that the strangers did not respect the peace they had made, which afterward proved a great misfortune. After this was over, it began to snow . . ."

Coronado had sent his prisoners, Bigotes, Cacique, Turk, and Ysopete, under strong guard, to witness the carnage in the hope that they would be convinced that a similar fate awaited them, and would reveal the whereabouts of the golden bracelet. The scheme failed, for there was no golden bracelet.

On to Moho!

The main army had arrived at Alcanfor, and Coronado organized a strong striking force, which he would lead himself. He had a surprise coming.

Moho was far more inpregnable than Arenal. The largest of the Tiguex pueblos, it stood on an elevation overlooking the Rio Grande. The walls were massive and high, the entrances narrow and twisting.

Coronado established his camp at a nearby spring, and then made a personal appeal to the people crowding the terraces to surrender and guaranteed them amnesty. His pleas were greeted with obscene gestures and filthy oaths shouted at him by both men and women. The people of Tiguex had had all they wanted of Spanish promises. They were prepared to fight to the death, and that was what they did.

The battle of Moho began late in December. Unlike Arenal, which had been destroyed in little more than two days, it soon changed from a continuing fight to a siege. Castaneda said it "lasted fifty days, during which time several assaults were made." Actually, however, it lasted some eighty days, and none of the assaults were successful.

Bolton, drawing on numerous sources, wrote of the initial attack: "The Spaniards first attempted to open a breach in the pueblo wall. Having broken through the outside coat of mortar, they discovered that the palisade was made of the trunks of trees firmly planted in the ground and interwoven with poles and willows, and so strong that it withstood blows they gave it with crowbars, logs or anything else available. Meanwhile, ladders were placed against the walls, and some fifty Spaniards, in the face of desperate resistance, and fighting their way every inch, managed to clamber up to the terraces. The Indians, preparing for just such an emergency, had assembled a large supply of stones, which they now hurled at the invaders so effectively that many were stretched on the ground."

The terraces, moreover, were not continous, but had gaps in them. This clever design made it impossible to go from one terrace to another without entering the pueblo, a feat none of the attackers was able to accomplish. Arrows rained on the Spaniards from wall slits and portholes, so well aimed that many were quickly wounded, and all soldiers who had managed to scale the wall were forced to retreat.

Then it was discovered that the arrows were poisonous, for wounds began to fester, and wounded men retched and screamed in agony before they died. Castaneda, who took part in this fight but was unscathed except for bruises, said nearly a hundred Spaniards were struck by arrows. Another account states that the venom was "thought to have come from rattlesnakes . . . for the Indians shut vipers in willow vessels and poked them with arrows so they would bite the points and make them poisonous."

The weather was very cold, and snow storms came frequently; the soldiers huddled about their campfires, which encircled the pueblo, and bitter winds swept over the great mesas and through the canyons. The Rio Grande was a river of ice, and their misery and frustration were unrelieved as the first weeks of the new year slowly dragged away.

Pueblo shamans and "doctors" were in many respects as skillful as the so-called physicians and surgeons of the sixteenth century who participated in Spanish conquests. Indeed, in treating some ailments—and, in particular, wounds—they were more knowledgeable and successful.

Constant burning sunlight, dry desert air, and a nourishing diet of proteins, fats, vegetables, and wild fruits contributed to the normal good health of the Pueblos. Viral and communicable diseases, such as smallpox, measles, scarlet fever, diphtheria, tuberculosis, and syphilis, were unknown among them until after the invasion of their country by Europeans and Mexican Indians who had been exposed to these virulent afflictions. The Pueblos, however, were no more free of native illnesses than any other Indians. They were not, for example, immune to arthritis, neuralgia, pleurisy, pneumonia, and various functional disorders. Ophthalmic conditions due to smoke and sand, and osteomyelitis and periostitis due to bone injury and infection, were suffered by them.

The culture of the Pueblos was advanced far beyond that of many tribes, and they displayed practicality and common sense in their medical treatments. Their knowledge of the medicinal qualities of indigenous plants was extensive. The Spanish learned much from them.

Through communications with Mexican Indians and as a result of long experience, the Pueblos possessed many effective remedies for internal disorders. According to Quebbeman, they applied splints to fractures and dislocations, cleansed wounds with water or the decoction of some plant, and employed dressings of lint and leaves. They had antidotes for snake bites and the stings of poisonous insects, curing potions for ague, inflammatory fevers, sore throat, indigestion, convulsions, and toothache, and herbal prescriptions used especially for the relief of women recently delivered. They could save a person from rattlesnake bite, but apparently this miraculous remedy was not made known to Coronado's men wounded by arrows poisoned with rattlesnake venom in the battle of Tiguex.

Several types of deadly poison were applied to arrowheads. The Spaniards had no really dependable cures for any of them. Castaneda tells of one instance when several soldiers shot by arrows dipped in the sap of a venomous tree died in horrible agony, their flesh swiftly rotting and falling from their bones. Indian medicine, however, saved others from a similar fate. He cites the case of a soldier named

Mesa who was wounded by an arrow, "but did not die, although it was a deadly wound infected with the fresh poison and it was more than two hours before he was attended to . . ." The cure, obviously supplied by friendly Indians, was quince juice. Mesa lived, but the poison "had left its mark upon him. The skin rotted and fell off until it left the bones and sinews bare, with a horrible smell. The wound was in the wrist, and the poison had reached as far as the shoulder when he was cured. The skin on all this fell off."

"Sixteenth century surgeons cut for stones," says Quebbeman, "did trephining operations, excised external cancerous growths, repaired anal fistulas, drained plural exudate, and dressed wounds. Some patients survived."

When it came to wounds, however, methods of treatment used by the Spanish surgeons were no more advanced than those of the Pueblos. Missionaries and Spanish doctors were greatly impressed and frequently astounded by the efficacy of the Pueblos' ministrations. Indians gave to the world's pharmacopoeia such invaluable drugs as cinchona, cacao, ipecac, jalap, cobaiba and sarsaparilla.

Neglect of problems of sanitation cannot be cited as a major cause of disease among the Pueblos. They were not unclean, either in their persons or in their manner of living. Numerous early documents attest to the cleanliness of their dwellings. Pueblo women generally took pride in their housekeeping, and prevented refuse from accumulating in their apartments.

"The villages are free of nuisances," wrote Castaneda, "because they go outside to excrete, and they pass their water into clay vessels, which they empty at a distance from the village."

The Spanish believed that plague was an act of God and punishment inflicted upon them for their sins. They were no more able to halt its ravages than they were able to cure the other deadly diseases they brought to the Indians. Prayers for forgiveness were their only hope of salvation, but fervent pleas to their Almighty God did not always, to say the least, bring desired results.

One would not be justified, it seems to me, in charging the Pueblos with being more superstitious than their conquerors. Suffering from afflictions for which there were no obvious causes, they reacted in the same manner as the Europeans—they called upon the supernatural beings of their pantheon for help with their complicated religious ritual.

---

1 5 4 1

Coronado had believed that the people of Moho would be forced to capitulate before much time had passed because of a lack of water. This came very near to being the case, but timely snows saved the defenders on several occasions. What he did not know at the time was that the Pueblos, fearful that not enough snow would fall to meet their needs, had made an attempt to obtain a water supply by digging a deep well. While the diggers were at work, the sides of the excavation suddenly caved in, burying alive thirty of them. There was no shortage of food, for the storehouses of Moho had been stocked in preparation for the usual long winter, and shortly after the well disaster a series of snow storms occurred.

The siege went on until at last, late in February, Coronado found his position rapidly becoming untenable. "Seeing that they would not surrender," said Cardenas, "that the winter was severe, and that the Spaniards could not endure it any longer, the general ordered that they be attacked." After a day of fierce fighting, during which a number of men on each side were killed and wounded, the Spaniards were again repulsed.

Coronado sent contingents of soldiers to Zia and other pueblos, and they confiscated badly needed foodstuffs and robes. Not all these raids were successful, however, as some of the pueblos chose to fight, and Coronado was obliged to lay siege to them. The matter of retreating to the more comfortable quarters still being held by some soldiers at Alcanfor was discussed. The decision was to continue the fight. Defeat by a few hundred savages was unthinkable to the officers; moreover, spring could not be far away.

It was lack of water, not Spaniards, that brought the fall of Moho. By the middle of March, the snow was gone. The headmen of the pueblo signaled a request for a conference, and it was granted. When the emissaries had assembled, Coronado was told, according to Castaneda, that as the Indians believed the Spaniards "would not harm the women and children, they wished to surrender their wives and children, because they were using up their water. It was impossible to persuade them to make peace, as they said the Spaniards would not keep an agreement . . ." Coronado assured them their wives and children would not be mistreated, "so they gave up about a hundred persons . . . who did not want to leave them."

As the days passed and the countryside began to display the delicate first greens of spring, the thirst of the people in Moho became unbearable. The effort to escape the torture was launched shortly before dawn on a late March day. To protect them, women were placed between lines of men, and the dash from the pueblo began.

The first alarm was sounded on the side where the cavalry was stationed, and, according to Castaneda, the fighting was quickly underway. One soldier was killed and several were wounded, but the Indians "were driven back with great slaughter until they came to the river, where the water flowed swiftly and very cold. They threw themselves into this, and as the men had come from the whole camp to assist the cavalry, there were few Indians who escaped being killed or wounded."

In the early daylight, soldiers crossed the Rio Grande and came upon many Indian men and women who had collapsed from wounds, exhaustion, and exposure. Coronado soon received word that detachments he had sent to other pueblos, and whose demands for food and clothing had been rejected, had succeeded in killing a large number of Indian men and women who had tried to flee. These were Keres. Several score had been captured and were being brought back to become slaves of their captors. Those who had by some miracle survived at Moho also were enslaved.

The victory was complete. Spring had come. Coronado could lose himself once more in the great dream, and he was soon making preprations to start for the fabulous country of Quivera and all the other rich provinces beyond the eastern horizon.

It is not possible, of course, to determine with accuracy the population of the Pueblos at the beginning of the historical period. Sixteenth-century documents are unreliable regarding this subject. They may state how many "houses" a pueblo contained, but not how many people lived in them. Going to the other extreme, they may credit certain towns with having populations of ten to fifteen thousand, patently absurd figures. Not until several decades after the colonization of New Mexico were demographic reports within the realm of reasonableness. However, these did not reflect the size of the population at the beginning of the historical period, for they were prepared long after thousands of Pueblos had been slaughtered by the Spanish. They must, moreover, be considered suspect to some extent, because Spanish governors sought to impress the royal government with the extensiveness and complexity of their own problems, and missionaries, anxious to secure appropriations for missions, were not hesitant about exaggerating the number of pagan souls to be saved.

Based on analysis of the available sources, the following estimates of the sixteenth-century Pueblo population are probably realistic, if perhaps conservative or somewhat too high in some categories:

Zuni	4,500
Hopi	3,500
Tiwa	13,000
Jemez	4,000
Tewa	6,500
Piro	9,500
Total	41,000

1 5 4 1 *(cont.)*

After the fall of Moho, all the pueblos of Tiguex and many others in the surrounding country were deserted.* Dazed by the catastrophe that had struck them, the people had fled their homes, vanishing into the wilderness, suffering their grief, and wondering what evil would befall them next. Spaniards searched the empty pueblos and rode far through the country to towns in which some people still cowered in fear, confiscating foodstuffs and other articles, meeting no

---

*Castaneda said that they were never reoccupied as long as Coronado was in New Mexico.

resistance. The resources acquired were not inconsequential, for within two or three weeks, Coronado had supplies he deemed sufficient to meet the needs of his entire force for thirty days. Certainly Quivera would be reached long before that period had expired, and he felt even more certain that there he would be able to replenish his stores for the return journey with the great resources that awaited him.

After enduring so many hardships, and meeting with so many disappointments, not all the officers were as convinced as Coronado that the Quivera venture would be profitable. Some of them were openly skeptical of Turk's tales, and some did not hesitate to brand him a magician, a witch doctor, and a diabolical liar. These suspicions were augmented when Turk's jailer swore that he caught him talking with the Devil in a jug filled with water. Moreover, Turk had stated almost exactly how many Spaniards had been killed at Moho, although it was impossible that anyone could have supplied him with the information, unless it came to him from the Devil in the jug. Coronado's ears were closed to such gossip and charges. His mind was made up. They were going to Quivera, and he was more than ever encouraged by Turk's latest story. It said that Quivera was governed by a powerful ruler, King Tatarrax, who was "bearded, rich, grey-haired, wore golden garments, prayed from a book of hours, and worshipped a woman who was the queen of heaven."

The New Mexico spring was in its full glory. In the long column that crawled out of Tiguex late in April were more than fifteen hundred persons, including the entire army, Mexican Indian helpers and the newly acquired Tiwa slaves, a thousand horses, five hundred cattle, five thousand sheep, and pack trains of supplies and equipment. Great dust clouds stood up to a turquoise sky, and the bawling of animals and the shouting of wranglers and the rattle of arms created a bedlam that reached back for miles behind Coronado and his staff, wearing gilded helmets and plumes and armor that caught the sun.

The trail followed was the same as that taken by Alvarado and his men the previous summer. It ran from the Rio Grande around the end of the Sandia Mountains, eastward across Galisteo Valley, and through Glorieta Pass to Pecos Pueblo on the Pecos River, altogether a distance of about twenty-five leagues from the starting point. En route numerous ruined pueblos were seen. Others were occupied, among them Los Silos and Galisteo, but the terrorized inhabitants remained behind barricaded gates, despite Coronado's assurances that as long as they were peaceful no harm would come to them.

The people of Cicuye, or Pecos, shouted and danced with joy at the sight of their leaders, Bigotes and Cacique, whom they had feared were dead. Coronado magnanimously freed them in a scene of wild rejoicing, and in return was presented with all manner of gifts and foods.

After a respite of a day or two, the great procession crawled on, descending the right bank of the Rio Pecos for four days. Where the trail crossed the river, which was roaring with the spring flood, a wooden bridge was constructed so that the animals and pack trains might be taken across with ease and complete safety.

Eight or ten days beyond the Rio Pecos—progress was slow because of the herds—they looked out on the unbelievably flat reaches of the Llano Estacado, the plains of the buffalo fading into the horizon. The land of the Pueblos was behind them, and before them were the seas of grass over which roamed the Apache, who, as Castaneda would write, lived like Arabs.*

*The story of Coronado's fruitless journey across the Great Plains belongs to the history of the Apache and other plains tribes dwelling in eastern New Mexico,

The aspens on the mountains were turning gold when Coronado rejoined his men on the Rio Grande. For him and all his once powerful army—now tattered, weary, and completely dispirited—the great dream had been destroyed by stark reality. He wrote truthfully of his failures to Viceroy Mendoza and dispatched couriers to Mexico with the letter. There was nothing else to be done but wait through another bitter winter in abandoned Tiguex until the arrival of spring, when he could start on the long and sad ride back to Mexico.

Not everyone with Coronado, however, had failed to find treasure. Fray Luis de Escalona, Fray Juan de la Cruz, and Fray Juan de Padilla considered themselves fabulously rich, for they had been permitted by God to go to a country containing innumerable souls to be saved, where the banners of Christianity had never flown, where the story of the Savior had never been heard. Coronado granted their requests to remain. They would be the first missionaries stationed in the Southwest.

Fray Luis de Escalona selected Pecos Pueblo. There he lived in a little hut. How long he survived is not known, for he was never seen again by white men, and later explorers could learn nothing of his fate. Fray Juan de la Cruz remained at Puaray, a pueblo near Bernalillo. He was slain, probably at the instigation of jealous medicine men. Fray Juan de Padilla, the former army officer, went back across the Great Plains to Quivera. He was killed by an Indian war party.

---

the panhandles of Texas and Oklahoma, and Kansas. In Texas the main army was sent back to the Rio Grande, and with only a small company, perhaps no more than thirty horsemen, Coronado pushed on until he reached the Smokey Hill River in the vicinity of Lindsborg, Kansas. There he gave up—he had found nothing but cattle and sky. Turk, still in chains, had reached home, but he benefited not at all from his deceptions. He was garroted. Ysopete was freed.

1542

A little more than two years had passed since Coronado had ridden out of Compostela, with banners flying and armor gleaming, for the Seven Cities of Cibola.

On a day early in April, he freed all the Indians he had enslaved and rode out of Tiguex for Mexico, a broken, sick man.

Until Cibola had been passed, Pueblos watched the column pass along the trail. They could live once more as they had always lived, but they could never forget the tragedies and the terrors they had suffered, and even though they held vivid memories of the magic they had witnessed, of the wonders of the Iron Age they had briefly known, each memory would be forever invested with a new hatred and a new anxiety. They could hope, always hope, that the incomprehensible strangers would never come again, but that would not be enough to keep them from gazing fearfully toward the horizon.

The Pueblos are characterized as "peaceful Indians." That is a generalization that demands qualification. They were not as warlike as the tribes surrounding them, the Apache on the east and south, the Navajo on the west and north, the Yuman tribes of the Colorado Basin, and the Ute also on the north. However, the Pueblos were organized to wage both defensive and offensive warfare, and without military actions they probably would have been annihilated before the first Spanish conquests.

"All the Pueblo villages," says Driver, "had a war priest who was ranked with the head civil priest in executive authority, and the two were responsible to a council whose

unanimous decision controlled the affairs of the pueblo
... The warrior sodality served as a police force within the
pueblo and a military force without ... The war priest and
the warriors' sodality formed a permanent group ready to
cope with violence at any time. Each pueblo embraced people from a number of internally related but externally unrelated kinship groups, so that conflicts between pueblos
can scarcely be called feuds. In size they fit the term raid,
yet their organization suggests the term war."

Hostilities between pueblos were sometimes caused by
fear of witchcraft or the leveling of evil supernatural powers
by one pueblo against another, but, as Driver states, "reprisals against raids initiated by enemies probably account
for more Pueblo forays than any other motivation ... the
Pueblos usually waited until they were attacked before they
fought."

The rich culture of the Pueblos was highly developed
long before the Athapascan Apache and Navajo reached
the Southwest from the far north. The Apache settled in the
plains and deserts and mountains east and south of the
homelands of the Pueblos, and the Navajo, choosing to
follow a course through southern Colorado, halted their
migration in a land they named Dinetah, in the San Juan
River drainage of northwestern New Mexico. Some
Navajo, according to their traditions, which are probably
accurate, came from the north by way of California.

Although climatic and environmental conditions differed
in numerous ways, both of the regions selected by the
Apache and Navajo contained bountiful natural resources,
game, grasses, seeds, wild fruits and nuts, and forests on the
higher elevations. Most of these things they had come to
know well and to make good use of in their wanderings, but
in New Mexico they found something they had never
known.

Having always lived a few steps ahead of hunger, and often with it, the life of the Pueblo Indians represented a security and plenty inconceivable to them. In amazement they gazed on irrigated fields of maize, pumpkins, beans, gourds, and a wonderful fiber—cotton. They saw fine pottery decorated with geometric designs of many colors. They saw superb woven baskets, rectangular and round, large and small. They saw ingenious tools, large flint knives, needles, rubbers, scrapers. They saw feather-cloth robes, and ponchos, blankets, and clothing of cotton. They saw mosaics, ornaments, and beads of turquoise and other beautiful stones, and they saw astonishing articles made of sea shells.

A new culture was born. Elements of the far northern woodlands, of the plains, of the mountains, and of the deserts would be preserved in it, but also woven through it—vital strands in its texture—would be many of the customs and beliefs of the Pueblo town dwellers whose wealth, sophistication, and beautiful, exciting religious ceremonials inspired the wanderers from the north.

The Athapascans were by nature neither peaceful nor sedentary. They were wild, unpredictable, and cruel. They wanted both the freedom of the wind and the rewards of the patient Pueblo laborer. They wanted to continue to revere their own gods, but they were willing to pay obeisance to the gods of the Pueblos, if by so doing they could gain benefits for themselves.

They saw only one way to acquire the luxuries and the knowledge and the skill of the Pueblos—by plundering them. To the Navajo, irrigated farming meant they could establish permanent communities and have a stable food supply and an easier life. Agriculture did not have as much appeal to the more nomadically inclined Apache, but they craved other advantages, especially useful possessions and skills, enjoyed by the Pueblos.

The warfare that would endure for centuries began. Raiding was a cornerstone of the economies of the Athapascans, a defensive weapon of the Pueblos. The Apache and Navajo stole any material thing they could get away with —food, clothing, skins, jewelry, utensils, weapons—but they also stole craftsmen and young women. The captive men were abandoned or even killed when they became useless as producers, but the young women captured were adopted, and through marriage became members of a clan, and they bore children to whom they passed on their industrial and artistic skills.

Yet, not all Pueblo articles acquired by the Athapascans, nor all knowledge of Pueblo ritual absorbed by them, were gained through banditry. Some pueblos, notably Taos and Pecos, were trading centers in which the Apache tribes regularly appeared with beautifully tanned robes, skins, and other products of the buffalo plains. Commerce was conducted between some pueblos of the Rio Grande and those farther to the west with the Navajo. And there were occasions on which Pueblo peoples, faced with adversities too great for them to overcome, sought sanctuary among the Navajo, who invariably welcomed them. Some of these refugees did not return to their former homes, even though they were given the opportunity.

But the actions and reactions of the Apache and Navajo were unpredictable. No pueblo could let down its guard, and any number of the ruins seen by the early Spanish treasure hunters who penetrated the Pueblo country were monuments to deadly Apache and Navajo aggressions.

PART TWO

New Trails: Exploiters and Martyrs

1581

It was almost as if nothing had ever been known about the country to the north, about the Pueblos who lived in it, almost as if no part of the northern mystery had been solved by Nunez Cabeza de Vaca, Estevanico, Cardenas, Alvarado, and Coronado. Indeed, it was true that more had been forgotten than had been remembered in the forty years that had passed since Cibola and Tiguex and Quivera had been disturbed by the pounding of horse hooves, the call of a trumpet, the thunder of a musket.

There were several reasons why the northern country had been neglected all this time, but the fact that Coronado had failed to find treasure there was not one of them. It was doubtful if most persons in Mexico knew he had been there. Castaneda and a few others who had taken part in the great venture had written about their experiences, but their manuscripts were buried in the disorderly archives of Spain, and if any copies had been made of them, they had not reached Mexico City. Actually, except for some religious tracts, there were few printed books to be found in all Mexico. Exposure to histories, biographies, narratives of adventure, and scientific works was a privilege enjoyed only by ecclesiastics, the wealthy, and the nobility in Europe. Most of the people of the provinces lived in literary ignorance.

In the four decades since the Coronado debacle, however, many things had happened which in themselves would have dominated the thoughts of enterprising, ambitious men, either educated or uneducated. Mexico, in many respects, had become a land of turmoil. Indian uprisings, political dissensions, the discovery of rich silver mines, the opening of vast new grazing and farming areas, and defiance of royal decrees and other forms of lawlessness had created internal problems that required the full attention of the provincial government, if not higher authorities in Spain. The frontier had been pushed steadily northward from central Mexico. Towns mushroomed, missions and convents were established, and soldiers were sent to protect them. Although they fought desperately to defend themselves and their resources, the Indians were crushed by the insuperable pressure, and, in violation of Spanish laws, uncounted thousands of them were enslaved and forced to work for mine owners, cattlemen, ranchers, and mills and other private commercial enterprises.

Nueva Viscaya (now the state of Chihuahua) was one of the booming frontier regions, of which Santa Barbara, a dirty, shabby, lawless town on the Rio Florida, was the trading center. Fabulous strikes of silver and other metals had been made nearby, and in the surrounding country were immense ranges of grass. Men of all stamps had appropriated these resources, and Santa Barbara and other settlements were filled with miners, cattlemen, farmers, slave traders, outlaws, and padres.

Fray Augustin Rodriguez had been one of the first missionaries stationed in the area. He lived among the Conchos Indians, and he had been eminently successful in winning converts and in protecting many of them from being carried away into the hell of a slave's life. From his trusting and loyal neophytes he had heard that far to the north, in a country unknown to white men, were a large number of Indians who had never heard of the Christian God. For years Fray Augustin had known a consuming desire to go in search of the idolatrous tribes, and, although he hated to leave his Conchos, he at last submitted to it.

The stampedes and wild, uncontrolled growth in northern Mexico had prompted the enactment of new laws prohibiting the exploitation of nature's bounties and the establishment of settlements and missions without royal permission. The statutes also contained the provision that only persons of good character, known to be devout Christians, and who could be relied upon to treat Indians with kindness and justice, would be permitted to lead expeditions of discovery. There were not many men on the frontier who could qualify under the new code except missionaries, and it was required that even they must be protected by soldiers on any venture they wished to undertake. Sending padres and soldiers into the wilderness was expensive, and the provincial government was not enthusiastic about such projects, for the money to pay for food, equipment, and livestock, as well as wages for the military and any Indian or white servants who might be employed, had to come out of its treasury, which seldom if ever contained sufficient funds.

Complying with the law, Fray Augustin wrote to the viceroy proposing that he and two other padres, Fray Francisco Lopez and Fray Juan de Santa Maria, be allowed to carry the word of God to the lost souls who, his Indians assured him, dwelt somewhere in the far north. After a wait of only a few months—perhaps he had friends in Mexico City who acted in his behalf—his plan was officially approved, and Captain Francisco Sanchez Chamuscado, a veteran frontier officer, was assigned to accompany the three friars with a military escort.

The Rodriguez-Chamuscado expedition, which started from Santa Barbara in June, would break a new trail to Pueblo country.

Besides the three padres, the little company was comprised of eight soldiers under Chamuscado, nineteen Indians engaged as packers and wranglers, ninety horses, and some six hundred head of livestock. Captain Chamuscado's aide, Hernan Gallegos, was assigned the duty of writing a diary, and he would record in an account that greatly enriched the history of the time that the purpose of their journey was to go "where God our Lord was pleased to direct them, in order that His Holy Faith might be taught and His gospel spread throughout the lands which they . . . might thus discover in His holy service and in the service of the royal crown."

Going down the Rio Conchos to the Rio Grande, they turned north. In this vicinity, the first noteworthy event of the march occurred. In an Apache town, Fray Augustin inquired if the people had ever seen a white man. The reply he received astonished everyone. He was told that a very long time ago four Christians, three white and one black, had passed that way. Nunez Cabeza de Vaca, Dorantes, Castillo, and Estevanico still lived in the memories of the Rio Grande Apache after the passage of forty-five years.

Above El Paso del Norte they entered country never before traversed by Europeans, but that did not mean that the Piro, the first Pueblos encountered, did not know white men existed. They had heard of Coronado's trail of blood and death, and they wasted no time getting out of sight. Fray Augustin was able to find some of the Indians and convince them that he wanted nothing but their friendship. Swiftly the "news that we were coming in peace spread so widely that there was not a day or night when we were not surrounded and accompanied by more than three hundred souls."*

The first Piro pueblo they saw was in ruins—probably destroyed by Apache raiders—but Gallegos thought it "must have been inhabited by a large number of people,

*See bibliography under Rodriguez-Chamuscado.

who must have been very advanced, judging by the buildings, and whose discovery would be of great importance, if they could be found. Here we halted for the night." They named the ruined pueblo San Felipe, and on August 21 took possession of the "entire province, on behalf of his majesty." They were the first Spaniards to reach the Piro country from the south. Some of Coronado's men had seen the most northern Piro pueblos. Now the gap between the two *entradas* would be closed.

San Felipe was located on the Rio Grande just south of San Marcial, New Mexico. Going on upstream a short distance, they came to the first inhabited Piro town, naming it San Miguel. The people "had left the night before, because they had noticed our approach." The friars, looking about, found some of the refugees and were able to persuade them to return to their homes. They learned that the province contained "twenty-odd pueblos."

The first written description of the Piro's way of life, penned by Gallegos, is regrettably brief: "In the houses we found many turkeys and much cotton and corn . . . in the valley many cornfields like those of Mexico, and also fields of beans, calabashes, and cotton. We did not dare to take any of the goods, for we wanted the people to know we did not intend to harm them. We found the houses very well planned and built in blocks, with mud walls, whitewashed inside and well decorated with monsters, other animals, and human figures. There were many curious articles in these houses, more neatly wrought than those of the Mexicans when they were conquered. The inhabitants have a great deal of crockery, such as pots, large earthen jars, and flat pans, all decorated and of better quality than the pottery of New Spain."

Some forty to fifty miles south of the future site of Albuquerque they entered the country of the southern Tiwa.

Up to this time, in September, they had met with no serious difficulties. On the surface, at least, the Tiwa displayed a friendly attitude. While the memory of their extreme suffering at the hands of Coronado's powerful force must have been vivid, and still a subject often discussed in kiva meetings, they could reason that the new intruders were not only few in number but gave no indication that they were searching for treasures that did not exist, and they made no excessive demands. The Tiwa could afford to wait to see what developed.

There were many large Tiwa pueblos "three and four stories high, whitewashed inside and with many well-squared windows. All the houses were decorated in many designs and colors. We journeyed through the territory of this nation for four days, always passing numerous pueblos —indeed, we sometimes passed through two a day—continuing until we reached the frontier of another nation . . . we learned more of what there was in the interior, and that it was thickly populated, news which gave us much satisfaction . . . The people . . . make tortillas and corn-flour gruel, have buffalo meat and turkeys . . . There is not an Indian who does not have a corral for his turkeys, each of which holds a flock of one hundred birds. The natives wear Campeche-type cotton blankets, for they have large cotton fields. They raise many small shaggy dogs . . ."

An interesting commentary on Pueblo social customs is contained in a passage of Gallegos's account. When the Spaniards were offered food, "We took a little, so that they should not think we were greedy nor yet received the impression that we did not want it; among themselves they consider it disparaging if one does not accept what is offered. One must take what they give, but after taking it may throw it away wherever he wishes. Should one throw it to the ground, they will not pick it up, though it may be something they can utilize. On the contrary, they will sooner let the thing rot where it is discarded. This is their practice. Thus, since we understood their custom, we took something of what they gave us. Moreover, we did this to get them into the habit of giving freely without being asked. Accordingly, they all brought what they could. The supply of corn tortillas, corn-flour gruel, calabashes and beans which they brought was such that enough was left over every day to feed five hundred men."

Gallegos thought that "for barbarians" the Pueblos were well groomed and well dressed; ". . . the men cut their hair short and leave on top—I mean on the crown of their heads —a sort of skull cap formed by their own hair, while others wear their hair long, to the shoulders, as the Indians of New Spain formerly did. Some adorn themselves with pieces of colored cotton cloth three-fourths of a *vara** in length and two-thirds in width with which they cover their privy parts. Over this they wear, fastened at the shoulders, a blanket of the same material, decorated with many figures and colors, which reaches to their knees . . . Some, in fact most, wear cotton shirts, hand-painted and embroidered, that are very pleasing. They use shoes. Below the waist the women wear cotton skirts, colored and embroidered; and above, a blanket of the same material, figured and adorned like those used by the men. They adjust it after the fashion of Jewish women, and gird it with embroidered cotton sashes adorned with tassels. They comb their hair, which is worn long."

He praised the industriousness and the craftsmanship of the Indians, presumably in this instance speaking of the Tiwa: "Only the men attend to the work in the cornfields. The day hardly breaks before they go about with hoes in

*A Spanish unit of length equal to about thirty-three inches.

their hands. The women busy themselves only in the preparation of food, and in making and painting their pottery and *chicubites* [baking pans], in which they prepare their bread. These vessels are so excellent and delicate that the process of manufacture is worth watching: for they equal, and even surpass, the pottery made in Portugal. The women also make earthen jars for the carrying and storing of water. These are very large, and are covered with lids of the same material . . . These Indians are very clean people. The men bear burdens, but not the women."

Now it was revealed that carrying the gospel to pagans was not the sole objective of the Rodriguez-Chamuscado expedition. At the Tewa pueblo of Malpartida (San Marcos, in the Galisteo Valley), ". . . we asked if there were many minerals in the vicinity, showing the natives the samples we had taken along for that purpose and requesting them to lead us to the place where such riches might be found. They immediately brought us large quantities of different kinds, including some of a coppery steellike ore. This mineral appeared to be rich and assayed about twenty *marcos* per hundredweight. The others assayed less. When we asked them where they obtained the ore, they gave us to understand that there were many minerals near the province and pueblo . . . We went to investigate and discovered mines of different ores. The natives *indicated that the Indians in the region of the buffalo had given them a part of the ore."*

Well may one wonder if the stories of Turk about the gold to be found on the Great Plains were still remembered, and the Tewa were using similar fables to lure the Spaniards out of their own land. They may have forgotten, if they ever knew, about Turk's unhappy end. In any case, they fed the same old narcotic to their visitors, who soon found it irresistible. "When we heard this and the report on the buffalo, we decided to find the herds and to explore the land in which they lived. . . ."

The plan was not acceptable to Fray Juan de Santa Maria. The others could go off into the wild blue yonder to see buffalo, if they wished, but he intended to go back to Mexico "to give an account and report of what had been discovered to his prelate, and to his Excellency, the viceroy."

Everyone was astounded and "condemned the decision as inadvisable, for he would not only endanger his own life, but imperil the soldiers, and in addition would jeopardize further explorations of the land. We urged him to wait until we had inspected everything . . . and had gone to see the buffalo . . ." Father Juan de Santa Maria's mind was made up, and on a September day he started back along the trail to Mexico—alone.

The company was gone about a month on the side trip to the Great Plains. They passed a number of towns, including the immense pueblo of Pecos, and may have reached tributaries of the Canadian River, but their rewards, besides the pleasure of eating good buffalo meat, were the same as those gained by Coronado—cows, endless plains, and sky.

Bad news and brewing trouble were awaiting them when they returned to the Galisteo Valley about the third week in October. Fray Juan de Santa Maria had been killed. The Tewa, cold and inhospitable, were plotting to attack them.

It is probable that their own Indian servants obtained this sad information, but that is a question Gallegos does not answer. He simply states that when the Tewa saw the friar leaving alone, "they became alarmed, believing he was going to bring more Christians in order to put them out of their homes . . . They followed the friar and killed him after two or three days of travel . . . in the sierra, which we named the Sierra Morena."*

Showing no fear, the Tewa did not deny that they had committed the murder, and "seeing . . . that they had killed

*The Manzano Mountains.

him so easily, they thought they would kill us just as readily
. . . we decided to withdraw gradually."

Before they had gotten away, however, some Indians
from a pueblo they called Malagon (San Lazaro, near San
Marcos) stole several of their horses. Captain Chamuscado,
Fray Augustin, and Fray Francisco, putting their heads together on the serious matter, devised a somewhat elaborate
scheme. The horse thieves must be taught a lesson that
would not be forgotten by the people of Malagon. This
could easily have been accomplished by some gunfire, but
such a simple precedure might endanger the plan the two
friars had decided to carry out. It was their intention to
remain among the Pueblos and establish a mission in some
suitable location. Violence was to be avoided at all costs, yet
the thievery could not be ignored.

Thus, it was decided to send five soldiers to Malagon,
recover the stolen animals, and bring the culprits back to
camp under a threat that they would be executed. Then,
when they were about to be separated from their heads, the
friars would rush out, tussle with the executioners, "and
snatch the victims away . . . in order that the Indians might
love their rescuers, who were resolved to remain in the
land."

Things did not work out as they were intended, and for
a time it appeared that the Spaniards were in greater jeop-
ardy than the thieves. Arriving at Malagon, the soldiers
came upon scattered pieces of slaughtered horses. In spite
of the evidence, the natives shouted from the pueblo roof
that they had "committed no such deed . . . we discharged
the harquebuses to make the Indians think we were going
to kill them, although we incurred great risk in doing so,
for we were only five men facing the task of attacking eighty
houses with more than a thousand inhabitants."

Most of the people concealed themselves in the pueblo,

but some men remained on the roof. Three soldiers entered the plaza and were told "that it was Indians in the next pueblo who had killed the horses, thinking they were animals like the native buffalo." This lame excuse did not work. The soldiers again fired their weapons, and a small stampede followed, with a number of warriors running "into the open in an attempt to escape." Two soldiers "rushed after them and each seized an Indian by the hair. The natives were very swift, but the horses overtook them." The two prisoners were taken back to the Spaniards' camp "to be punished, in view of their crime and as an example to the others."

Captain Chamuscado ordered that they be beheaded. A block was prepared, the prisoners were forced to put their heads upon it, and the executioner raised a machete. Thereupon, the friars, displaying no little talent as actors, rushed forward "in flowing robes and saved the captives from their perilous plight."

If the script sounds as if it were prepared for a modern-day horse opera, staging the melodrama brought the desired results. The next morning the people of Malagon appeared "heavily laden with turkeys and other food for our use, entreating us not to be angry with them . . ."

The Pueblos, however, demonstrated that they themselves were not incapable of doing a bit of acting. As the Spaniards moved on, they soon became aware that word of their approach had gone ahead, and that groups of Indians had "assembled for the purpose of killing us . . . that the people of the entire region were gathering for this purpose." Careful watch was maintained, the weapons were kept ready, and as the threats increased, "we determined to attack and kill them, and to burn some of their small pueblos even though we should perish in the attempt . . . We challenged them many times so that they might know there was no cowardice in us. But as the friars had decided to remain . . . we sometimes—in fact, most of the time— relinquished our rights . . . Nevertheless, their decision to stay was against the judgment of all, because the natives had killed the other friar and because they were to remain among such great numbers of idolatrous people."

Peace, if precarious, prevailed. They went on as the winter approached, following Coronado's trail westward from the pueblos of the Rio Grande to Acoma and Zuni. They heard of the Hopi towns, but they did not visit them. The snow was deep and the cold severe as they turned back, Chamuscado and his soldiers deciding to "return to the land of Christians before any misfortune should befall them and before the natives should attempt to carry out their evil plan." The new year had begun when they reached the Tiwa pueblo of Puaray, on the frozen Rio Grande, not far from Alcanfor in which Coronado had spent so many miserable winter months.

1582

Fray Augustin Rodriguez and Fray Francisco Lopez had selected Puaray as the station in which they would begin their missionary work. And on the last day of January, the two padres stood in their tattered robes before the pueblo gate, made the sign of the cross, and waved good-bye to their companions.

Gallegos wrote that Captain Chamuscado and his men were determined to return quickly to Mexico "in order to bring help for the conversion of these natives." His relation indicated, however, that they deviated from the main trail several times to look for minerals. Hammond and Rey suspect that they followed this practice throughout their journey, making side trips that were not recorded. Gallegos does say that in one place, "twenty leagues from Puaray, we discovered six mineral deposits." His description of the location suggests that they may have wandered considerably west of the Rio Grande, into the Magdalena Mountains, although the distance from Puaray would have been more like forty than twenty leagues. His estimates of distances, however, were notably inaccurate. The deposits, he wrote, were "in a very fine locality with abundant water and timber; the veins are rich and well provided with supporting walls. In the opinion of all our men—who were nearly all miners and knew about mines, veins, and minerals—the deposits were, and are, excellent." Captain Chamuscado, acting as leader and magistrate of the expedition, formally took possession of the mines and "recorded" them. Indians they encountered, presumably Piro, told them of "six or seven" more mines in the area, "but because the supply of iron for horseshoes had been exhausted, we did not go on to explore them . . . God willing, we shall locate them when the land is settled, for such an abundance of mines is indeed marvelous."

Somewhere along the Rio Grande, either in southern New Mexico or northern Mexico, "God willed that Captain Chamuscado should be stricken with an old ailment." Suffering great pain and partially paralyzed, the veteran frontier soldier, who was "sixty or seventy years of age," courageously kept on. They decided that bleeding him might bring some relief, but as the "equipment had been left with the friars, we proceeded as soldiers do in time of need when they draw blood with a horseshoe nail and apply the medicines by means of a horn." The ministrations were ineffectual. With his hands and feet useless, Chamuscado was unable to stay in his saddle. Several stops of three and four days'

duration did him no good. A pole litter, covered with the
hide of a horse killed for the purpose and some buffalo
robes, was slung between two horses. It was hoped that by
this means their commander could be taken "to Christian
hands where the holy sacraments could be administered
. . . Burdened by this device, we traveled with great difficulty."

Captain Chamuscado died in March, and was buried beside the trail that ran along the Rio Conchos, only thirty
leagues from his home.

On Easter morning, early in April, the residents of Santa
Barbara were startled by the sound of guns being fired at
the edge of town. They saw a ragged group of horsemen
and Indians approaching, and "we were given an especially
warm welcome because the inhabitants had thought us
dead."

How much of the contents of his notebooks Gallegos
made public is not known. He may have revealed very little
of what had been discovered, but someone—perhaps the
soldiers—talked about the mineral deposits and about the
richness of the country. Whatever or however much was
disclosed, it was enough to give birth to rumors that the
expedition had found fabulous quantities of gold and silver
and other metals, that the friars and the dead Chamuscado
had taken possession in the name of the king of an immense
unknown territory that not only held no end of treasures
but contained limitless grass pastures, lush valleys, immense
forests, and an incalculable number of heathen Indians, all
of whom were eager to become Christians. Gallegos, gossip
had it, had slipped away to Mexico City to give the viceroy
incredibly rich samples of ore—and that, at least, was true,
but the fact would not be known in Santa Barbara until
much later. It did not matter. What was known there, or
rumored there, was more than enough to fire the blood of
any adventurer.

Perhaps others contemplated forming expeditions, but the first definitely known action resulting from the glowing tales was taken by a young mine owner and cattleman, Antonio de Espejo.

In the ten years he had been in Mexico, Espejo had acquired considerable wealth and property, not all of it by legitimate means. He had been sent out from Spain at the age of twenty-nine as a confidential officer of the Inquisition. Although the post was lucrative—he was not above taking advantage of the opportunities for blackmail it opened to him—he was driven by an ambition to make a much greater fortune than was possible by exposing, or threatening to expose, heretics and officials disloyal to the church. Possessed of a complex character, he was highly intelligent and clever, tough but seldom crude, and he could be persuasive, diplomatic, and socially charming.

His first business enterprise in Mexico City was a cattle-trading company. When a number of his prime beeves were stolen and sold to a butcher, he dramatically demonstrated his inherent courage and his ability to safeguard his own interests. With two vaqueros to help him, he boldly entered the slaughterhouse and recovered the animals at gunpoint. He was arrested and thrown into jail, but the authorities quickly released him when he warned them that information he had obtained as an Inquisition spy would be injurious to certain officials if publicly disclosed.

The northern state of Nueva Viscaya appeared to offer greener pastures, and he and his brother Pedro, a thorough ruffian, acquired mineral property and grazing ranges in the Santa Barbara vicinity. They became successful as mine operators and cattle ranchers, but even in the wild country, where law enforcement was weak at best, the ruthless and violent methods they employed got them into serious trouble. Antonio murdered an Indian vaquero whom he accused of laziness, and both he and Pedro were involved in several other encounters in which blood was shed. During a roundup, several of their Spanish cowboys deserted after Antonio threatened their lives. A gunfight followed in a nearby settlement, and Pedro killed one of the deserters and wounded another. Both Espejos were charged with murder and taken to Mexico City for trial. Pedro was sentenced to a term in prison, but Antonio, who was still an investigator for the Inquisition, was only given a fine. Instead of paying, he fled back to Nueva Viscaya. Although he was a fugitive from justice, no attempt was made to rearrest him.

The report accredited to Gallegos that the country farther north was rich in undeveloped minerals inspired in Antonio de Espejo a shrewd scheme. He held no doubts about his own chances of obtaining permission to undertake an expedition—for a man with his unsavory record, they were nil. However, he had another card to play, and it gave him a winning hand. Aware that the Franciscans were profoundly anxious about the two priests who had remained at Puaray, he offered to underwrite the expenses of an investigation to determine their fate. The missionaries of Nueva Viscaya were eager to accept, but they were unwilling to ignore the statutes governing such matters. They dispatched fervent letters to Mexico City requesting viceregal approval of the proposal. Months passed, but their pleas remained unanswered.

At last, disgusted with the red tape and delay, Fray Bernadino Beltran, who had been chosen to represent the order on the venture, announced that he would obtain the necessary permit by other means. He got it, but just how he accomplished the feat is uncertain. One account indicates that it was obtained from his superior. Another records that it was issued by the lieutenant governor of Nueva Viscaya. Still another states that a Captain Juan Ontiveros not only granted Fray Beltran's request but authorized the formation of a military escort composed of soldiers who wished to volunteer their services, all wages and expenses to be paid, of course, by Espejo. In either case, issuance of the permit was not in compliance with the law, but that was a point the Franciscans chose to overlook. Nor did Espejo concern himself with this phase of the matter. He was, so to speak, merely going along for the ride. The permit did not bear his name. If there were repercussions, the onus would be on the Franciscans, and it was doubtful that they would be penalized for trying to find out if two of their colleagues were still alive.

The Espejo expedition has been called a "rescue mission" by most historians. That is a convenient label, but it is inappropriate, as events demonstrate. More properly, the journey should be described as a daring and important exploration, for regardless of Espejo's private motives, he traversed regions never before penetrated by white men.

Three other friars were to have accompanied Fray Beltran, but a confusion of orders resulted in their dropping out. The start was made November 10 from the Valle de Allende, a short distance east of Santa Barbara. Espejo had hired fourteen soldiers and a number of Indians to care for a small supply pack train and a herd of one hundred horses. It was a company prepared to travel with speed, and it did.

Diego Perez de Luxan, an educated officer who was Espejo's chief aide and who exhibited great loyalty to him, kept a journal of the expedition. It was submitted to the viceroy, but like so many invaluable historical documents of the time, it was buried among the masses of state papers that accumulated in the archives of Mexico City and Seville. It was "discovered" and copied some years later after the less honest reports written by Espejo had received wide circulation.*

In December, they were traveling up the Rio Grande above its confluence with the Rio Conchos. They, too, were told how Nunez Cabeza de Vaca and his companions had passed along the same trail. In one pueblo, "we were met by a friendly Indian whom the Spaniards [Rodriguez-Chamuscado expedition] called Juan Cantor. He had been taken as an interpreter by Father Fray Augustin and on the way back had remained there because it was his land. He was versed in the Mexican language, was an uncle of the interpreter he had brought along. . . ."

Previously, a report had been circulated by Conchos Indians that the friars at Puaray had been killed, but the friendly Indians, "and especially this Juan Cantor, told us that the report that the friars were dead was false; that on the contrary they were alive."

On this cheering note, the year ended.

1583

Late in January, continuing northward along the Rio Grande, they were among the Piro, passing through "a mountainous district close to said river. This ridge contains numerous veins of silver, which extend for more than ten or twelve leagues." In certain religious ceremonies, Piro

---

*Appended to the Luxan journal is this statement: "I, Martin de Pedrosa, royal notary, certify that having been ordered by his lordship, Count of Monterrey, viceroy of this New Spain, to search among the papers left by Francisco Dominguez, cosmographer of his Majesty, for those which in any way might relate to the expedition to the provinces of New Mexico, I did so and found this report in precisely the form in which it is transcribed . . . I so certify. Mexico, May 14, 1602."

men adorn their penes with feathers, and, apparently, the Spaniards reached them while these rites were being held, for Luxan noted that "men tie their privy parts with a small ribbon," or "with small pieces of cloth; others leave them uncovered, tied near the prepuce with a cord of maguey fiber."

In February, they had almost reached the territory of the Tiwa when "the Indians told us by means of signs that the friars had been killed." Some of the men wanted to turn back, and some advocated that a fort be constructed and that seven soldiers remain in it while the others go on to Puaray to learn the truth. Espejo, who had been elected leader and chief magistrate of the expedition, refused either to turn back or divide the company. Rescuing the friars, he declared, had been only one purpose of the journey. He had become excited by Indian tales that rich provinces lay to both the east and west, and in several places he had found "many ores of different colors." He insisted, moreover, that "this was a good opportunity for me to serve his Majesty . . . while incurring no expense to him . . . ," and he would admit in time that he was also harboring the hope that his discoveries and explorations would influence the court to grant him a pardon for his crimes. He was, after all, still a fugitive from justice.

The weather was very cold and the country was covered in deep snow. It was late in February when they reached Coronado's Tiguex, near Bernalillo, and found that Fray Augustin and Fray Francisco had been slain.

No consideration was given to attempting to punish the murderers. Indeed, their identities could not be learned, although there seemed little doubt that the inhabitants of Puaray (which they called Puala) were guilty. Fray Augustin sang mass, and bestowed upon the pueblo the name of Puala de los Martires.

Puaray and most of the other adjacent pueblos, some

thirteen in all, were deserted. Luxan thought that the "inhabitants of all these settlements had fled to the sierra [the Sandia Mountains] because all had taken part in killing the friars. Some Indians soon came to find out what we wanted to do and we sent them to bring the others in peace." The Tiwa were fearful of returning, however, and "we decided to seek them in the sierra . . . where we saw seven or eight thousand Indians. We appealed to them in a friendly way and dismounted from our horses. Then some came down and asked for peace by means of signs, agreeing to return to their pueblos because they said their women and children were suffering greatly from cold." All the pueblos were well stocked with food, and "we provisioned ourselves well." The Tiwa were "neat and cleanly people, for so they are in eating and sleeping." The inhabitants of Puaray, however, remained hiding in the hills.

Again some of the company proposed returning to Mexico, but Espejo convinced them once more that dividing the little force might be disastrous. He had, moreover, been told by the Tiwa that two other prosperous Indian kingdoms lay to the west, and he was eager to visit them.

The vagueness of both Luxan's and Espejo's accounts leaves some doubt as to the route followed. Apparently they went westward from the Rio Grande to Zia, and then turned south to Acoma. Although both the Coronado and Rodriguez-Chamuscado expeditions had passed through this region, the Espejo company, as far as is known, was the first to meet Navajo. The encounter occurred at a settlement not far from Acoma, when a band of Navajo came down from the higher country in the vicinity of Mount Taylor, ostensibly on a trading mission. These "peaceful mountaineers" gave the Spaniards tortillas and other things, "even though we did not need them as we had abundant provisions." The "tortillas" were probably some kind of corn cake which the Navajo had learned to make from the Pueblos. Curiosity and perhaps apprehension undoubtedly caused them to approach the Spaniards bearing gifts. Such a gesture, unless employed to throw intended victims off guard, was seldom made by Navajo. Luxan recorded nothing more about the meeting, but Espejo would write that the Navajo, whom he called Querechos, "held a solemn ceremonial dance for us . . . dressed gaily and performed juggling tricks, including some with live snakes that were quite elaborate, all of which was most interesting to watch." These performances, however, seem more like something witnessed in a Hopi town. Espejo's memories may have been confused. He also remarks that the area occupied by the Navajo "gave promise of mines and other riches, but we did not go to see them as the people from there are many and warlike. The mountain people came to the aid of those [Pueblo] settlements."

Zuni was reached late in March. There, still standing, were crosses erected by the friars with Coronado, and there they found three Mexican Indians, Andres, Gaspar, and Anton, who had been servants with the Coronado expedition. They had in their possession "a book and a small old trunk left by Coronado . . . We could understand each other, but the Indians spoke Spanish with difficulty."

In Zuni there was again "much controversy." Fray Beltran and several others refused to go any farther, declaring that the mission undertaken had been completed. In vain Espejo pleaded with them to continue, and at last told them they could remain in Zuni or go back to Santa Barbara if they wished, but that he was going on to the province of Mojose—the Hopi.

With Espejo when he left Zuni for the Hopi towns in the middle of April were nine soldiers. Fortunately, one of them was Luxan, who kept an account of the journey. The

Zuni had warned that the Hopi would attack the Spaniards, and Espejo accepted the offer of the Zuni to send a hundred and fifty warriors with him.* Luxan thought the Zuni were spoiling for a fight and "showed a fine spirit, saying they wanted to die wherever the Castillos died . . ." The Spaniards "cut up pieces of red felt and put a colored sign on each man's head so that all could be recognized, and determined to attack unless the enemy [the Hopi] submitted peacefully at once. There were games and a playful spirit among the friendly Indians."

The report that a battle could be expected proved to be without foundation. When the first Hopi pueblo was reached, "even though it was almost sunset, so many people came out in a short time with tortillas, tamales, roasted green corn ears, and other things," for both the Spaniards and the Zuni, that "half was left over. The Hopi asked for peace, and with trembling said it was a rumor falsely raised against them that they wanted to make a war on us.

"The Lord willed that the whole land should tremble for ten lone Spaniards, when there were over twelve thousand Indians in the province, armed with bows and arrows . . ." This, of course, was a gross exaggeration. If there had been twelve thousand Hopi present who were determined upon launching an attack, none of the ten Spaniards would have survived to tell about it.

During several days of feasting and festivities in various Hopi pueblos, Espejo was told that "great riches of gold" were to be found to the southwest. In a consultation with his men, it was decided that he and four soldiers, with Hopi guiding them, should go in search of the mines. The others would return to Zuni with the company's baggage, equipment, and surplus horses.

---

*Luxan said the number of Zuni who accompanied them was thirty, and another document recorded the figure as eighty.

Espejo's daring was never better demonstrated than on the last day of April when he and four chosen companions, men no less courageous than he, rode out of the Hopi country in the face of a warning from their guides that "the mines were far away, that there was a scarcity of water, and that the route was over difficult ridges."*

Now Espejo took his place in history as a true discoverer. No white man had ever traversed the trail which crossed the Little Colorado River where Winslow, Arizona, stands today, and went on past places bearing the modern names of Salt Creek Canyon, Chavez Pass Canyon, Jay Cox Tank, Hay Lake, Cow Lake, Beaver Creek, and Montezuma's Castle, through a magnificent, rugged land, crisscrossed by gorges and immense ridges that swept against a blue spring sky. In the country through which the Verde River boiled in a tortuous course, they were in the homelands of several bands of Western Apache. These people had never seen a Spaniard, but it was obvious that they knew something about them and understood why they had come there, for Luxan wrote of them that they had "crosses painted on their foreheads, even the children . . . They gave us ores as a sign of peace and many came to show us the mines . . . we met many mountain people who received us well."

Near a "black peak" a few miles west of the Verde River, they found the mines about which the Hopi had told them. After an investigation, a deeply disappointed Luxan described them as being "so worthless that we did not find in any of them a trace of silver, as they were copper . . . and poor. We therefore determined to return at once." Espejo, in his own account, however—which was written after he

*The men with Espejo were Diego de Luxan, the chronicler, Gregorio Hernandez, Bernardino de Luna, and Francisco Barreto. Returning to Zuni were Gaspar de Luxan, a brother of Diego, Pedro Hernandez de Almansa, Alonso de Miranda, Juan Lopez de Ibarra, and Pedro Hernandez.

had returned to Mexico and was designed with the hope of securing a license to develop the mineral resources of New Mexico—disagreed sharply with Luxan's analysis. "I found the mines," he said, "and took from them with my own hands ores which, according to experts on the matter, are very rich and contain a great deal of silver."

The fact was that they had discovered the great mines near Jerome, Arizona, which in later years would yield immense fortunes in copper and silver. Espejo was right in his judgment of them, but he would never know how right he had been. Nor would Luxan ever know the magnitude of his mistake.

The route they followed in returning to Zuni remains in doubt. Luxan indicates that they traveled by way of some Hopi pueblos and "reached Zuni on the seventh of May. Here we found our companions in good health and well treated . . ." Estimating the distance from the mines to Zuni to be about seventy leagues, Espejo stated, "We wanted to return by a different way so as to have a better opportunity for observing and appraising the characteristics of the land, and I found a route more level than the one followed in going . . ." He added that the men at Zuni had been "provided with all the food they needed. We all rejoiced greatly at being together again."

However, if Fray Beltran and the others left at Zuni had suffered no hardships, they were far from content, and were more than ever determined to go home. Espejo was no less set upon traveling homeward by way of Tiguex, the Rio Grande, and the buffalo plains, for he was still convinced that more mines were to be discovered in those regions, and he argued that if they were not located, "the land could not be settled nor all of these many souls saved." The dispute reached a crisis after mass on Trinity Sunday.

Fray Beltran declared flatly that he would look no more

for minerals or any other treasures. Several others took the same stand, one of them being Gregorio Hernandez, who had gone with Espejo to the Arizona mines but had now decided to join the faction advocating an immediate return to Mexico by the most direct route. Luxan branded him a "leader of this discord," and charged that Hernandez "told everybody it was possible to escape from the land alive, and in this manner he was trying to promote his own interests and sow dissension among all. Hence he rebelled and raised the flag, demanding that the captain and the other comrades follow the king's standard." Emotions were at a high pitch, with the Zuni interested spectators to the row. Hernandez was ordered by Espejo "under penalty of death, loss of property, and conviction of treason to continue the discovery of the land, for which purpose he had been given the said flag and had taken the oath of loyalty. Since he would not desist but insisted on leaving, the flag was taken away from him by force." Calm was restored, however, and Hernandez "was not arrested or punished, because we were so few, and also because we did not wish to cause disturbances among the natives."

The violent disagreement was finally resolved by the unceremonious departure of Fray Beltran, six soldiers, and several Indian servants. The wife of one of the soldiers, a Spanish woman, was pregnant. When or where her child was born, or if it lived, are not matters of record. Some of the Mexican Indians also were accompanied by their squaws.*

Espejo left Zuni on the last day of May. The soldiers who

---

*Fray Beltran's party would reach Mexico in safety. In order to avoid the unfriendly people of Puaray and other Tiwa pueblos, they may have turned down the Rio San Jose in the vicinity of McCartys, New Mexico, to its confluence with the Rio Grande, then have followed their outbound trail to Santa Barbara. However, no account of their homeward journey is known to have been written.

had elected to remain with him were Diego de Luxan, Gaspar de Luxan, Bernardino de Luna, Pedro Hernandez de Almansa, Juan Lopez de Ibarra, Alonso de Miranda, Francisco Barreto, and Juan Fernandez. "We nine men were left alone in the land, with more courage than strength . . . ," wrote Luxan. A number of the Mexican Indian servants also had remained, but some of them soon demonstrated that they could no longer be trusted.

On the fourth of June, the little company passed Acoma, "where we found the people of the pueblo in rebellion." The next night four Mexican Indians deserted, "laden with blankets and clothes," namely, "a free Indian servant of Captain Espejo, two servants of Diego de Luxan, and two Conchos Indians, Juan Garcia and his wife Lucia." A search was made for them, but they were not overtaken. Lucia, however, reappeared and said the people of Acoma had killed her husband "because they wanted to steal what he carried."

Gaspar de Luxan and Barreto were assigned to confirm the death of Juan Garcia, "but as it was night they were unable to find him." When morning came, "they found him alive, with three arrow wounds, from which he died that day." Juan Garcia confessed on his deathbed "that he had fled, incited by Fray Beltran, who personally had asked him to do so with the promise that they would wait for him on the road and would give him horses . . . The people of Acoma kept shouting at us from the hills night and day."

Near Acomita, an outlying settlement of Acoma, "when we saw the impudence of the Indians, we decided to give them a surprise" at daybreak. But the Indians had anticipated the trick, and "they surprised us with a shower of arrows and much shouting . . . we rushed to the horses, firing our harquebuses." The Indians succeeded in wounding "only one horse. . . . Half our men with all the servants went to the rancheria and set fire to the shacks. We destroyed also a very fine field of corn . . . something they felt a great deal . . . The next day we destroyed another Indian cornfield, although the natives defended it with a fusillade of arrows." Luxan expressed the belief that all the trouble had been caused by Fray Beltran "and the rebellious ones with him," but events do not support such a contention.

Apparently the soldiers had not failed to satisfy their sexual desires, and several of them had acquired mistresses. Now followed scenes which, except for the presence of elements of serious violence, might well have been contained in a comic opera with lascivious overtones. Just where the staging took place is uncertain, but the company evidently had encountered another band of Navajo, called Curechos by Luxan. As he tells the story in his own inimitable manner and odd linguistic form, "there were peace parlays . . . ," but exchanging women apparently was the chief topic under consideration.

It seems that two of the soldiers had obtained possession of two Navajo women. One, a captive of the Hopi, had been given to Francisco Barreto, and the other had been secured somewhere along the trail. Barreto's woman had managed to escape and return to her people, but the other was not so fortunate. In the "peace parlays," it was agreed that Barreto's female chattel should be restored to him, and in return the Spaniards would surrender the girl they still held.

The Navajo, however, "determined to put over a wicked plan. It was as follows: as they had sent the Indian woman belonging to Barreto to her land, they took one of their relatives [probably a captive from some other tribe] and sent her over, wearing her feather crest so that we should not recognize her, with the intention of recovering their own girl and giving us nothing but a discharge of arrows.

This was planned with the help of the interpreter, who was another Indian woman belonging to Alonso de Miranda and who was trying to escape. The Navajo were clamoring to make the exchange, and Barreto took the woman interpreter as well as the one who was to be exchanged, tied with two maguey ropes. He was accompanied by another companion on horseback.''

The Navajo had positioned themselves on a hill, and "did not wish to come down, pretending they were afraid of the horse and that Barreto should ascend the sierra a short distance, after which they would make the exchange. Barreto told his companion to go back, that he wanted to carry out the business alone; and although there was much talk back and forth, the companion obeyed. When Diego de Luxan saw this, he realized the intentions of the Indians, mounted his horse, and went to join Barreto. The latter had left his sword and harquebus and had the Indian woman tied to his body, as a man inexperienced in war, although a good and brave soldier. He asked Diego de Luxan to go back. After much discussion, Luxan took the woman interpreter, and left his harquebus in the saddle tree, much against his [own] will, but at the entreaty of Barreto, who, being a Portuguese, thought that all the Indians in the world would not be sufficient to harm him."

Now both Barreto and Diego de Luxan were on foot, without arms, and being surrounded by Navajo with the disguised woman. Realizing that they "would not fare well" if they went any farther, Diego de Luxan suddenly "made a leap, seized the disguised Indian woman by the hair, and at the same time let loose the woman held by Barreto. The Navajo shouted at Diego de Luxan, who ran down the sierra with both Indian women. The woman interpreter wrestled with him, took from him a knife that he carried in his boot, and threw it to the Indians. Then, like a lioness, she grasped his sword, seizing it by the guard,

which Diego de Luxan could not prevent without letting
the two Indian women escape, because his hands were occupied in holding them. He threw them to the ground and
dragged them down the hill, even though the Indians shot
many arrows and threw many stones to force him to let the
women go. Then Barreto came and seized the disguised
woman, but there was such a discharge of arrows that two
pierced his right cheek and right arm. When they had
reached the plain, Espejo and other companions came to
help. With all this, Barreto had to let go of the disguised
woman; if he had not done so, the soldiers might have fared
much worse; nevertheless, they regretted very much having
lost her in the skirmish."

Evidently, the senseless brawl ended at this point, with
neither side the victor. Two days later the Spaniards were
camped on the Rio Grande not far from Puaray. They were
greeted by the Tiwa with scorn and shouts of derision.
Their requests for food were refused, and it was decided
that "unless we administered some punishment they . . .
would soon try to kill us."

Puaray was deserted, except "for some thirty Indians on
the roof. When we asked them for food . . . they mocked
us like the others. In view of this, the corners of the pueblo
were taken by four men, and four others with two servants
began to seize those natives who showed themselves. We
put them in an estufa [kiva] . . . We set fire to the big pueblo
. . . where we thought some were burned to death because
of the cries they uttered. We at once took out the prisoners
[from the kiva], two at a time, and lined them up against
some cottonwoods close to the pueblo, where they were
garroted and shot many times until they were dead. Sixteen
were executed, not counting those who burned to death
. . . This was a remarkable deed for so few people in the
midst of so many enemies."

The route taken from the Rio Grande to the Pecos River

is not clearly identified, but the group most probably followed the customary trail across the upper Galisteo Basin. As they were searching for mines, however, they may have deviated from this course in several places. News of the destruction of Puaray had spread "throughout the provinces and the people were very much afraid and regaled us." This situation, however, did not prevail at the immense pueblo of Pecos, "which must have contained two thousand men armed with bows and arrows." When the Spaniards asked for food, the Pecos inhabitants replied with surliness that they had none, and "thereupon six armed men entered the pueblo, determined to burn it, and the people were so frightened that they gave us the food against their will."

They left Pecos Pueblo on July 5, taking with them "two Indians by force [a man and a woman] to direct us to the buffalo." As they descended the Pecos River in the weeks following, Espejo and his company were once more traversing country never before entered by white men. They were in the realm of the Plains Apache, but they encountered none of these Indians. Luxan wrote that the "land was all very level, containing fine pastures and many waterholes . . . we found many buffalo tracks as well as bones and skulls," but "in all this trip we did not find any buffalo," and "we were greatly troubled by lack of food." These statements were in direct conflict with the report of Espejo, who said they had seen "great numbers of native cattle." Luxan's account, of course, is demonstrably more reliable.

They followed the twisting course of the Pecos River until the eighth or ninth of August, when they were near Toyah Lake in western Texas. Fortunately for them, they met three friendly Jumano Apache, and by drawing maps in the dirt and by signs were able to make them understand that they wanted to go to the junction of the Rio Grande and the Rio Conchos. With similar means the Jumano made it clear to them that if they continued down the Pecos they would be going far out of their way. The Jumano offered to guide them directly "by good trails" to their destination, and "this brought us no little joy."

When some days later they reached the confluence of the Rio Grande and Rio Conchos, called the La Junta area, "the people there gave us a great reception . . . and presented us with quantities of ears of green corn, cooked and raw calabashes, and catfish. They put on a great dance and festivities . . . Our feeling of security was so great that we went about almost in shirt sleeves."

On the tenth of September, they rode into the Valle of Allende, where they had started. They had been gone approximately ten months.

Espejo's report to the Spanish sovereign, which he wrote immediately after returning to his ranch, contained even higher praises for the land of the Pueblos than the account submitted by Gallegos, and it left no doubt as to Espejo's personal ambitions. In part he told King Philip:

"The natives of all those provinces are large, more vigorous than the Mexicans, and healthy, for no illness was noted among them. Their women are fairer than the Mexican women, and they are an intelligent and orderly people. There are attractive pueblos with plazas and well-arranged houses. This indicated that the inhabitants would learn quickly any matter dealing with good government.

"In the greater part of those provinces, there is an abundance of game beasts and birds: rabbits, hares, deer, buffalo, ducks, geese, cranes, and pheasants . . . There are also fine wooded mountains with trees of all kinds, salines, and rivers containing a great variety of fish.

"*Carts and wagons can be driven through most of this region;* and there are good pastures for cattle as well as lands suitable for vegetables or grain crops, whether irrigated or depending on seasonal rains.

"There are many rich mines, too, from which I brought ores to be assayed and to determine their quality.

"I brought also an Indian man . . . and an Indian woman . . . so that they might enlighten us regarding those provinces and the road to that region, if its discovery and colonization are undertaken anew in the service of his Majesty. . . ."

The highest officials of the Spanish government were fully informed of the exciting tales about the country of the Pueblos that were circulating throughout New Spain. Communications from provincial authorities supported the optimistic opinions of frontier residents and priests that settlement and development of the north would not only return fortunes to the Spanish treasury but would bring countless thousands of heathens into the Catholic faith. The archbishop of Mexico told the Council of the Indies that if half of what he had heard were true, a new world had been discovered.

Yet it was not these reports, encouraging though they were, that were entirely responsible for reviving the interest of the sovereign and his foreign affairs advisers in colonizing New Mexico, a subject to which little thought had been given for several decades. Now a series of menacing international incidents demanded that serious attention be paid to guarding the northern flank of Spain's immense New World dominion. British raiders had struck along the Pacific Coast, threatening the lucrative commerce which had been established between Mexico and the Orient. Explorers from other European nations were probing the opposite side of the continent. There were rumors that the Strait of Anian, believed to reach from the Atlantic to the Pacific across northern North America, had been discovered, and that England was planning to fortify it, and thus would control a new and shorter route from Europe to the Far East.

Several months before Espejo had returned to write of the wondrous resources he had discovered, King Philip had revealed his desire that practical measures be taken toward the founding of a permanent colony, appropriately garrisoned, in the undeveloped region north of Mexico. In a royal cedula to the viceroy of Mexico, he had stated the belief that the best procedure, and perhaps the most economical, would be to contract with some reponsible person to undertake the conquest, a man who was not only wealthy, devout, and of good repute but who could be depended upon to obey the laws controlling colonization and who had fully demonstrated his ability to serve as the first governor of the new province of New Mexico.

Only a saint could have come anywhere close to meeting these specifications, and there were not many identifiable blood and flesh saints in Mexico. There were, however, any number of men who, if their records for integrity and responsibility were somewhat stained, could qualify as being wealthy and prominent, and anyone could swear to uphold the laws and attend mass on holy days.

Proprietors of great estates, mine owners, magnates of commerce, political and military officials—indeed, the affluent and the distinguished in every state of Mexico—were soon engaged in a feverish competition for the coveted post. Fearing royal displeasure, and far more cognizant than the sovereign in far off Seville of the tremendous organizational, legal, and political complications involved in such an immense project, the viceroy and his confidants were careful to make no hasty decisions. In fact, they indulged in such thoughtful deliberations, were so extremely cautious, and argued so much among themselves, that nothing at all was accomplished.

1584

Espejo had the temerity to offer to "pacify and settle" New Mexico at the same time he pleaded with the king to "mercifully pardon" him for murdering two vaqueros. He advocated that he be "accompanied on this expedition by twenty-four Franciscan friars who can remain in the various provinces opened to colonization . . . the friars are to be sent entirely at your Majesty's expense." He would, declared Espejo, "recruit four hundred men, one hundred of them married, with their wives and children," as the nucleus of the colony, and supply a thousand mares, the necessary number of stallions, four thousand cows and bulls, eight hundred horses, one thousand male and female sheep, dried beef from five hundred cows, fifty pack animals laden with provisions, wagons and carts, and a quantity of iron bars and tools.

There are indications that because of his experience as an explorer, frontier cattleman, and mine operator, Espejo's proposal was given serious consideration on high levels. However, competition was keen, pressures on officials were great, and the machinery of the Spanish government often was stalled by aggravating breakdowns. These were caused not so much by political dissensions, religious squabbles, and administrative negligence as by slow and unreliable communications. Ships were freqently lost, and the royal mail went down with them and their crews. Under the most favorable conditions, an exchange of dispatches between Mexico City and Seville took a year.

1585

Applicants waited in vain for a decision on the New Mexico colonization project.

1586

Espejo received word that he ranked high among the contenders. Confident that he would be victorious if he could plead his case personally before high officials in Seville— and perhaps be so fortunate as to be granted an audience by the king—he sailed for Spain. He died in Havana.

1587–1589

The files of the Council of the Indies bulged with communications regarding the northern conquest. Numerous meetings were held at which the matter was thoroughly discussed, but no recommendation of a leader was made.

1590

The New Mexico problem became a major burden of a new viceroy, Luis de Velasco. Despite the growing urgency, he refused, on the grounds that he was unfamiliar with the problem, to make blind decisions, or even to acquiesce to the opinions expressed by his predecessor. He would announce his views in due time, but only after conducting his own investigation.

Undoubtedly a number of men, some of whom had lived for six years with the hope of being chosen, had been tempted to take matters into their own hands, much as Espejo had done. But the risks were many, the costs would be extreme, and there was no assurance that success, great as it might be, would relieve them from suffering penalties. Certainly they would not escape the wrath of other contenders, and many of them were men with political influence.

Gaspar Castano de Sosa was a pioneer in the northern Mexican state of Nuevo Leon. He had founded several settlements, had been the first alcalde of Monterrey, and later had become lieutenant governor and captain general of the state. As unscrupulous as he was aggressive, he had acquired, by both legal and illegal means, mining properties and ranches, and he had engaged in the Indian slave trade.

Twice, at great expense to himself, he had sent emissaries to Mexico City to plead for his appointment as colonizer of New Mexico, to no avail. The only reply he had received had infuriated him. The viceroy had commanded him to stop capturing and selling Indian slaves, and had warned him not to leave Mexico without permission. Although he realized no less than did his competitors for the New Mexico office the perils inherent in an unauthorized conquest of such magnitude, he permitted his greed to overcome his good sense. Visions of accumulating great riches blinded him, and he devised a scheme for grasping the great opportunity before someone else fell heir to it.

Castano was the owner of extensive cattle ranges and agricultural lands in the vicinity of Monclova, his home. He invited townspeople and tenant farmers, all of whom were mired in the state of poverty in which he kept them, to a fiesta. After stuffing his ragged guests with good food and wine, he revealed his plan. He had learned confidentially, he informed them, about bountiful lands to be taken for nothing, and he proposed that they join him in an expedition to occupy them. Everyone who went would become the owner of a large farm, but there would be even greater rewards. So rich was this northern country in minerals that with little work they would all become inconceivably wealthy. To prove that he was telling the truth, he displayed some pieces of extraordinarily high-grade silver. It had been taken, he swore, from unowned deposits on the upper Rio Grande.

The silver trick worked. Dancing for joy, the ignorant peons, who had no hope of possessing more than a mud hut, a straw bed, and a few animals, agreed to go with him to the land of promise.

The Castano expedition is historically important for three reasons: (1) it was the first attempt to establish a permanent colony in the country of the Pueblos, indeed, in the entire American Southwest; (2) the first wheeled vehicles ever seen by southwestern Indians were those of Castano's settlers; and (3) the expedition was the greatest debacle to occur since Coronado and his men put Cibola behind them, a half-century earlier.

In the terrible heat of August, a long column composed of one hundred and seventy men, women, and children— virtually the entire population of Monclova and its environs —a train of supply wagons, a herd of horses and cattle, and two wheeled brass cannon crawled in a cloud of choking dust toward the Rio Grande. Riders were sent ahead to capture some Indians and enslave them. Now the peons had their first taste of the great affluence they would enjoy— they had servants, wranglers, and camp tenders, all their own.

Castano, completely a victim of his own illusions, disdained to follow the long-established trail along the Rio Conchos. He harbored the idea that if he opened a new route he might come upon people and treasures earlier explorers had missed. As a result, it took the slowly moving company six weeks to find a passage to the Rio Grande. The river was crossed with great difficulty at some point between the present Texas towns of Del Rio and Eagle Pass. So exhausted were the colonists and animals that they were obliged to spend another two or three weeks recuperating from the ordeal.

Starting early in October, they soon found themselves in country that in places was impassable. At last, after several more weeks of struggle, they reached the Rio Pecos. Turning north, they found a more feasible trail through the immense plains of the Llano Estacado. It was the trail over which Espejo had returned.

The author of a *Memoria* of Castano's exploits has not been definitely identified, but the account remains the chief source of information of this phase of Pueblo history.* In November, the company was in the country of the Jumano Apache. Espejo, traveling with only a few men, did not mention having any difficulties with Indians in this region, but Castano's large force encountered serious trouble. The *Memoria* relates that on one occasion several men "who were leading the way, crossed the [Rio Pecos] river upon reaching an impassable spot, at which moment they saw a group of Indian men and went toward them. We all began to talk to the group by signs, some from one side of the river and some from the other. Our men drew away . . . but Juan de Vega, himself a native [Mexican Indian], lagged behind. Some of the Indians, seeing he was alone, seized him, took some ropes away from him, threw him into the river, and

*See bibliography under Castano-Morlete.

shot him with three arrows. The next morning a large number of natives appeared, and the lieutenant governor tried in every way to get them to come to the camp, but to no avail.

"While we were at this place . . . the men in the camp noticed the Indians driving away some oxen. The lieutenant governor, seeing their shameless behavior, ordered Cristobal de Heredia and five soldiers to go after the thieves. During the pursuit, Heredia and his men encountered a group of Indians, who, they said, attacked them with arrows. Our men in self-defense killed some of the assailants, apprehended four, and brought them to camp . . . the lieutenant governor ordered that one of the prisoners be hanged as punishment and that the other three, since they were mere youths, be kept as interpreters . . . Despite our extreme care they escaped with an ox . . ."

From this point forward the account contains numerous entries regarding food shortages: "We found quantities of mesquite,* which the humbler members of the party ate, thus saving us some provisions; this was much appreciated, as the supplies were getting low . . . we caught a goodly number of fish, which we considered a great treat, aside from the fact that the catch relieved a pressing need . . . the abundance of mesquite . . . was eaten not only by the humbler members of the expedition but also by the rest of us . . . there was so much mesquite that occasionally it spared us the need of slaughtering . . . there were many wolves, which killed some of the goats that had strayed . . . By now our provisions of corn and wheat were well-nigh depleted. Since we had plenty of fish and mesquite, the lieutenant governor ordered that each person be given only

---

*A leguminous shrub that bears pods rich in sugar, an important food of range cattle and other animals.

one small tortilla for each meal, but that two pounds of meat be distributed also to every individual per day."

Early in December, Castano estimated that they were close to territory in which the Rodriguez-Chamuscado and Espejo companies reported large pueblos. He ordered Heredia and eleven men to reconnoiter the country ahead, instructing them "to make every effort to find some Indians and to bring one or two back to camp, so that we could learn from the captives whether there were any settlements in the vicinity. Our men were *not to enter any town* . . . because the governor wanted to do so himself with his wagons and his entire force united in one body."

The scouting party departed, and the column continued to advance slowly up the Pecos. During the next fortnight, Heredia twice sent men back for supplies, reporting that no settlements had been found. Castano sent them word to continue their search.

On December 23, Castano and a companion, riding in advance of the main company, saw in the distance a group of men approaching. Some were on foot, a few were riding bareback, and most of them were without weapons. Hurrying forward to meet them, Castano learned of the sad experiences of Heredia and his scouts. They had not only disobeyed their instructions by entering a settlement, but they had come perilously close to being annihilated.

They had found the great pueblo of Pecos. As they had sighted it ahead near the end of a day, "they had camped for the night and the next morning went toward the pueblo and were forced to enter it because the weather was so bitterly cold and the land was covered with snow. The Indians . . . received them in a friendly manner, giving them food for that day and some eight or ten fanegas of corn."

The next day Heredia asked for more supplies to take back to the company. He and his men "walked securely about the pueblo, relying on the good will of the inhabitants. All of a sudden the natives began to shout, and, at the same time, to hurl stones and shoot arrows. Faced with this attack, the men fell back as best they could to the place where they had left their arms." They found only five harquebuses; the other guns had already been stolen by Indians. Three of the Spaniards had been wounded, but all of them managed to get away. Left behind in Pecos were "five harquebuses, eleven swords, nineteen saddles, nine sets of horse armor, and a quantity of wearing apparel and bedding."

Heredia and his men fled southward along the Pecos trail, expecting at any moment to be overtaken and slain. For three days they traveled through the snow "without a morsel to eat. Then God willed that they should meet an Indian woman on the plain who gave them some corn flour and beans, so little that it hardly amounted to a handful for each person; but had it not been for this aid they would have perished from hunger, cold, snow, and fierce winds . . ."

In accordance with the custom generally followed by Spanish expeditions of the time, Castano assembled his lieutenants to discuss a course of action. It was decided that he should take a force of the ablest men and proceed ahead to recover the stolen goods and punish the thieves. A cheerless Christmas, without festivities or religious services, was spent preparing for the offensive. On the next morning, Castano started. He had with him nineteen heavily armed men, seventeen Mexican Indian servants, and the two wheeled cannon.

Castano's assault on Pecos began in the early morning of the last day of the year.

"Going forward . . . his men in formation and with flag unfurled, the governor, as we came in view of the pueblo, ordered the buglers to blow their trumpets. When he reached the town, he noticed that the natives were in battle array, men as well as women standing fully prepared on the terraces and down below." Camp was established at "a harquebus shot from the pueblo." The cannon were set up, and the cannoneers were told to keep fuses lighted, and Castano "urged us to be very alert and to conduct ourselves like brave soldiers, as we were accustomed to do."

Preparations for battle completed, Castano "called to the Indians in sign language, but none would leave his dwelling or come out from behind the barricades, trenches, or ramparts which the pueblo maintained for its defense at the most vital points."

Castano rode closer to the walls and again "called to the Indians and told them he would not do them any harm or injury, but this failed to calm them. On the contrary, they hastened to pile up stones on the terraces. The stones were brought by the women, for the men were all armed, at their posts, and shouting lustily at us."

Four or five times during the day Castano, with two or three soldiers, "circled the entire pueblo in an effort to soothe the natives with kind words and by signs, to no avail." Nor were the gifts he offered accepted. "Instead of softening, the Indians shot arrows and hurled quantities of stone by means of slings."

At two o'clock in the afternoon, convinced that any further effort to induce the Indians to surrender would be useless, Castano ordered that one of the cannon be fired over the pueblo. When it became apparent that this had no effect on the defenders, the men began to advance, firing their harquebuses. Indians toppled from the terraces, but for each one that fell two or more others appeared in his place. Several Spaniards were badly hurt in attempts to climb the walls. Arrows and stones came in showers. The Indians, "realizing the strength of our onslaught, replied in kind. None of them abandoned his section or trench; on the contrary, each one defended the post entrusted to him, without faltering in the least . . . women showed fierce courage and kept on bringing more stones to the terraces . . . Such intelligence among barbarians seemed incredible."

No account depicts with greater clarity the ingenuity shown by Pueblos in constructing defenses than the *Memoria* attributed to Castano. It seems doubtful that any force of Indians using Stone Age weapons could have conquered Pecos. Against anything but guns and cannon, it would have been an impregnable objective.

Besides the outer walls and heavy barricades, the great pueblo was honeycombed with twisting, narrow tunnels. A section could be abandoned without danger to other sections. In each of the five plazas, invaders would be exposed to arrows and stones shot from parapets and roofs. Having gained a level with great difficulty, several Spaniards "were told to climb to the top . . . while others below protected their ascent . . . There did not seem to be as large a number of Indians at that spot as there were before, but the few who held their posts . . . defended the terraces very bravely . . . no one could climb to the top except by the slender wooden hand ladders, which only one person at a time could ascend. There were no doors leading from one room to another, but only hatchways just large enough for a single person; therefore our men, in order to get through them and climb to the terraces, had to ascend without sword or shield, after which they passed the weapons to one an-

other as they climbed." Castano, "perceiving the danger to
our soldiers, ordered the others to train their harquebuses
on the enemy . . ." Three warriors were brought down,
"with the result that the natives were forced to abandon the
barricade and our men took it." Piecemeal victories were
achieved by firing from positions beyond the reach of arrows. "Wooden corridors" extended along the "streets and
plazas between the houses. The natives pass from one house
to the other through these corridors, and also by means of
wooden bridges spanning the street from terrace to terrace."

In the fading light of the wintry afternoon, the insuperable weapons of the Spaniards won the fight. The shouting
and the tumult died, no arrows or stones fell, and a strange
silence fell over the pueblo, broken at last by the bugle calls
of triumph. Castano entered a plaza with several of his men,
and Indians gave him signs of peace; Castano told them
"that they should not be afraid. The natives understood him
clearly, and they soon brought out some food which they
threw down to us from the corridors, since none of them
dared to descend."

Pecos had capitulated, but the inhabitants remained concealed in their houses. An attempt was made to take some
of them prisoner, but none could be caught "because there
were many trap doors and hatchways, and because the area
was so burrowed with underground passages that it was a
real labyrinth."

Guards were posted "to prevent the Indians from leaving," and in the falling darkness of New Year's Eve, the
other Spaniards withdrew to enjoy the warmth of their
campfires.

1591

Castano paid a New Year's call at the pueblo, and "many people came out and made signs of friendship." Some men, carrying torches, "entered the underground passages where the natives had hidden the day before, and they found many tunnels leading to other blockhouses and to underground estufas . . . there were no people at all in the area searched." As the entire pueblo was calm, Castano ordered the sentries removed.

When the Spaniards entered it on January 2, "not a single inhabitant was to be found." Overnight the entire population had vanished in complete silence into the surrounding mountains.

Pecos storehouses were "provided with such an abundant supply of corn that everyone marveled. There were those who maintained that the total must amount to more than thirty thousand fanegas . . . all of excellent quality. Moreover, there was a good supply of beans. In their houses, the natives also store . . . herbs, chili, and calabashes. After sending a large quantity of food back to the main group, Castano made preparations "to visit some other pueblos." His real purpose, of course, was to look for mines. He had shown samples of minerals to the Indians with whom he had talked at Pecos after the battle, and they had told him that similar ores were to be found among people to the west. The soldiers who would accompany him "were displeased . . . on account of the hardships involved, and because, instead of returning to the headquarters of the expedition, they would have to go in search of a road . . . for the route we were following could not be traveled by wagons." But neither snow, nor ice, nor freezing winds, nor forbidding canyons and mountain passes could have stopped Castano from attempting to fulfill the dream that fired his blood and dominated his thoughts—the dream of finding gold and silver.

As they were ready to leave Pecos on January 6, two Indians wandered into the pueblo and were seized. One was sent to inform the people that they could return to their homes in safety, but the other was held as a guide. Shortly after the party had started, another Indian was captured, and he, too, was forced into service.

News of the fall of Pecos undoubtedly had preceded Castano, and the inhabitants of numerous pueblos he visited agreeably supplied him with food. As these settlements are not named in the *Memoria,* his wanderings cannot be delineated with accuracy. Descriptions of the terrain traversed, however, indicate that he followed a trail through Glorieta Pass to the Santa Fe area and the Rio Grande. Camps were made at numerous pueblos, probably Tesuque, Nambe, Cuyamunque, Pojoaque, and Jacona. Crosses were erected in each town, and Castano conducted ceremonies designed to impress upon the Pueblos that they had become subjects of the province of New Mexico, which he was establishing in the name of the Spanish king. He appointed Pueblo governors, alcaldes, and other officials, and "all these acts were performed with appropriate ceremonies, marked by the blowing of trumpets and the firing of harquebuses."

The *Memoria* speaks of a pueblo (probably San Juan) "situated in a valley between sierras" that was "buried under snow a yard in depth by actual measure, such as we had never seen before; it was so deep that the horses could not travel. Consequently, when we arrived no one came out to meet us . . . The very sight of us frightened the inhabitants, especially the women, who wept a great deal."

After traveling for some distance up the Rio Grande,

Castano turned about and followed the river to Cochiti, Santo Domingo, and San Felipe. He left the river in several places to explore the surrounding mountains and valleys. No trouble with Pueblos arose, and "it seemed as if the lieutenant governor was especially endowed by God to win allegiance to his Majesty from these barbarians, so that by the divine will they might be brought to a knowledge of the Catholic faith. The governor had a cross with an image of God our Lord, and whenever he came to a pueblo he held it in his hands while he and his companions knelt reverently to kiss the crucifix, at which the barbarians marveled. Moreover, he induced the Indians in all these peublos—men, women and children—to do likewise."

Late in January, Castano started back to the Pecos to bring the main group of the expedition to the more populated area of the Rio Grande. On the last day of the month, the entire expedition moved forward through the Galisteo Valley. The weather continued cold, the streams were frozen, and progress was achieved with great difficulty and suffering. The animals could quench their thirst with snow, but fodder was difficult to obtain, and on some day they went without food of any kind. Stops were made in the pueblos of San Cristobal and Galisteo, in each of which they were "well received."

By February 23, the company had advanced only as far as San Marcos. Castano decided that it might be prudent for him to return to Pecos Pueblo and "reassert Spanish authority." He left San Marcos on March 2, taking nineteen men with him. Several soldiers were sent ahead "to check the flight of the people if they should try to escape." When Castano arrived, he found the people of Pecos ". . . all assured and calm; many came out to meet him . . . no one left . . . To reassure them further and overcome all fear, we paraded through the town on horseback, with trumpets blowing, which greatly pleased the Indians . . . The next day the lieutenant governor assembled them all and named their governor, alcalde, and alguacil; and we raised a large cross . . ."

Castano had selected Santo Domingo Pueblo as the "capital" of his colony, and on March 9 the entire expedition arrived there. He soon resumed his tireless search for the treasures he believed were to be found but which thus far had eluded him. With twenty men he went first to the area between the Sandia and Ortiz Mountains. He came upon two pueblos, Paa-ko and San Antonio, which had been recently destroyed by Plains Apache. They "could see plainly that it was true, because there were signs of many having been killed. In these towns we found an abundance of corn and beans."

Returning to the Rio Grande, Castano and his gold hunters continued on to the pueblos "whose people had killed the friars"—Puaray and the other Tiwa towns in the Bernalillo area. For ten days or two weeks, they continued to explore, but no mineral veins were discovered, and they turned back toward Santo Domingo deeply disappointed. They had nearly reached the "capital" when Indians informed them "that many other Spaniards had arrived [in Santo Domingo], which pleased us all very much."

Their pleasure was of brief duration. Going on, they soon met three colonists who were looking for them with bad news. Captain Juan Morlete, with a force of fifty cavalrymen, was waiting in Santo Domingo to arrest Castano.

When Morlete left Nuevo Leon is not certain, but he probably started sometime in the previous December, as it has been ascertained that early in January he "camped on the Rio Grande" in southern New Mexico. The orders he carried from Viceroy Velasco were dated October 1, 1590, but it would have taken some time for him to organize his

expedition—he was authorized to recruit his company—
and to have reached northern Mexico.

The main purposes of Morlete's mission, said the viceroy's instructions, were "to put a stop to the expedition
planned and undertaken by Gaspar Castano and his men in
contravention of my specific order as well as the general
orders of his Majesty; to check the injuries and excesses
against the poor natives which have done such great disser-
vice to God our Lord and his Majesty; and to insure the
punishment of those who perpetrated the offenses, as well
as giving satisfaction to the Indians for abuses already suffered . . .

"When by God's favor you reach Gaspar Castano and his
people, you will use every mild and prudent means you can
to persuade them to give up their expedition and return
with you . . . you will bring them back in reasonable comfort; but you must always remember that you are conducting them as prisoners whose lack of conscience and evil aims
you cannot trust . . . you will impound all goods belonging
to the prisoners. . . . you will bring everything to this
capital, including all their wagons. If there are women in
the company of the accused, you will see to it that they are
well treated and made comfortable, and that their personal
decency is respected . . . This same kindliness and good
treatment shall be shown to any children . . . you will take
away from Castano and his people any slaves they have
seized and will return these slaves, as you proceed to the
places whence they were removed or wherever they wish
to go."

Captain Morlete was in the plaza of Santo Domingo when
Castano and his men arrived. The lieutenant governor rode
up to him and dismounted, and the two men, with typical
Spanish courtesy, greeted each other warmly and em
braced. Morlete then drew from his pocket "a royal decree

. . . which he read aloud word for word," and requested Castano to submit to arrest. According to the *Memoria,* Castano "replied that he was quite willing, if that was the wish of his Majesty, for he was entirely subject to his authority. Then all of them walked to the tents, and Morlete gave orders that the lieutenant governor should be shackled . . ."

Santo Domingo was the first "permanent" Spanish settlement in the land of the Pueblos, but it existed hardly more than a month. On an April day, when the valley of the Rio Grande was beautiful with the full flowering of spring, the weary and discouraged colonists, the trail-worn livestock, and the creaking wagons, all guarded by Morlete's cavalry, started down the long trail to Mexico.

Castano was never released from the irons. During the days when the column rested, he busied himself in writing a long letter to the viceroy, proclaiming his innocence of any wrongdoing and appealing for mercy. His efforts, he told Velasco, "will greatly facilitate the execution of your Grace's plan for settlement of the land, as his Majesty has urged you to do . . . The many things I saw in the said land . . . will prove most effective in encouraging many people to go there; for I have traveled over it with wagons, and all that was seen or reported in the past is negligible in comparison with what has now been brought to light." He was, said Castano, "sadly exhausted and broken in health . . . People will find that I am as obedient and humble now as I have always been and shall continue to be, not at all like the person pictured in the accusations heaped against me."*

*Castano was sentended by the Audencia (judical court) of Mexico to serve six years in exile in the Philippines. He was killed there in a revolt of galley slaves, unaware that the Council of the Indies had revoked the decision of the lower court and had found him innocent.

1592

No decision as to who would be given a contract for the colonization of New Mexico was made, although an announcement had been expected from day to day throughout the year. Rumors were rife, but little reliable information was obtainable from the high officials responsible for resolving the problem. Not many persons were privileged to attend the deliberations of the Council of the Indies, and even fewer shared in the private thoughts of the viceroy and the king. However, one thing was certain: each of the candidates was demanding extensive concessions and royal favors. This increased the difficulty of obtaining the approval by Philip II of recommendations submitted to him, for the sovereign, notoriously parsimonious, desired to achieve the conquest with little expense to the already overburdened treasury and without sacrificing prerogatives he felt properly should be retained in their full scope by the viceroy and the council. A man possessed of irrevocable authority and uncontestable rights in a remote place like New Mexico, the boundaries of which were not known, might assert himself in ways injurious to Spain's position as a world power.

1593

Despite the disastrous experience of Castano, there were still some men on the northern Mexico frontier daring enough to gamble their own freedom, and even their own lives, in an attempt to satisfy a craving for wealth and power.

One of them was Captain Francisco Leyva de Bonilla. In

February he was sent by the governor of Nueva Vizcaya with a contingent of cavalry to hunt for Indians who had been raiding cattle herds. This was the opportunity for which Bonilla had been waiting. Unbeknown to his superiors, he had been conspiring with a disreputable adventurer, Antonio Gutierrez de Humana, to go to New Mexico illegally and explore for silver mines. Now, with a heavily armed and well-supplied company under his command, he decided that the time was right for launching the scheme. Humana agreed, and somewhere in the barren country along the Rio Conchos, he joined Bonilla with a group of men and Mexican Indian servants he had secretly recruited for the venture. A few of the soldiers, who had been unaware of the plot, refused to become deserters and turned back, but most of them were induced to go along by promises of rich rewards.

The route taken by previous expeditions, down the Rio Conchos to the Rio Grande and up that river to New Mexico, was followed, and after nearly two months of hard travel and exploring, they established their headquarters in the Tewa pueblo of San Ildefonso.

In this area they must have encountered another Turk, who told them of the fabulous fortunes to be found in a province called Quivera. They swallowed the tale with no less gullibility than Coronado had shown more than half a century earlier. In May they had passed Pecos Pueblo, on their way to the Great Plains.

Beyond the Canadian River, in eastern New Mexico, they vanished into the sea of grass.

1594

Orders were issued by the provincial government in Mexico City for the arrest of Bonilla and Humana, but no force was sent to pursue and capture them. That would be a duty of the man who would lead the conquest of New Mexico, for it was no secret that the moment of decision was near. The king himself was becoming irritated by the delay, and had told concerned officials to settle the matter. It had, after all, been under consideration for nearly a decade, and the sovereign was disposed to think that any further postponement might prove to be unwise.

1595

The coveted post went to a man of enormous wealth, distinguished lineage, and the heart of a beast. He was Don Juan de Onate of Zacatecas.

Any hopes the Pueblos may have had of escaping further persecution by the Spanish were obliterated on September 21 when Viceroy Velasco's signature and seal were affixed to the lengthy document granting Onate the authority "to carry out the discovery, pacification, and conquest of the provinces of New Mexico."

In seeking the appointment, Onate had enumerated personal qualifications that were not only impressive but met most of the reqirements specified by the king. Although the date of his birth is not known, some indication of his age is suggested in his statement that in going to New Mexico he would be continuing what "I have been doing for more than twenty years in fighting and pacifying" Mexican Indian "nations in the kingdoms of New Galicia and New Vizcaya, at my own expense—emulating my father, Cristobal de Onate, who, as captain general in the Kingdom of New Galicia, conquered, pacified, and settled the greater portion of it at his own cost . . . and in which he followed in the footsteps of his forefathers, who as knights and gentlemen, always devoted themselves to the service of the royal crown of Castile . . ." Cristobal de Onate had served under Cortes, conqueror of Mexico, had distinguished himself as a military officer, and was one of the discoverers of the famous silver mines of Zacatecas.

Juan de Onate's wife was Dona Isabel de Tolosa. Her father was a renowned conquistador and mine owner, Juanes de Tolosa, and her mother was a daughter of Cortes and a granddaughter of the Aztec emperor, Montezuma. Much of Juan de Onate's fortune had been inherited from his father and his wife's family, but he had greatly increased his wealth by his own enterprise. He had acquired vast ranches, and claimed to have discovered at his own expense a number of mines that had "yielded millions in royal fifths to the crown," and, of course, millions to himself.

Viceroy Velasco's family—his father had been the second viceroy of Mexico—had been socially intimate with the Onates for many years. This close friendship undoubtedly influenced Velasco to be more generous in the agreement he signed with Juan de Onate than he might have been with another man. However, approval of Onate's contract was one of Velasco's last official acts in Mexico City. He had been notified of his promotion to the viceroyalty of Peru. His successor, the Count of Monterrey, already had arrived from Spain.

Onate's contract gave him extreme powers. He was in almost every sense a dictator. His title was Governor and Captain General of New Mexico. He was also the highest judicial officer of the colony, with the authority to deliver

unappealable decisions in civil and criminal cases, not ex-
cluding those punishable by death. All patronage was under
his jurisdiction. Besides the making of appointments, he
was authorized "to distribute among the soldiers, conquerors, and settlers who may go on the said expedition . . .
pueblos and vassals" as he deemed proper, and these *encomiendas,* these gifts of Indian towns, farmlands, water
rights, and grazing ranges, were to be enjoyed by the recipi-
ents and their heirs for four generations.

Onate would receive an annual salary of six thousand
gold ducats of Castile—an unusually large income—and he
was permitted to borrow a similar amount from the provincial treasury, "upon furnishing guarantors to repay the
money." He was granted the privilege of "taking up mines
or shares in mines," but instead of the customary "royal
fifth," he would be required to pay to the sovereign only
a "royal tenth" of any gold, silver, or other metals and
precious stones recovered. He requested that the king be
persuaded to reduce this dividend "to one-twentieth for a
period of fifty years." He was given the authority "to levy
the tributes which the Indians will have to give, according
to the fruits of their land," not only tributes to the king but
to himself and all other *encomenderos* having suzerainty over
natives.

For his own private estate in New Mexico, Onate could
appropriate thirty square leagues of land (more than
150,000 acres), "wherever I shall select, including all the
subjects who may live within the said territory. If any
pueblo which is a capital should fall within these boundaries, it shall be understood that the other pueblos under the
said capital, even if they should fall outside the thirty
leagues, shall be added to my *repartimiento,* including the
lands, pastures, waters, and woods of the districts where the
said subjects may happen to be."

Two other provisions of the contract were extremely

significant. He could establish a Treasury of New Mexico over which he had absolute control, and he would be accountable for his actions only to the Council of the Indies in Spain. He had bluntly demanded these terms "so that none of the viceroys of this New Spain or neighboring *audencias* may meddle in the jurisdiction of the New Mexico government."

Onate guaranteed to recruit at least two hundred fighting men, as many families of settlers as possible, contribute some seven thousand head of livestock (cattle, sheep, goats, oxen, and horses), grains for sowing, tools, equipment, carts and wagons, building materials, gifts for Indians, clothing, medicines, and all food supplies that would be needed for the long journey. Except for the money he had borrowed, all expenditures required to get the expedition under way had to come out of his own pocket, and he estimated that they would total more than half a million pesos. Affluent as he was, such an amount would be a strain on the immediately available resources of his family.

Perhaps it was the appointment of a new viceroy, Monterrey, whom he did not know, that stirred doubts in him as to the wisdom of assuming such a heavy financial burden before being assured that Velasco's successor would unqualifiedly support the great project. That could not be determined at once, of course, and he was eager to get started. He could, however, take at least one step that would provide protection in the event developments inimical to his interests occurred.

He inserted the following stipulation in the agreement approved by Velasco: "If, after I have made this contract with your lordship and you have signed it, there should arrive from Spain someone with a contract from the king for this project and should bring a cedula and orders that your lordship support him, in such case these orders are not to invalidate the contract I may have signed with your lordship

or annul the rights of those representing me . . . and inasmuch as I shall be incurring great expense from the outset
. . . for this reason if what I have contracted and agreed
upon should turn out valueless and someone else shall be
entrusted with the expedition, I shall be reimbursed from
the royal treasury for all that I may have spent in the expedition and its equipment, as well as for any losses or dam-
ages."

To which Velasco appended the understanding:
". . . should the contingency he mentions come to pass, in
so far as the expenditures and provisions he may have made
for the expedition are concerned," it would be Onate's
right "to recover his losses from the person who may try to
take the contract away from him."

Hoping to start early in the coming year, Onate proceeded to organize the expedition. He soon discovered
how wise he had been to include the protective stipulation
in his agreement.

1596

The work of recruiting colonists and assembling equipment
and supplies for the expedition was well under way when,
in February, Viceroy Monterrey wrote the king that he had
found it necessary to abrogate some of the concessions
granted Onate. One of his chief objections to the Onate
contract was the provision which placed Onate beyond the
jurisdiction of his own office and the courts of Mexico. Not
even viceroys enjoyed such freedom from restraint, and he
thought it was "proper for the security of your majesty's
royal conscience" that the viceroy of New Spain, as well as
the Council of the Indies, retain the power to censor and
punish Onate for violations of the ordinances governing

new discoveries and colonization. He also deprived Onate of the power to appoint royal officials in New Mexico, and to determine the amount of tribute to be extracted from Indians.

Onate and his supporters, most of whom had invested money in the enterprise, vigorously protested the changes, but at last, believing that in spite of them fortunes could be made, ceased their opposition.

Suddenly a more menacing situation arose in another quarter. The Council of the Indies denounced Onate as totally unfit to command the expedition, charging in an April letter to the king that Onate "had so mismanaged his estate that he now owes more than thirty thousand pesos in bad debts, that he is holding back his creditors by deceit, and that in another expedition that he made, the soldiers did not think much of him but disobeyed him." Reliable persons who knew Onate well, declared the council, had stated that "it will be impossible for him to obtain the objectives of this expedition, for not only does it require great financial resources, which he does not have, he being a private person, but no man of importance will want to follow him or be under his government. So, the only people who will join him will be outcasts and vagabonds, who serve only to cause disgraceful disturbances and riots."

Now it was disclosed that Onate had a new and formidable rival. He was Don Pedro Ponce de Leon, a member of one of the oldest, most distinguished, and most influential families in Spain. The council strongly favored canceling Onate's contract and giving a new one to Don Pedro.

Meanwhile, Onate's assembled forces, supply wagons, and livestock herds were pushing toward Santa Barbara, the frontier outpost from which they would start their conquest. They had reached the Nazas River in September when they were staggered by a message from Viceroy Monterrey. It informed Onate of the king's order that "he was to halt at once and proceed no farther . . . with the expedition, but, on the contrary, delay it until he receives further orders from his majesty . . ."

The king vacillated on the situation, in one moment favoring Don Pedro but never ordering the cancellation of the Onate contract. At last fate decided the problem for him. Don Pedro, a man in middle age, became ill. Moreover, he was having financial troubles, and when he asked the king for a loan, his prospects as a conqueror quickly sank below the horizon. Getting money out of the pinchpenny Philip was a feat achieved by few persons, regardless of friendship or prominence.

At one time Onate had been fully prepared to start for New Mexico, but the king's command to delay the expedition pending further orders had caused some colonists and soldiers, as well as several priests, to return to their homes. Onate, however, refusing to admit defeat, went about filling the vacancies with new recruits. The next move was up to the king and the viceroy, and he would remain with all his company on the Rio de las Nazas until informed of their final decision.

In December, investigators sent by Monterrey arrived to make a thorough inspection and inventory the expedition's equipment and supplies.

1597

If the viceroy had expected that his auditors would find that Onate had failed to fulfill the terms of his contract, he was disappointed. Every bushel of grain, every sack of flour, every vial of medicine, every gun, every tool, every head of livestock, every horseshoe nail was counted. Every colonist and soldier was interviewed and physically described in the report. Other priests had taken the places of those who had decided not to go.

The expedition was ready.

After several months of hesitating, the king finally decided on a course of action in February, unaware, of course, of what had taken place on the Rio de las Nazas. Keep Don Pedro Ponce waiting in the wings with hopes of regaining the spotlight, the sovereign instructed the Council of the Indies, but secretly inform Viceroy Monterrey to let Onate proceed. If it was found that Onate had not fulfilled the terms of his agreement, some other decision would be made. Don Pedro was out.

These royal instructions did not reach Mexico City until summer, and it was fall by the time the joyful news was transmitted to Onate. Now Monterrey feared that during the long delay the high standards which the expedition was required to meet might have fallen below acceptable levels. He ordered that another exhaustive inspection be conducted, and sent agents to perform the duty.

The site chosen by the viceroy's chief investigator for the inspection was a barren desert area a few miles from Santa Barbara. The tedious work of counting and examining and listing every article began on December 18. The ordeal was still going on when the year ended.

PART THREE

*Colonization:
The Sword and
the Cross*

1598–1609

On a May day, the Piro Pueblos gazed in wonder and fear at a great dust cloud moving slowly toward them from the south along the trail that followed the west bank of the Rio Grande. Many of them gathered what possessions they could carry and fled into the hills, but some were bold enough to stay in their homes. They had seen Spaniards in small groups, but now they witnessed a sight that not only surpassed anything they had ever known, but anything that the wildest imagination was capable of conceiving.

The awe-inspiring cloud darkening the sun was caused by nearly a hundred heavily loaded wagons, troops of horsemen, and an unbelievable herd of more than seven thousand animals strung out in a ragged pattern for more than four miles. In the column were one hundred and thirty families, women and children clinging to the sacks and crates piled above the creaking wheels. There were two hundred and seventy single men—soldiers, craftsmen, farmers, hopeful young adventurers—eleven Franciscan friars, and scores of Mexican Indian and Negro servants, wranglers, and camp tenders. Leading the long parade, and the most impressive and colorful of all its segments, was a group of men on fine horses, all splendidly arrayed in shining armor, plumed helmets, silk and lace shirts, and Cordovan boots with tasseled spurs.

Three weeks earlier, near El Paso del Norte, Governor and Captain General Don Juan de Oñate had taken possession "of all the kingdoms and provinces of New Mexico" in the name of King Philip, and there had been "a sermon, a great ecclesiastical and secular celebration, a great salute and rejoicing, and, in the afternoon, a comedy."

Now, along the Rio Grande between San Marcial and Socorro, he saw for the first time Pueblo people over whom he would rule, and as they were filled with terror, he "reassured them with trinkets," and he did not invade their homes, but camped on the bank of the river.

The abandonment of numerous pueblos by people struck with terror at the sight of the great cavalcade convinced Onate that it would be wise for him to proceed in advance of the main expedition with only a small number of men, dispel the fears of the natives, and obtain their promises to remain peaceful and obedient. The plan was successful from the outset.

Onate took with him his two nephews, Vincente and Juan de Zaldivar, two friars, Alonso Martinez and Cristobal de Salazar, and several soldiers and servants. He met with no difficulties. In at least a score of pueblos he was hospitably and ceremoniously received, and on each occasion Pueblo leaders solemnly swore allegiance and vassalage to their new conquerors, the Spanish king, the Christian God, and the governor of New Mexico.

One of the largest and most important councils was held in Santo Domingo on July 7. By this time, several other officers and officials of the expedition had joined Onate. Among them was His Majesty's notary Juan Perez de Donis, who recorded that the conference was attended by "captains and chieftains" and a multitude of "common people" from more than thirty pueblos.

Fortunately for history, Onate had found two Mexican Indians who had come north with the Castano expedition, and somehow had managed to escape being returned to Mexico with the other disappointed colonists of that company. Their Spanish names are given only as Tomas and Cristobal. Both spoke the "Mexican tongue," and both had acquired enough of Pueblo languages to serve as competent interpreters. Without these two men, the notary's valuable accounts of such proceedings could not have been in any degree reliable.

The report of the Santo Domingo meeting is typical of all other similar conferences Onate held with Pueblos as he passed for the first time through their country. It preserves for posterity outstanding examples of the hypocrisy, humbuggery, and unqualified dishonesty employed by Spanish officials and countenanced by Spanish priests.

"All the aforesaid captains of the various nations," wrote Juan Perez de Donis, "were sent for and assembled by the governor, Don Juan de Onate, and, after attending mass, his lordship asked them to meet him in the great kiva of this pueblo.

"He told them that he had been sent by the most powerful king and ruler in the world, Don Philip, king of Spain, who desired especially to serve God our Lord and to bring about the salvation of their souls, but wished also to have them as his subjects and to protect and bring justice to them, as he was doing for other natives of the East and West Indies. To this end he had sent the Spaniards from such distant lands to theirs, at enormous expense and great effort. Since, therefore, the governor had come with this purpose, as they could see, it was greatly to their advantage that, of their own free will and in their own names and in those of their pueblos and republics, as their captains, they render obedience and submission to the king, and become his subjects and his vassals, as had the peoples of the kingdoms of Mexico, Tezcuco, Michoacan, Tlaxcala, Guatemala, and others. By so doing they would live in peace, justice, and orderliness, protected from their enemies, and benefitted in their arts and trades and in their crops and cattle.

"They replied to this through the interpreters, all in agreement and harmony and with great rejoicing. One could easily see and understand that they were very pleased with the coming of his lordship. After deliberation they spontaneously agreed to become vassals of the most Christian king, our lord, and as such they immediately rendered their obedience and submission. The governor explained to them that they should realize that by rendering obedience and vassalage to the king our lord they would be subject to his will, orders, and laws, and that, if they did not observe them, they would be severely punished as transgressors of the commands of their king and master, and that, therefore, they should reflect on what they wished to do and what to answer. They replied that they understood and that they wanted to submit to his majesty and become his vassals. They insisted that they spoke the truth, without deceit or reservation."

Onate then told the assembled Pueblos "that since they were rendering obedience and vassalage to him of their own free will and had seen that he caused them no harm or allowed the soldiers to do so, they should fall to their knees, as a demonstration that the Spaniards and they were now all one people. . . . Then they arose and began to kneel on the ground before the governor, who at this point told them to wait while he explained to them that the main reason which had moved the king to send him to this land was the salvation of their souls, because they should know that their bodies had also souls which did not die even though the bodies did. But if they were baptized and became good Christians, they would go to heaven to enjoy an eternal life of great bliss in the presence of God. If they did not become Christians, they would go to hell to suffer cruel and everlasting torment. He told them that this religion would be explained to them more at length by the most reverend father commissary and the friars, who were present, and who came in the name of his Holiness, the only universal pastor and head of the church, the Holy Father at Rome . . . therefore it was important that in spiritual matters and in things pertaining to their salvation they should acknowledge God and his vicar on earth . . . and they should fall on their knees, as a sign that it was indeed true and as proof of vassalage and submission, and kiss the hand of the father commissary . . ."

Purportedly the Pueblos replied that they understood, but if they did then surely a miracle that all Christians might well remember in their own thoughts had occurred. But true or not, "the chieftains in turn knelt and kissed the hand of the father commissary and rendered obedience to the governor, who ordered me to draw up a sworn statement of the ceremony . . ."

Three days after leaving Santo Domingo, Onate and his retinue rode into the pueblo of Ohke, which stood on the east bank of the Rio Grande about twenty-five miles northwest of the future site of Santa Fe. On every side beautiful hills and mesas rolled away, as if in support of the turquoise sky, and along the river fields of maize and other crops were ripening in the summer sun.

After a council in which the inhabitants pledged themselves to obey the governor and revere God, Onate ordered them to vacate their homes. The Spaniards moved into the pueblo, and the inhabitants moved out into the country.

Ohke, proclaimed Onate, would be his capital. But the name did not please him. And he changed it to San Juan de los Caballeros. Everything found in the pueblo was confiscated, and the former inhabitants were left to depend for survival on their neighbors, to manage as best they could.

For a month the Spaniards lolled in the San Juan plaza, enjoying the scenery, the pleasant weather, and the bountiful food, until the main expedition rolled up to the gate. The thousands of animals turned the fields into barren ground, but there was grass in plenty on the surrounding ranges, and horses, cows, sheep, oxen, goats, and mules were soon fat and contented. Such was not the case with the Spaniards, however, now crowded into the small pueblo.

Onate sent scouts out to locate a larger place which also proffered adequate fields and grazing grounds. The pueblo of Yunque at the confluence of the Rio Chama and the Rio Grande, which contained more than "four hundred houses," was selected. The inhabitants were ousted, and the Spaniards moved in bag and baggage. Onate did not think Yunque an appropriate name for the new capital, and he changed it to San Gabriel. Here the first Christian church in the Southwest was built. With everyone helping in the construction, it was completed in a few weeks and dedicated with lengthy ceremonies, religious services, and pageantry.

Onate divided New Mexico into mission districts, and appointed priests to stations in them. The assignments were:

1. The Jemez and all of the Apache of "the neighboring sierras and settlements" to Fray Alonso de Lugo. These Athabascans were the Navajo, of whom almost nothing was known.

2. The most northern pueblos, Picuris and Taos, as well as "all the Apaches from the Sierra Nevada toward the north and east," to Fray Francisco de Zamora. These Apache were the many groups living on the Great Plains.

3. The great pueblo of Pecos and others of the surrounding region to Fray Francisco San Miguel.

4. The Keres pueblos of San Felipe, Santo Domingo, Cochiti, and several others to Fray Juan de Rozas.

5. Zia, Acoma, the Zuni, and the Hopi to Fray Andres Corchado.

6. The pueblos of Tiguex in the Bernalillo area to Fray Juan Claros.

7. San Juan and other Tewa pueblos to Fray Cristobal de Salazar and Fray Juan de San Buenaventura, a lay brother. The father commissary, Fray Alonso Martinez, and another lay brother, Fray Pedro de Vergara, also would make their headquarters in the first capital.

These ecclesiastical duties completed, Onate gave his full attention to fulfilling the dream which had brought him to New Mexico, the dream of finding treasure. It was his feeling that he had carried out the main provision of his contract by founding the colony—an enormous realm of plains, mountains, and deserts, the boundaries of which, except for that on the south, extended only God knew how far. Now was the time to begin to discover what riches it contained, and he did not propose to allow himself to be distracted by routine social and economic problems. He had brought with him aides whom he believed were fully capable of assuming these burdens. As far as he was concerned, only one task confronted him—determining the richness of the prize he had won over the many contenders in Mexico. His plans were soon completed.

In the early fall, his nephew, Vincente de Zaldivar, was far out on the plains of eastern New Mexico with a company of sixty men, assigned to investigate the region of the "cattle."*

Early in October, Onate set out with a strong company,

---

*Vincente de Zaldivar would attempt to capture a herd of buffalo with the purpose of driving the animals back to San Gabriel and domesticating them, an idea that for ludicrousness would be difficult to match, as he soon learned. As the adventures of this expedition took place outside the Pueblo country, however, they will not be recounted.

perhaps a hundred men, on an extensive exploration. He left his other nephew, Juan de Zaldivar, in command at San Gabriel with instructions to follow him with thirty men as soon as Vincente had returned from the buffalo plains.

Onate had three purposes in mind: to look for metals, to obtain pledges of obedience from a number of pueblos not yet visited, and to open a trail to the Gulf of California, at the mouth of the Colorado River, from which place it was hoped that communications by sea could be established with Mexico. How he expected to accomplish this feat is not known, but Clause 22 of Onate's original contract with Viceroy Velasco states: "That I be allowed to bring two ships per year, free of taxes and import duty, to provision the land and exploit the mines that may be discovered." There is no record, however, that Onate had made any such plans; moreover, his own actions strongly indicate that he had not.

From San Gabriel, Onate traveled south, passing through Galisteo and along the eastern slope of the Manzano Mountains. After examining the famous salt beds east of Estancia, he visited the Piro pueblo of Abo and some settlements of the Jumanos, and "these pueblos of the salines and the Xumanas [Jumanos] all rendered obedience to his majesty."

Doubling back, Onate crossed the Rio Grande at Puaray (Bernalillo) and followed the ancient trade trail to Acoma, where the inhabitants "furnished us liberally with maize, water, and fowls. . . . Here we rested for one day." Onate's requests for robes and other articles were graciously fulfilled, and the inhabitants "also rendered obedience to his majesty." Ironically, it was the generosity of the Keres of Acoma that would be the cause of one of the most atrocious episodes in the history of the Pueblos.

In the first week of November, Onate reached Zuni. At Hawikuh, Coronado's headquarters in the summer of

1540, the people "treated us very well with maize, tortillas, calabashes, beans, and numerous rabbits and hares, which are very abundant . . . We found crosses in all these [Zuni] pueblos. The Indians show great devotion for them and often offer them what they offer their idols, such as flour [sacred cornmeal], sticks painted in various colors [prayer sticks], and feathers of native fowls.

"These Indians speak some Mexican words because two of the Indians who came with Coronado remained there. They were now dead. One of them, named Gaspar, left two sons. We saw the one named Alonso. He used a few Mexican words, but did not understand any. At this place each house gave an istle blanket [made from yucca], which makes good clothing."

Leaving Hawikuh on Sunday, November 8, Onate reached the Hopi pueblos about a week later, and the "natives came out to welcome us with tortillas, scattering powdered flour over us and our horses as a sign of peace and friendship." As they had done with Espejo, the Hopi told Onate that mines were to be found some distance to the southwest and offered to guide the Spaniards to them. Onate at once assigned Captain Marcos Farfan de los Godos and eight soldiers to investigate the deposits and determine their value. The day after Farfan departed, Onate started back to Zuni, planning to wait for him there.

Farfan was gone three weeks, but he brought back "alluring reports of fine mines which they had found . . ."* They brought very fine samples of ores from which silver was later obtained in numerous and diverse quicksilver assays, and all the men "who were languishing for want of metals to smelt were reanimated."

Farfan's official report stated that in one place at the

---

*These were the same mines Espejo had discovered near Jerome, Arizona, and which Luxan had pronounced worthless.

mines "we found an old shaft, about eighteen feet deep, from which the Indians obtained the metals for daubing themselves and painting their blankets, for in the said mine there are brown, black, yellow, blue and green ores. The blue is so intense that some of it is thought to be enamel. . . . This vein was very wide and rich and extended over many ridges." At various places they staked out some seventy claims "for ourselves and for those who had remained in the camp to accompany and protect the governor."

It was December, the weather was bitterly cold, the snow lay deep over the mesas, and Juan de Zaldivar had not arrived as planned. For these reasons, Onate decided to return to San Gabriel, and, after spending the Christmas holidays there, to "make the expedition to the sea with all the forces necessary for the purpose." He had been traveling only three days toward Acoma when he met several soldiers who were looking for him. They brought bad news.

Obeying orders, Juan de Zaldivar had set out from San Gabriel with thirty men soon after his brother had returned from the buffalo plains. The company had reached Acoma on December 1, and Zaldivar asked that the men be furnished blankets, clothing, and provisions for the journey to overtake his uncle. The Keres explained that after supplying Onate with large quantities of such things only a short time earlier, they could spare no more. Zaldivar told the Indians that the Spaniards needed flour more than anything else, and they replied that if he would wait two days, they would grind it for him.

According to Captain Gaspar Lopez Tabora, Zaldivar "went with this witness and seventeen companions" to get the promised flour, and "when we had reached the top of the pueblo, Zaldivar ordered everyone to remain in sight, both soldiers and servants, in order not to molest the Indians in any way. It was done so, and Zaldivar assured his men that the natives would furnish the flour readily in trade for hatchets and the other articles he had brought them. The Indians accompanied him in large numbers and led him from one small, narrow plaza to another until they had Zaldivar and his soldiers in a very narrow place on a high cliff where they had no room to fight or defend themselves.

"By this time the Indians had given them some flour and maize, although not as much as was needed . . . Zaldivar sent Captain Diego Nunez de Chaves with six men to get the rest of the provisions at the places indicated by the Indians. He went, and a short time later Zaldivar asked this witness to find out what the captain was doing. This witness went to Captain Nunez, who told him that the Indians would not give anything . . . Zaldivar sent six more men to gather flour in other places and to finish quickly."

Suddenly, loud yells were heard "from the direction of Captain Nunez. What had happened was that the Indians, as soon as they saw that the forces were divided, began to attack and kill. So this witness fell back immediately with his soldiers to rejoin Zaldivar, followed by Indians. . . . They pursued the Spaniards in large groups, and began to hurl countless stones, arrows, and clubs, not only from the ground but from the terraces, both men and women participating in the attack.

"The Indians were so numerous, threw so many stones, and shot so many arrows that they forced the Spaniards to a high cliff where they killed Zaldivar, Captains Felipe de Escalante and Diego Nunez, [eight] other soldiers and two servants. This witness escaped down a cliff . . ."

Several other Spaniards were wounded in fighting near the pueblo. After dark, the survivors divided into two groups, some starting back to the capital, and others being sent to find Onate.

Filled with fury and grief, Onate traveled swiftly back to San Gabriel. The people of Acoma, he declared with tears running down his face, must be punished, not only to avenge the death of his beloved nephew but to teach them and all other Indians the folly of defying the "Christian representatives of the Spanish King."

It was a sad holiday season in San Gabriel.

Before many days of the new year had passed, the Pueblos would fully comprehend the meaning of "rendering obedience and vassalage" to the king of Spain and the governor of New Mexico, and "acceptance of the true faith and revering the Christian God in heaven."

After long and exhaustive judicial proceedings, during which the testimony of the survivors of the battle of Acoma was recorded in minute detail, Onate, to complete the record which must be sent to the viceroy, asked the father commissary for "an opinion on what constitutes a just war; and, if it is a just war, what disposition may be made of the vanquished and their property."

Fray Alonso Martinez's response also was recorded. A just war, he stated, "requires, first, the authority of a prince with supreme power such as the Roman pontiff, the emperor, the kings of Castile who enjoy the imperial privilege of not recognizing a superior in temporal matters . . . No private individual may declare war, as this requires the organization of armies, which is the function of a prince only . . .

"Second, it requires a just cause, which may be any one of four: to protect the innocent who suffer unjustly and whom the prince must defend whenever he can; to restore goods unjustly seized; to punish transgressors of the law, if they are his subjects, or of the laws of nature, even if not his subjects; and lastly and above all to attain and preserve peace, which is the main purpose of war.

". . . the vanquished and their property are at the mercy of the conqueror . . .

"If the cause of war should be the punishment of the delinquent and guilty, they and their goods would be at the mercy of the victor, in accordance with the just laws of his kingdom, if they are his subjects. If they are not, he may force them to observe the divine and natural law, using all means that he may justly consider expedient."

Admitting that the father commissary's "ideas were generally accepted," Fray Claros thought it should be understood, however "that the reference to compelling the guilty-vanquished to observe divine law, if they are heathen, shall be by admonition and persuasion." Further, Fray Claros agreed with Fray Martinez's opinion "provided it is an offensive war, and provided that we take into consideration at all times the degree of intelligence of the offenders, so that when proceeding against them it may be done in accordance with the seriousness of their offenses. If, however, the war should be defensive, it needs no authority from prince or anyone else, because it is the natural law that anyone individually or in common with others may defend himself from those who attempt to harm or injure him."

Father Martinez agreed that "such self defense is blameless—*cum moderamine inculpata tutela.* So whether the defense is by one or many it finally devolves on the individual or private person."

Onate had the support of the priests, who thought that punishment of the people of Acoma was "a just war."

Vincente de Zaldivar was accorded the honor of commanding the punitive expedition. Onate's orders to him said:

". . . in the discharge of your commission to the pueblo of Acoma, you should make more use of royal clemency than of the severity that the case demands, take into serious consideration the stupidity and incapacity of the Indians, if that is what they showed in this case rather than malice . . .

". . . summon the Indians of Acoma to accept peace, once, twice, and thrice, lay down their arms, and submit to the authority of the king our lord, since they have already rendered obedience to him as his vassals.

"You will ask the people of Acoma to surrender the leaders responsible for the uprising, and the murderers, assuring them that they will be justly dealt with.

"The Acomas must abandon at once the fortified place in which they live and move down into the valley, where the ministers of the holy gospel . . . may be able to teach them more easily the matters of our holy Catholic faith.

"If the Indians come down and submit peacefully, you will keep them under strict guard and bring them before me in order that we may hear their pleas and administer justice.

"After the Indians have been removed . . . you will send back to the pueblo as many soldiers as you deem necessary, burn it to the ground, and leave no stone on stone, so that the Indians may never be able again to inhabit it as an impregnable fortress.

"If God should be so merciful as to grant us a victory, you will arrest all of the people, young and old, without sparing anyone. Inasmuch as we have declared war on them without quarter, you will punish all those of fighting age as you deem best, as a warning to everyone in this kingdom.

"All of those you execute you will expose to public view . . . as a salutary example.

"If you should want to show lenience after they have been arrested, you should seek all possible means to make the Indians believe that you are doing so at the request of the friar with your forces. In this manner they will recognize the friars as their benefactors and protectors, and come to love and esteem them, and to fear us.

"To execute this punishment as you see fit, I grant you the same powers I myself hold from his majesty."

Acoma and the great mesa on which it stood were etched against a clear sky on the wintry afternoon of January 21 as Vincente de Zaldivar halted his force at the foot of the narrow path that twisted its way up the heights to the narrow entrance of the pueblo. The brilliant sunlight glistened on the armor and weapons of the seventy cavalrymen who sat their horses in a semicircle about him. Farther out on the snowy plain where water was available, camp tenders, servants, and vaqueros were busy unloading pack trains, setting up a camp, and building fires.

Obeying Zaldivar's instructions, the interpreter, Tomas, called upon the Keres with signs and words to surrender, but "the Indians, fortified on the *penol,* all shouted loudly, raised their swords on high, and presented themselves in the coats of mail and other pieces of equipment taken from the Spaniards whom they had killed . . . calling us whoremongers."

After posting guards about the mesa, Zaldivar retired to his camp.

The Pueblos "spent all that night in huge dances and carousals, shouting, hissing, and making merry, challenging the army to fight." Despite the guards, two horses were killed by warriors who crept within arrow shot of the grazing herd through an arroyo.

On January 22, more appeals to the Pueblos to lay down their arms were answered with "showers of arrows, stones, pieces of ice, and curses." Zaldivar gave the order to attack, and "on this day, feast day of Saint Vincent, at three o'clock in the afternoon, the battle began."

Under a murderous deluge of rocks and arrows, dismounted cavalrymen attempted to climb the mesa slopes, but were forced to withdraw, many of them suffering wounds and bruises. However, harquebusiers maintained a steady fire, and many defenders were seen to drop on the terraces. Dusk was falling when Zaldivar ordered the siege to be maintained "and all the soldiers to be on the watch, fully armed, throughout the night."

On January 23, "San Ildefonso's day, the Indians on the rock continued the battle with determination and fury. The fighting proceeded from early morning, with many Indians killed or wounded. Then Zaldivar spoke to them through Tomas, the interpreter, and urged them to consider the number of their dead and not to persist until all were killed, promising that he would do justice to all who surrendered and placed themselves in his care. They replied that they and their women and children wanted only to die . . ."

During the afternoon, a number of soldiers, covered by heavy gunfire, managed to reach the top. Several houses were set on fire, and as the Pueblos retreated, more Spaniards came up and were able to entrench themselves behind walls. Indians took refuge in kivas, and others "broke away through many tunnels . . . which opened out into adjoining rooms."

The Sky City, impregnable under any assault by Indians, could not stand before the onslaughts of men armed with guns, before the devastating destruction of lead and powder. Signals of surrender and pleas for mercy came from the houses. The firing died away. Men and women emerged offering blankets, robes, food. Disdaining the gifts, Zaldivar ordered them to descend to the plain, where they would be held as prisoners. A line of men, women, and children, many of them wounded, moved down the twisting path.

But hundreds more were still cowering in the estufas and other parts of the pueblo. Zaldivar sent soldiers to bring them out one by one. As they were dragged before him they were hacked to pieces, and limbs, heads, and bodies were thrown over a sheer cliff.

The light of the winter day was fading before the slaughter was completed, and Zaldivar "ordered the estufas and living quarters to be set on fire. Many were burned alive in these places, men and women, some with children in arms; others were suffocated by the smoke. All their provisions were likewise burned, except the blankets, buckskins, skins, and fowls, because these things were all plundered by order of Zaldivar."

Some eight hundred Keres died at Acoma.

More than five hundred Keres men, women, and children were taken under guard to Santo Domingo, where the governor was waiting to congratulate his nephew on the great victory.

On February 12, Onate, sitting as a one-man supreme court of New Mexico, announced the punishment to be suffered by the prisoners:

"The males who are over twenty-five years of age I sentence to have one foot cut off and to twenty years of personal servitude.

"The males between the ages of twelve and twenty-five I sentence likewise to twenty years of personal servitude.

"Two Indians from the province of Moqui [Hopi] who were present at the pueblo of Acoma and who fought and were apprehended, I sentence to have the right hand cut off and to be set free in order that they may convey to their land the news of this punishment.

"All the children under twelve years of age I declare free and innocent of the grave offense for which I punish their parents . . . I place the girls under the care of our father commissary, Fray Alonso Martinez, in order that he, as a Christian and qualified person, may distribute them in this kingdom or elsewhere in monasteries or other places where he thinks that they may attain the knowledge of God and the salvation of their souls.

"The boys under twelve years of age I entrust to Vincente de Zaldivar . . . in order that they may attain the same goal.

"The old men and women, disabled in the war, I order freed and entrusted to the Indians of the province of the Querechos that they may support them and may not allow them to leave their pueblos."*

Internal troubles began to arise in the colony. Most of the settlers were deeply disappointed by New Mexico. The country was not at all as they had expected it to be. It was bitterly cold in winter, extremely hot in summer, swept by blizzards and dust storms and torrential rains. Onate appeared to be uninterested in their welfare and consumed by his hope of finding treasure. It was almost as if he did not understand that dire economic problems existed. No large-scale agricultural projects were undertaken. No efforts were made to maintain reserve food supplies. The colonists, especially those with families, lived in constant fear of Indian attacks in retaliation for the barbaric treatment of the people of Acoma, but Onate seemed unconcerned, and no adequate defenses were constructed.

To all complaints Onate reacted by inflicting stricter disciplinary measures. It was his conviction that with so many pueblos in the country, the colonists could obtain sufficient necessities to supplement what they could provide for themselves. He inaugurated systematic looting, and set the amount of tribute each town was required to meet. Some Pueblos were soon living in abject poverty.

On Vincente de Zaldivar's journey to the buffalo plains, several campsites which Indians identified as belonging to the Bonilla-Humana company had been seen. These were

---

*The Querechos were Plains Apache. In other words, the old men and women of Acoma were given to them as slaves.

the first clues to indicate the route taken by the expedition of 1593, but they helped Onate not at all to carry out his orders to arrest Bonilla and Humana for their illegal exploration. Their whereabouts remained unknown.

The mystery was suddenly solved in part, however, by the appearance in San Juan de los Caballeros of a Mexican Indian named Jusepe, who claimed that he had been "recruited" by Humana to serve him as a personal servant on the northern treasure hunt.

Taken before Onate, Jusepe stated that after passing Pecos Pueblo, the company traveled generally northeastward for about thirty days, when they came to "two large rivers, and beyond them many Indian villages with a large number of inhabitants." Farther on, in a plain, they came to a very large settlement. One of the rivers they had crossed previously flowed through this town. In some places between the houses, which were "built on a frame of stakes with straw roofs, like jacales," were fields of maize.

These Indians could have been Wichita, Kansa, or Osage, and the two large rivers could have been the Arkansas and the Smokey Hill or the Kansas and the Republican. Bonilla and Humana may have traveled farther north than Coronado, for Jusepe mentioned journeying on for a considerable distance beyond the heavily settled region. It is not improbable that the men were the first Spaniards to enter Nebraska.

In any case, somewhere in the heart of the Great Plains, Bonilla and Humana had a falling out, the cause of which is not known. After a bitter quarrel, Humana sulked in his tent. At last he sent a servant to summon Bonilla, "who came dressed in shirt and breeches. Before he reached the tent Humana went out to meet him, drew a knife from his pocket, unsheathed it, and stabbed Captain Bonilla twice, from which he soon died. He was buried at once."

Humana appeared to have gone mad, and fearing for

their own safety under the leadership of the brutal outlaw, five Indian servants deserted. Four of them apparently had met death while attempting to return to Mexico. The other, Jusepe, had been taken prisoner by Lipan Apache. After being held captive for a year, he had escaped and had found his way to Pecos Pueblo, where he had remained for some time. When, eventually, he heard that Spaniards had established a settlement on the Rio Grande, he had set out to find them.

Jusepe had no knowledge of the fate of Humana and the men with him. Thus, Onate was not relieved of his obligation to apprehend them.*

Onate gave up—at least for the time being—his plan to travel to the South Sea. He contemplated making explorations in other directions, especially to the north and east, which he thought might prove more profitable. The assignment of finding a trail to the Gulf of California was given to Vincente de Zaldivar. He left San Gabriel sometime in July, 1599, with thirty soldiers, but very little is known

---

*Onate would be told by Plains Indians that the Spaniards had been wiped out by a large band of warriors, whose identity remains uncertain, but he would obtain no material evidence to substantiate the report. Rumors also would be heard that, fearing to return and face punishment, they had gone farther north and had joined bands of other Indians, but the falsity of these tales would be established in time. One story, however, seems to have a foundation of truth. It reports that Humana, after murdering Bonilla, traveled toward the southwest, and eventually he and his men reached a small stream in the area that would come to be called El Cuartelejo, and which embraced southeastern Colorado and extreme western Kansas. One night, presumably early in 1594, they were attacked by Indians, most probably Apache. One version of the story states that a man and an Indian woman of the company escaped, but another says that all were killed.

Whatever the truth, several years later a party of Spaniards came upon a number of badly rusted guns and swords in a cottonwood grove beside the El Cuartelejo stream. A padre gave it the name of El Rio de Las Animas Perdidas en Purgatorio —"the River of Lost Souls in Purgatory"—for the rusted weapons allegedly were identified as having belonged to Humana and his companions.

about this expedition. If an account of his journey was written, it has not been found. Fragmentary information indicates that he and his men wandered through the deserts of western New Mexico and Arizona, and at last, their horses exhausted and their supplies depleted, turned back. They were gone more than three months.

It has been definitely established, however, that on the first part of their journey they traveled southward, east of the Manzano Mountains, to the Piro pueblos in the vicinity of Abo and probably visited some settlements of the Tompiros. They found the people rude and inhospitable, and Zaldivar's requests for food and blankets were bluntly refused. Apparently because the Indians greatly outnumbered the small force he had with him, he decided not to press his demands and went on, but he did send a message to Uncle Onate about the "insulting treatment" he had received.

Onate was soon on his way with a company of cavalry "to punish the Indians for their insolence toward Zaldivar." The vagueness of the record leaves in doubt the identity of the people who rebuffed Zaldivar. It states merely that they were "Jumanes." They may have been Jumano, but it is more likely they were Tompiros. However, Onate went to a settlement "to collect the tribute of the blankets." Only twelve or fourteen were given to him. He was "not satisfied with this pittance," but the Indians told him they had no more to give him. Thereupon, the houses were fired, and as the inhabitants sought to flee, six were killed and a number wounded by soldiers. Because Onate thought the interpreter had not translated his words correctly, he executed him. Then, apparently believing he had taught the Indians a lesson, and that thereafter they would be more respectful, he rode back to San Gabriel.

He was wrong. A short time later, five soldiers deserted

and set out for Mexico. Two of them were killed in the vicinity of Abo; the other three managed to save themselves and return to San Gabriel, no doubt praying that Onate would forgive them. What punishment they suffered is not known, but because of the slaying of the two deserters, Onate declared war on the Piro of the salines. Vincente de Zaldivar had returned from his wanderings in search of the South Sea, and he was commissioned to conduct the offensive.

The Tompiros had been warned by scouts of the approaching Spanish force in time to assemble some eight hundred warriors from a number of pueblos. Zaldivar, in command of a hundred mounted men, found them waiting for him "at the pueblo of Agualagu."*

Zaldivar narrowly escaped injury under a barrage of arrows as he made an effort, through an interpreter, to persuade the defenders to surrender. He wasted no more time in negotiations. Stationing his men in strategic positions about the pueblo, he ordered them to fire at will at any Indians who showed themselves on the terraces and rooftops.

For six days the Tompiros stubbornly held out, repulsing every attempt of Spaniards to scale the walls, but paying a terrible price for their bravery. Guns, of course, won the battle in the end. Zaldivar augmented the reputation he held as butcher of the Acomas. In the fighting, he and his soldiers killed six hundred Indian men, women, and children, burned Agualagu and two other adjacent pueblos, and took four hundred prisoners. Each soldier was awarded a male slave "as compensation for the hardship he had endured." The living women, children, and elderly persons

*The location of this pueblo is not known. The name has no similarity to the names of identifiable towns in the area. It was, however, near Abo.

were set free, as feeding them presented a problem with which the colony would have been unable to cope, and a surplus of servants already existed in San Gabriel and each mission station. Perhaps for this reason, little effort was made to hold the slaves given to the soldiers. In any case, not many days had passed before all of them had escaped.

Oñate vigorously defended his administration and praised New Mexico as a highly valuable province in reports to the Count of Monterrey, but despite his efforts to gloss over them, the stains of the colonists' discord and dissatisfaction seeped through his professed optimism. He had strenuously sought to prepare the people for the rigors and hardships and frustration they would encounter, he told the viceroy, but "the devil, who has always tried to prevent the great loss he would suffer through our coming, resorted to one of his usual tricks with the mutiny of more than forty-five soldiers and officers, who in anger at not finding bars of silver on the ground right away and resentful because I did not allow them to abuse the natives either in their persons or property, became dissatisfied with the land, or rather with me. They tried to band together and escape to New Spain, or so they said, but their intention, as became clear later, was rather to take slaves and clothing, and to commit other outrages." He had seized several of the culprits and was prepared to garrote them, but because of "insistent requests of the friars and of the entire army, I gave up the idea of punishing them." He did not mention that the loss of so many soldiers not only would have dangerously imperiled the safety of the colony but would have prevented him from taking a strong force on the exploring expeditions he planned to undertake.

In an absurd outburst of enthusiasm, Oñate swore that, if given adequate support, the pacified worlds he would give His Majesty would be far greater than those secured by Cortes. (All Hernan Cortes had done was to conquer Mexico, a land immeasurably richer in every way, and containing at least fifty times as many Indians, than the province of New Mexico.) All Onate needed, he claimed, was more money, more colonists, more provisions, more tools—indeed, more of everything—and he was confident that the viceroy would not fail to fulfill his requests.

Although the sources from which great returns would be derived were "numerous and diverse," he believed that he need emphasize to the viceroy only four, as "the others were commonplace and well known." First, there was "the great wealth that the mineral lodes have begun to reveal, and the large number of them in the land, from which royal fifths and other benefits will be derived."

Actually, the minerals discovered amounted to very little, with the exception of the mines in Arizona, and these were too remote to be developed without enormous expenditures for machinery, manpower, and transportation, all of which was beyond the realm of possibility. Silver and other precious metals were known to exist in New Mexico only in negligible quantities.

"Second, the certainty of the nearness of the South Sea, whose trade with Peru, New Spain, and China should not be underestimated, for with the passing of time it will be the source of profitable and continuous customs revenues. . . . What I consider important in this respect is the trade in pearls, the report of which is so reliable, as I have stated, and we have seen their shells here with our own eyes."

The nearest possible seaport on the Gulf of California was six or seven hundred miles away from San Gabriel, and the only route to it was across almost impassable deserts. The Pacific coast was even farther away. Who were the people who would purchase goods from China and Peru and New Spain, and pay customs duties? The Indians?

"Third, the increase in vassals and tributes, together with the increase in revenue, whereby the prestige and power of our king is also augmented, if that is possible."

Little revenue and even less prestige would accrue to the king from the simple economy of the Pueblos or any other Indian peoples.

"Fourth, the wealth from the rich salines and the mountains of rich sulphur, of which there is more than in any other province. Salt is a universal article of commerce among these savages and a part of their common food."

True, but the Indians and the colonists got the salt for nothing. How could it—or the sulphur—be of commercial value to Spain? Transporting it in ox-drawn carts fifteen hundred miles to Mexico City or Veracruz would make its cost prohibitive.

Onate sent three officers he considered loyal to him to carry "reliable information" to the viceroy and to plead that more settlers be granted permission to emigrate to New Mexico. To Mexico City he also sent the little children of Acoma "to satisfy the royal conscience and for their safety . . . May your lordship honor them, for they are going to the house of God."

While others may complain, he told Monterrey, "I prefer to bear my difficulties, to being burdensome to his majesty or your lordship, confident of meeting the needs of many poor people who may wish to join me . . . I renew the request for abundant, adequate, and speedy succor, in priests as well as settlers and soldiers."

Onate said nothing to the viceroy about the tributes he had levied on the Pueblos and the brutal methods employed in exacting them. But others did, and eventually the cruelties of the system he had initiated would be revealed to authorities in Mexico City, to the Council of the Indies, and to the king.

Whenever Onate dispatched messengers to Mexico City —which was not very often—colonists and soldiers were granted permission to send letters to their families and friends. Not all of these personal communications reached their destinations. Onate opened them and destroyed any that were critical of him or contained complaints about the hardships of life in the colony.

Captain Luis Gasco de Velasco, who had contributed considerable money and property to the Onate expedition, felt duty bound to inform the viceroy of the true state of affairs in New Mexico. Surreptitiously he arranged with a priest who was going to Mexico with a messenger to carry a letter to Monterrey.

"The Indians fear us so much," the captain told the viceroy, "that on seeing us approach from afar, they flee to the mountains with their women and children, abandoning their homes, and so we take whatever we wish from them.

"We have been here three years, hoping to discover something of value and importance, which has not been found up to the present.

"The system employed during this time to feed more than five hundred persons, men, women, and children, has been to send people out every month in various directions to bring maize from the pueblos. The feelings of the natives against supplying it cannot be exaggerated, for I give your lordship my word that they weep and cry out as if they and all their descendants were being killed. But, in the end, necessity has compelled us to do this to keep from starving to death . . . I have even seen that the natives pick up the individual kernels of maize that fall to the ground . . . During Lent we ate meat three days in the week for lack of anything else . . . Our supply of everything is decreasing daily, to such a point that we fear we will soon be entirely wanting."

Practically all the Indians, said Velasco, were naked, but despite this poverty, the tribute was collected with "such severity that it availed them nothing to say that they had nothing but what they had on. The Spaniards seize their blankets by force, sometimes even when it is snowing, leaving the poor Indian women stark naked, holding their babes to their breasts."

The colonists were more fearful of Onate than of Indians or wilderness perils. The governor had come to fancy himself a supreme potentate, possessed of powers equal to a king; indeed, he demanded that he be addressed on certain occasions as "His Majesty." Several times Onate had ordered that the royal standard of Spain be lowered before him, and this had "happened once when the whole force was attending high mass."

Persons who voiced complaints were "labeled as traitors. The fact is we are all depressed, cowed, and frightened, expecting death at any moment." Several men had paid with their lives for trying to escape, and some had been killed for asking permission to return with their suffering families to Mexico. Four soldiers who had left were pursued. Two of them were thought to have reached Mexico in safety, but the other two were overtaken by Onate's guards and executed on the spot.

Captain Velasco related two harrowing murder tales. Pablo de Aguilar, "a truthful man, very well liked and honorable," incurred the enmity of Onate when he protested the severe treatment he and his family had suffered. Accompanied by several of his personal Negro and Mexican Indian servants, all armed with butcher knives and swords, the governor went to Aguilar's quarters. Captain Velasco and several other men were present. Aguilar was seized, "the governor himself giving him a push, knocking him over some boxes, and right there they stabbed him.

Onate himself thrust a sword through his body. And even though the poor man implored for mercy, saying that he was married, and though he asked for confession, they granted him nothing. When Father San Miguel came in to confess him, Aguilar was already breathless and in convulsions, his teeth set, his eyes staring at the governor. They cut off his head, not satisfied with the many wounds, each one mortal, that covered his body."

Alonso de Sosa Albornoz, "seeing that, on account of the poverty of the land, he would not be able to provide for his wife and children there, urgently begged the governor to grant him permission to go back with his family." The permission was granted, and Albornoz "prepared a cart and got everything in readiness for the moment that he should be ordered to start out."

While waiting to leave, Albornoz was sent with several others to round up horses. In a ravine a short distance from San Gabriel, he was attacked by "Vincente de Zaldivar and some of his followers. They stabbed him to death, without giving him an opportunity to confess . . . His widow was left with a large number of children . . . the relatives of Albornoz did not ask again for permission to leave."

One of Onate's Mexican Indian servants ran away, and when he could not be found, the governor "hanged two Pueblo chieftains, claiming that they knew where he was . . ." One day Onate went "in person to a pueblo to seize their maize, and, as the Indians had concealed it in some small rooms he ordered the walls torn down. When an Indian reproved the act in his native tongue, the governor gave him a thrust and pushed him down the terrace. He fell on his back, and was instantly killed . . . Then the governor ordered a group of houses in this pueblo set on fire."

Onate's emissaries in Mexico had succeeded in recruiting

some eighty colonists, and they reached San Gabriel on Christmas Eve in 1601. With them were seven more friars. There was great rejoicing on Christmas, but trouble soon arose.

Some of the new men had been awarded commissions by the viceroy, and Onate considered this an intrusion on his rights as governor, captain general, and adelantado. Refusing to acknowlege the commissions, he shouted angrily: "Tell them to wipe their behinds with them."

The very word *Quivera* seemed to be a magnet with irresistible powers. Onate probably heard from Indians all the fables that had lured his predecessors on futile journeys in search of treasures on the Great Plains. Jusepe, who had been with Humana, added a few enchanting details to the stories, but without a dishonest motive in mind. He was merely telling what he had seen with his own eyes. The Bonilla-Humana expedition, he related to Onate, had traveled through a land teeming with buffalo, containing innumerable rancherias and abundant food supplies. One settlement "must have extended for ten leagues, because they traveled through it for two days, and it must have been two leagues wide, more or less . . . there were numerous plum and walnut trees . . . the climate was more temperate than in New Mexico." To an Indian, a land with such resources would have been a paradise. To Onate, these embellishments only gilded his dream and kindled new hopes. Surely such a bountiful place must contain treasure.

Yet, it was not only the expectation of finding gold that took Onate to Quivera. There is evidence indicating that he was eager to ascertain how far the land extended to the north, and that he believed he might be able to open a route to the North Sea, an accomplishment that would have been of incalculable benefit to Spain and which would have brought him great honors as well as monetary rewards.

He left San Gabriel in June 1601, with seventy men, two padres, and a number of Indian servants, pack trains, and several large carts drawn by horses and mules. They would be the first wheeled vehicles on the central Great Plains.*

As both he and his nephew Vincente de Zaldivar would be absent on the Quivera exploration, Onate had named Francisco de Sosa Penalosa to act as lieutenant governor. Penalosa soon found himself confronted with an uprising. The longsuffering settlers, as well as most of the soldiers and some of the officers and priests, were openly demanding that the province of New Mexico be abandoned without further delay.

Penalosa made no effort to resolve the crisis with threats of violent reprisals or legal actions against anyone who deserted. Yet it was necessary that he protect himself. It took little imagination to envision himself before a Mexico City court on charges of failing to act responsibly and to perform his duty as a colonial officer of the king. In a democratic procedure that Onate would never have tolerated, he summoned priests and officers to a public meeting, announcing that all of them would be given an opportunity to express opinions and advance proposals. The statement of each speaker would be recorded by notaries and its accuracy would be attested by witnesses.

The results of the council placed the colony on the brink

*Onate's expedition to Kansas has no direct bearing on Pueblo history. On the journey, his company was attacked by a large force of Plains Indians, and came perilously close to being wiped out. In a report sent to Mexico City, the battle was termed a triumph for Onate, but it contained the admission that the Spaniards' victory "was granted by God our Lord. Without His aid it would have been practically impossible, in view of the way the natives kept increasing in number. . . ." Besides the aid of the Lord, Onate and his soldiers enjoyed a large measure of good luck. For an unknown reason, the Indians had chosen not to pursue them as they fled homeward in disorder.

of complete disaster, but Penalosa had the record that would absolve him, and others who remained loyal to Onate, from any possible charges of dereliction in office or of treason.

The testimony taken revealed tragic and hopeless conditions in the land of the Pueblos.

Fray Francisco de San Miguel stated that instead of preaching the word of God to the Indians, "he has seen the Spaniards blaspheme it." He always met with "great obstacles because of the bad treatment the Indians received from us. Our people do not leave them anything in their houses, either any living thing, food, or anything of value. For this reason the Indians run away." He had asked the governor "many times to have pity on the suffering of the natives and not to tolerate so many robberies and injustices. But as the country is so wretched and poor, the governor has not been able to effect any remedy, nor can he do so now.

"The fact is that in order to induce the Indians to furnish corn for food, it has been necessary to torture the chieftains, even to hanging and killing them. We find ourselves in extreme need of food and see the natives starving to death, eating whatever filth there is in the fields, even the twigs from the trees, dirt, coal, and ashes.

"If we stay any longer, the natives and all of us here will perish of hunger, cold, and nakedness."

The bad treatment of the Indians, said Fray Francisco de Zamora, had brought "great discredit on our teaching, for they said that if we who are Christians caused so much harm and violence, why should they become Christians?"

The Indians have been "stabbed and knifed when things were taken from them . . . not to mention the treatment of the Indian women . . . soldiers have violated them often along the roads." It was Fray Zamora's recommendation that New Mexico be abandoned "in order that we shall not all perish, particularly the women and innocent children." The church "was not gaining by our labors in this land, and in order that the word of God should not be further dishonored, nor his majesty deceived, as he has been to the present . . . we should leave this place."

Fray Lope Izquierdo testified: ". . . our presence in this land would only end in the death and extermination of our people, as well as of the natives . . . The only decent way to overcome the harm done the natives is to depart from their lands and leave them free, or to let our people perish when their provisions give out . . . many natives are starving to death . . . our men, with little consideration, took the blankets away from the Indian women, leaving them naked and shivering from cold . . ." In this condition, the Indian women "embraced their children tightly in their arms to warm and protect them, without making any resistance to the offenses done them, for they are an humble people, and in virtue and morality the best behaved thus far discovered. Falsehood, robbery, and other vices contrary to good habits of nature are unknown among them." By leaving, "we are not in any sense deserting the royal flag."

Alonso Sanchez, an administrative official of Onate's staff, had sold a prosperous cattle business and a farm in Mexico because he "wanted to serve the king, as my forefathers had done." He had also believed that New Mexico was a rich land, and that he might acquire a fortune in it. He had brought his wife and several sons and daughters with him, but now all he asked "in payment of his services, hardships, and privations, was permission to leave." He would be satisfied to depart in nakedness and extreme poverty. Moreover, there was no hope that gold or silver was to be found in the colony.

Captain Diego de Zubia, procurator general for Onate, declared that he realized "how little God and his majesty are being served," and stated that conditions had reached a point "where the army is on the verge of starving to death or dying at the hands of barbarous Indians, who will fall upon us when they see how helpless we are, without weapons, or anything else. . . . it is not just, nor will he allow, that this army, his wife, and children, shall perish."

So the testimony went, some officers and priests merely endorsing the statements of preceding witnesses, and some citing their own reasons for wanting to leave.

Down the long Rio Grande trail in the late summer of 1601 moved a caravan of desperate, ragged, hungry, and sick colonists. Had it not been for Indians along the route who furnished them with provisions and the wild game they were able to kill, it is doubtful if any of them would have reached Mexico alive.

Remaining in San Gabriel with Lieutenant Governor Penalosa were only two friars and perhaps twenty-five officers and administrative officials. Living in constant fear of being annihilated by Indians, they stood guard each night, and throughout each day sentries gazed toward the eastern skyline hoping to see Onate and his soldiers returning from Quivera. There was talk of leaving, but at last, in October, it was decided to send Captain Geronimo Marquez, accompanied by a few Mexican Indian servants, to Mexico City with a last fervent plea to the viceroy to send reinforcements.

". . . all the evils and ruin of this land," Fray Juan de Escalona wrote the viceroy, "have sprung from the fact that this conquest was entrusted to a man of such limited resources as Onate. The result was that soon after he entered the land the Spaniards began to perpetrate many offenses against the natives and to plunder their pueblos of the corn they had gathered for their own sustenance; here corn is God . . . Onate did not want to sow a community plot to

feed his people, although we friars urged him to do so
. . . all the provisions which the governor took along [to
Quivera] they took from the Indians. I was to have gone on
this journey, but on observing the outrages against the
Indians, and the war waged against them without rhyme or
reason, I did not dare to accompany the governor. . . ."
Onate also had taken sixty mules, six carts, and two Negroes
furnished to the friars by the Spanish government. If Onate
were to stay in New Mexico "twenty thousand years," declared Fray Escalona, "he could never discover what there
is to be discovered in this land, unless his majesty should aid
him and take over the whole project . . . His Majesty could
have discovered this land with fifty well-armed Christian
men" and the colony could have been "placed under the
royal crown and the conquest effected in a Christian manner
without outraging or killing these poor Indians, who think
that we are all evil and that the king who sent us here is a
tyrant."

Escalona excoriated Onate for writing untruthful reports.
The friar thought the Pueblos "the best infidel people that
I have seen; they govern themselves in an orderly manner
. . . No silver has been found . . . This I believe was ordained
by God so that the Spaniards, instead of remaining here,
would go forward . . ." Escalona, however, did not believe
the province should be abandoned, for he was convinced
that under proper management it could be developed and
thousands of souls could be saved.

Lieutenant Governor Penalosa was not as optimistic. He
bluntly stated in a letter to the Count of Monterrey: "All
will be lost if our Lord does not remedy the situation by
permitting Onate to discover something so important that
the men may overcome their indifference and lack of confidence in finding anything worthwhile in these lands. The
men with Onate went away so despondent over their priva-

tions that only the special grace of God will keep them here
. . . Those of us who remain here can bear it no longer
. . . I humbly beg you to succor us with the necessary things
to support life . . . If succor does not reach us within five
months we will be compelled to abandon this land, as we
are determined to do."

In a report to his prelate, Fray Escalona said: ". . . so as
not to abandon and desert this place entirely, I am staying
here, together with . . . a few other Spaniards, awaiting
instructions as to what we should do. We will stay four or
five months, about the time required for the return of those
who have gone to seek an answer . . . We remain here at
great risk, since we are so few and since there is no fortress
here where we can seek refuge, nor is there any wheat or
corn to eat. If we fail to receive an answer in this time we
will have to leave . . ."

A totally dishonest account of conditions in New Mexico
was prepared by some of the men remaining in San Gabriel
who were loyal supporters of Onate. Penalosa "accepted"
it without comment, and it was sent to the viceroy with
Captain Marquez. Fray Escalona undoubtedly had been
aware that the false statements were being prepared when,
in his letter to the Count of Monterrey, he referred to
communications that "do not tell the actual truth . . ."

The false report was signed by Captain Marquez, Cristobal Baca, Bartolome Romero, Alonso Gomez Montesinos,
Gonzalo Hernandez, Martin Gomez, Hernon Martin Ser-
rano, Juan Fernandez, Alonso de la Vega, Juan Luxan, and
Antonio Correa. These men swore under oath to the following:

1. There were more than sixty thousand peaceful people,
without any bad habits, in the pueblos.

2. No friar had gone as much as two leagues from San
Gabriel to preach the holy gospel. The natives would accept

Christianity readily if it were preached to them and explained.

3. When the colonists deserted, food supplies were abundant. There were on hand thousands of fanegas of corn and wheat, harvested in the colony's fields. The natives also were plentifully supplied. There was no danger of a famine. In the pastures of San Gabriel were more than three thousand head of cattle and sheep, and the gardens were filled with fruits and vegetables. They were fully capable of supporting themselves.

4. Before the arrival of the Spaniards, the Indians continually fought each other. Now they were at peace, and Spanish guns gave them protection they had never known. When the Pueblos heard that the Spaniards were leaving, they begged them not to go and offered to support them if they were in need of food.

5. San Gabriel was calm and peaceful when some soldiers plotted to desert. The friars gave support to the rebels, and exhorted everyone to leave. Some priests went about arousing people who were calmly and happily gathering their grain and tending their gardens. Only a short time before, however, in their sermons the friars had urged all to remain in the land because they were rendering service to God.

6. The Pueblos pleaded with the Spaniards to enlighten them regarding God in Heaven, and if the friars had been willing to teach them, they would all now be Christians.

7. Vincente de Zaldivar had fought the Acomas and the Piro only because they had attacked without provocation, repeatedly refusing to remain at peace.

8. In any clashes that had occurred, the Indians always had been the aggressors.

Onate returned to San Gabriel late in November 1601. Many of his men were still suffering from wounds received in fighting with Indians on the Plains, and others were ill.

Almost mad with anger, he issued formal charges of treason against the deserters. Vincente de Zaldivar and a few men were sent in pursuit of them, but they had reached safety in Santa Barbara before he could overtake them.

The viceroy, undoubtedly influenced by the reports he had received of Onate's brutalities and his failure to establish a prosperous colony, ruled that the settlers who had fled would not be punished, nor would they be forced to return to New Mexico. Zaldivar spared no efforts to secure more aid and settlers for the colony, and finally went to Spain to present the case to the Council of the Indies and the king. Both his pleas and those of Onate's supporters failed. The king, having seen Fray Escalona's letters, instructed the viceroy to conduct a thorough investigation into the affairs and conditions of the colony.

Not one but two investigations were made, with witnesses being called to testify in Mexico City. Evidence against Onate continued to mount. A new viceroy, the Marquis de Montesclaros, was scheduled to take office in the summer of 1603, and authorities in Spain decided to place the entire matter in his hands. Being unfamiliar with the problems involved, Montesclaros made no hasty decisions.

In 1604, Onate decided that he might be able to save himself and his colony if he could discover a good harbor on the Gulf of California to which ships from Mexico could bring supplies and reinforcements that would enable him to continue his expeditions into the vast, unexplored northern regions. This was not a new idea, but now he decided that it might influence the government to favor his appeals for support. He left San Gabriel on the expedition in the fall of 1604, taking with him thirty men and leaving fifty to guard the capital. Fray Escobar kept a diary of the journey.

Onate crossed Arizona and reached the gulf, locating what he considered to be a feasible port. He was back in San

Gabriel in the spring of 1605. Hammond and Rey write that he "decided to go to Mexico in person to make the best presentation of his discoveries. On August 7, he was in San Bartolome, Chihuahua, writing to the viceroy for permission to make the trip. But without waiting for an answer, he returned to San Gabriel, while Father Escobar, escorted by four soldiers, went on to Mexico with his own journal of the expedition and testified before the viceroy. One wonders why Onate did not go on himself, but perhaps he had received word from his relatives and friends in Mexico that it would be best for him to hurry back to San Gabriel or face the prospect of never being allowed to return."

It would not have mattered, however, whether Onate stayed in New Mexico or went to Mexico City. His sun had set.

After studying all the conflicting reports and listening to witnesses in Mexico City hearings, Viceroy Montesclaros admittedly was confused. He thought that "this conquest is becoming a fairy tale." In effect, he tossed the ball back to the king. Although he leaned toward the belief that further expenditures of effort and money would be wasted, or at best would be a gamble, he felt that His Majesty should make the final decision as to whether the colony should be maintained, and that he himself should do no more than "point out the inconveniences that are likely to ensue."

On the basis of the evidence available—all of which had been placed before both the king and the Council of the Indies—the viceroy held the opinion "that the documents concerning the charges against Onate do not at present justify any penalty on him personally and he should not be punished until he has been heard, but from what we know already in regard to these excesses, there is sufficient reason why your Majesty should not entrust the continuation of the expenditures to him." It would be "inconvenient," however, should Onate be charged with crimes, tried, and found not guilty. His Majesty also should not overlook another "inconvenience" that possibly could occur. It had to do with the royal conscience. With great religious zeal, priests had carried the word of God to the heathen of New Mexico, and the banners of Christianity waved over the vast province. Friars were still there and should be given protection. Although nothing of material value had been discovered, and the natives were "wretched in clothes and spirit," possessed no silver or gold, and dwelt in poor houses, and the number baptized was small, the viceroy thought that, nonetheless, if there should be only one lone Christian native in New Mexico; "your Majesty would be obligated through justice, conscience, and prestige to preserve him, even at great cost to the royal treasury."

After lengthy consideration of the New Mexico problem, the Council of the Indies informed the king in January 1606 of its conclusion that "it would be to the service of God and your majesty to order the viceroy of Mexico positively not to proceed further with the said discovery, but to command him to send for Onate on some plausible pretext, with discretion and tact, so that he may leave [San Gabriel] without causing any disturbance, and to detain him in Mexico, disband the army, and appoint as governor a reliable, prudent, and God-fearing man to govern what has been discovered in New Mexico and to maintain it in peace and justice, to protect and befriend the Indians, and to provide friars to teach them."

King Philip delivered the final blow to Onate in June 1606 by endorsing without qualification the recommendations of the council. When the sovereign's order reached Mexico City is not certain, but it was obviously several months after being issued in Madrid. Even after it had reached New Spain, it was not promptly executed. The delay undoubtedly was due to a change of viceroys. Montes-claros was removed and Luis de Velasco, the viceroy who had awarded the New Mexico colonization contract to Onate a decade earlier, was reappointed to the office. Perhaps Velasco did not approve of the trickery involved—that is, enticing Onate to Mexico with some "plausible excuse" and then detaining him.

However, in the summer of 1607, Onate was secretly informed, either by Velasco or some other friend in Mexico City, of the way the wind blew. Pretending that he knew nothing of the scheme to remove him, he resigned in August.

"Although I do not tire of waiting or of enduring the hardships that one encounters here, the soldiers are so worn out by seeing themselves put off for so long with mere hopes that they do not wish nor are they able to wait any longer. Nor do I find myself able to restrain them . . . Furthermore, the friars do not care to proceed with the baptizing of the natives until they know that the affairs of this land are settled, nor am I sure that they are inclined to remain here . . .

"Finding myself helpless in every respect, because I have used up on this expedition my estate and the resources of my relatives and friends, amounting to more than six hundred thousand pesos, and anxious that the fruits of so many expenditures and of more than eleven years of labor should not be lost, and especially because I am eager that our holy Catholic faith should be spread in these lands and that the king our lord should increase his dominions by the addition of great and rich provinces, which, according to our information, are at our threshold, I find no other means to attain all this than to renounce my office . . ."

Velasco had no alternative, of course, but to accept the resignation. This was done in February 1608, and Velasco named Captain Juan Martinez de Montoya, one of the officers still at San Gabriel, as acting governor. Onate was ordered to remain in New Mexico and to cooperate with his successor until December 1609, by which time a final decision as to the fate of the colony would be made. These instructions were sent to Onate in the spring of 1608.

How greatly religion influenced Spanish affairs of state was amply demonstrated in the deliberations which took place during the next year. New Mexico might well have been given up as a worthless land had it not been for the fact that some Pueblos had been baptized. As Hammond and Rey state, this was a problem "for which no one seemed willing to assume responsibility." To abandon the baptized Indians was unthinkable, but to "remove them bodily to some other place would cause great hardship and suffering, and to leave them to relapse into heathenism would place an unjust burden on the king's conscience."

The scales were tipped in favor of maintaining the colony by the arrival from San Gabriel of Fray Lazaro Ximenez. The missionary reported that seven thousand Pueblos had been baptized, and that hundreds more were eager to embrace the Catholic faith. Velasco and several members of the Audencia put their heads together in a determined effort to reach a decision. The conferences continued for weeks, but at last a unanimous agreement was reached.

The program that the viceroy and his judicial counselors devised called for the retention of New Mexico as a royal colony, but expenditures for its maintenance were to be heavily restricted. The garrison at San Gabriel would be limited to fifty married soldiers. Twelve priests would be stationed among the Indians to continue the conversions. No expeditions of conquest or explorations would be undertaken without authorization by the king. A man experienced in colonial affairs, who could be trusted to enforce all laws, and who would be sympathetic to the needs and problems of both friars and colonists, would be appointed governor.*

The man Velasco chose as governor was Pedro de Peralta, who, the viceroy declared, had served the crown long and faithfully as a government official. Peralta would receive an annual salary of two thousand pesos common gold and traveling expenses. He was not a wealthy man, and Velasco allowed him to draw one year's salary in advance "in order that you may be able to equip yourself with what you need for such a long trip."

The instructions given Peralta by the viceroy proffered no relief for the Pueblos. He was authorized to "allot Indians in *encomienda,* as many as he may think suitable, to persons who have served and are living in those provinces." The *encomiendas* granted by Onate were to be preserved.†
As the Pueblos were scattered over a large area, Peralta was to "congregate the dispersed and move those who are poorly situated to more appropriate and peaceful locations, which will promote the welfare of these Indians and facilitate their administration."

Peralta, accompanied by a contingent of soldiers and several priests, probably reached San Gabriel in the fall of 1609. Onate departed soon after his successor's arrival.‡

---

*When, in time, the king was informed of the plan, he accepted it in toto.

†Indians "allotted in *encomienda"* were in reality slaves, more often than not poorly clothed and fed. Missions were granted *encomiendas,* as well as ranchers and farmers. The *encomendero* was required under the law to provide his native labor with necessities and assure that they were converted to Christianity. Abuses were, in every respect, more the rule than the exception.

‡Charges of inflicting barbarities on the Pueblos, being derelict in duty, writing false reports, and committing sexual immorality were brought against Onate, Vincente de Zaldivar, and several other officers. After long delays won by politically influential friends, they were tried, convicted, and heavily fined. Besides being fined six thousand Castilian ducats, Onate was exiled for four years from Mexico City and stripped of his titles. After more than ten years of pleading that he had served his country well and should not be allowed to die leaving a blot of dishonor on the record of his family, he was granted a royal pardon.

The king had thanked Velasco for the "zeal with which he looks after matters pertaining to the service of God and the exaltation of the faith" in his determination not to abandon "the conversion of New Mexico." The colony was publicly described as a great missionary field. It was that, to be sure, but there was another reason besides the desire to convert Indians from paganism to Christianity that influenced the sovereign's attitude toward the New Mexico problem. It was power politics. Other European nations, notably France and England, had already challenged Spain's New World territorial claims. No attempt had been made by Spain to define the boundaries of New Mexico. Yet it had been established that north of it lay an enormous land mass that had been touched only along its edges. Under accepted international policies, as long as Spain maintained an armed force in the colony, even though a small one, it was justified in claiming possession of the vast uncharted northern realms.

But if the size of New Mexico was not known, the destiny of its Pueblo people had been settled.

PART FOUR

The Struggle for Supremacy: State versus Church

1610

Governor Peralta had been instructed to find a place more suitable for the provincial capital than the old and cramped town of San Gabriel. After examining the surrounding country, he selected ground close under the mountains east of the Rio Grande. It was in several ways a most desirable site. A dependable, clear, cold creek tumbling from the high country would supply water in plenty for both irrigation and domestic use. All the pueblos could be easily reached over ancient trails that ran down into the valley of the Rio Grande and into the Galisteo Basin.

In the summer, the building of San Francisco de la Santa Fe was begun. There would be a main plaza. On the north side would stand the Palace of the Governors, a long, low structure with a powder magazine and prison at one end and a chapel at the opposite extremity. Behind the palace would be a walled garden, and beyond it stables and quarters for the guard. Barracks for the garrison would be located west of the palace. To the east of the plaza, ground was set aside for a church and Saint Francis Convent, and south of the creek would stand the chapel of Saint Michael. An acequia madre would be constructed to carry water through the heart of the settlement. North, south, and west were good pastures and cultivable land. Most of the houses would be close to the plaza to afford protection for the colonists, but almost all of them would be adjacent to gardens and fields. Forced Indian labor built Santa Fe, and it was one project on which both the clergy and administrative officials cooperated. The harmony was brief, however, and would soon vanish in a storm of controversy.

Neither the New Mexican governors nor the Franciscans were victims of the internecine conflict for which they were responsible.

The victims were the Pueblos. Captives in their own country, indeed in their own homes, virtually every phase of their lives was dominated by one faction or the other, and not infrequently by both. Sexual intercourse, childbearing, and elimination were liberties generously granted them, but all other activities were subject to regulatory decrees that were rigidly enforced. They had no civil rights, no religious freedom, no political prerogatives.

The segments of the Pueblo population over which the priests claimed suzerainty worked long hours in the fields, vineyards, gardens, and factories of the missions. The fruits of their labors were euphemistically called contributions to God. Their only rewards were enough food to keep them alive, which they themselves produced, and a few garments and blankets they were permitted to keep out of the large quantities they were forced to manufacture. They could expect to receive greater rewards, of course, when they went to heaven.

Only one difference existed between the *encomiendas* of the missions and those under the jurisdiction of the governors. Profits from a chief executive's farms, ranches, and sweatshops went into his own pocket. God got no part of them.

Onate had made no attempt to develop agricultural or industrial projects. He and his cohorts had lived by confiscation while searching for treasures and defending Spanish honor besmirched by recalcitrant savages. New royal decrees, however, prohibited unlicensed explorations and directed both priests and political officials to concentrate on converting Indians and making the colony as a whole, and the missions in particular, fully self-supporting.

Obviously, no progress toward these goals could be achieved without adequate labor, and that was available from only one source—the Indians. It could not be obtained from such tribes as the Apache and Navajo, for they dwelt in wild freedom, wandered over vast regions, and were warlike and beyond possible control. Young people, and especially children, of the unsettled tribes had an intrinsic value. They could be sold into slavery in Mexico, or even held as slaves in New Mexico, but catching them was difficult and dangerous work. More male colonists and soldiers were needed before large-scale slave raids could be undertaken.

Unfortunately for the Pueblos, they were in the same position as the sedentary peoples of central and southern Mexico at the beginning of Spain's New World conquest. The early conquistadors had won swift and decisive victories with traditional European military tactics. Hernan Cortes and his soldiers, for example, encountered in the Aztecs, as Moorhead succinctly states, "a sophisticated Indian civilization concentrated in a relatively small area, tied by religious devotion to permanent temples, by economic dependence to tilled fields and established market places, and by social organization and sentimental attachment to fixed townsites. The defenders could not retreat." Moreover, the Spanish, "had horses for mobility; cannon for destruction; armor for personal protection; the strangeness that inspired fear; and a talent for creating confusion." This was precisely the situation in the Pueblo country.

From the day Governor Peralta took office, the cornerstone of the colony's economy was the free labor of the Pueblos, and the stage was set for the struggle between state officials and the clergy to benefit from it.

The causes of the controversy were commercial greed

and religious zeal, two forces that appear at first glance to be irreconcilable; closer scrutiny, however, reveals links that prevent them from being defined as completely unrelated elements. The priests dressed their greed in ecclesiastical garments, but the disguise in no sense weakened its virulence. Civil officials defended their brutalities, the levying of heavy tributes, and their corruption on the ground that they were acting in behalf of the state, maintaining the security of the colony among savage people who would overthrow it unless held in subjugation, and fulfilling their sworn duty to build an impregnable economic structure; but few, if any, contributions to the royal coffers were permitted to seep through the pores of the superficial facade.

The priests were saving souls, and the more snatched from the hands of the devil, the more favors they would receive in the heavenly paradise of the next world. The governors were saving money, and the more put away, the more they would enjoy life when they returned to Mexico.

The battle was joined. In one important respect, the church had an advantage. It controlled the only established transport service linking New Mexico with the outside world. Naturally, under such a monopoly, cargos for and from the missions received top priority. Normally, a caravan—thirty to forty wagons, each carrying two tons of merchandise and drawn by eight to ten mules—took a year and a half to complete the journey of three thousand miles, but accidents, and not infrequently attacks by Apache, disrupted operations for long periods.

Besides such commonplace items as pots, pans, dishes, nails, agricultural implements, and tools, the manifests of the northbound wagons included paintings of saints; heavy bronze church bells, altar supplies, and wall hangings depicting angels, the crucifixion, and religious events; silver and gold ornaments; life-size statues of Christ; and kegs of wines and other spirits. When they returned to Mexico, the wagons were laden to capacity with products from the missions, such as tanned buffalo and deer hides, pinon nuts, blankets, and other salable goods manufactured by the Pueblos.

Trudging along beside the creaking wheels of the southbound trains were files of captives—Navajo, Apache, and Pueblo men, women, and children lashed together, chattels of both the missionaries and the governors. The men would be sold to Mexican mine owners. The women and children would be sold as household servants. If they were attractive enough, young women might be purchased by operators of brothels.

Spanish law decreed that only Indians captured in warfare could be held as slaves. The statute could hardly be termed a handicap for anyone engaging in the vicious trade. Raids by Navajo and Apache on missions and ranches occurred with the regularity of the moons. Thus, as confirmed enemies of both church and state, they were fair game for slavers. But in times of quiet, it was easy to stir up trouble. All that priests and governors had to do was send a band of settlers out for the purpose of taking Navajo and Apache prisoners, and any defense attempted by the quarry could be termed an act of war. Dealing with recalcitrant Pueblos involved less effort. As they were already captives, they could be removed simply by branding them enemies of God and the king. Priests, of course, always baptized defiant Pueblos before sending them south to the flesh markets. The slave traffic increased with the passage of each year.

No regular official communication service existed between Mexico City and the provincial government. There was almost no chance that dispatch riders could complete the long journey unless they traveled in strength, and that was an expensive service. A contingent of soldiers always accompanied the mission supply trains, however, and government messengers, as well as incoming and outgoing officials, civil servants, and colonists, invariably traveled with them.

The mail pouches carried to Mexico City were filled with complaints and demands for relief from both factions. Governors complained that the clergy was preventing Indians from being employed on projects vital to the colony's development. The clergy complained that the governors were attempting to prevent them from extending the kingdom of God. The headaches increased and the confusion mounted in Mexico City, and neither archbishops nor viceroys appeared able to devise an acceptable compromise. Both sent orders and directives to no avail; indeed, their replies to the protests seemed only to augment the struggle for supremacy.

The penalties suffered by Onate and his lieutenants had in no way reshaped the mold for corrupt government that they had made and left behind in New Mexico, the die they had cast for injustice, for unconscionable social and religious practices, and it would be used by every Spanish governor to hold office in the next two centuries. The governors, lower officials, and settlers wanted only to get rich, and exploiting Indians was the one possible way to do it. The priests wanted to save souls, but they also wanted to gain riches for the church, if not for themselves. For them, too, Indians were the only source of revenue. New colonial statutes and royal cedulas designed to protect natives were meaningless, for the remoteness of the colony made it impossible for either church or civil authorities to enforce them, and both the clergy and the governors could ignore them with impunity.

"Violent name-calling, plotting, slander, and petty

treachery," Beck remarks, "can be understood, even if such conduct cannot be justified. When clerics, especially those belonging to the Franciscan order, engaged in similar practices, it can be neither understood nor justified."

With the help of Navajo raiders, most of the people taken prisoner at Acoma—including those who were maimed—had escaped even before Peralta took office. Bravely the Keresans commenced the restoration of their ancient pueblo on the high mesa. There was no feasible way of recapturing them, for the trails to the west were patrolled by Navajo, and there were not enough soldiers in Santa Fe to launch an offensive against them. Every trooper was needed to hold the Pueblos, and even that was a task which they failed to perform with success. Pueblos slipped away to the Navajo country or to Zuni and the Hopi towns and remote settlements of their own people. Some went north to find havens among the Apache of El Cuartelejo.

Official dispatches from Mexico City informed the king that depredations by Navajo and Apache—burning ranch buildings, killing settlers, and stealing livestock—were driving the colonists to despair. Moreover, New Mexico was contributing nothing to the Spanish treasury. Pueblos fled to the high country, beyond reach of the military, whenever tribute collectors appeared. Costs of maintaining the colony were rising steadily, with no possible relief in sight. The missions seemed to be prospering, but the New Mexico government and the laity were in desperate need—of everything.

No increase in expenditures was authorized, but an order did come from the sovereign for the Franciscans to make greater attempts to pacify the Apache and the Navajo. The friars were not enthusiastic about the idea, claiming that the atrocities of Onate and the punishments which civil officials and the military continued to inflict had inflamed all Indians to such an extent that "they spit on the cross." Officials and soldiers retorted that the friars were not interested in learning Indian languages, so the Indians could not understand them even if they were willing to listen.

The schism widened, and conditions deterioriated, until the debased emotions of both sides of the controversy destroyed any possibility of peace or compromise, and the result was uncontrollable violence.

1612

The church hierarchy in Mexico descended to a scheme that might have been expected of an outlaw junta but hardly of persons proclaiming their devotion to the principles of Christ. An arrogant, crude, intolerant man garbed in a Franciscan habit and giving the name of Fray Isidro Ordonez arrived in Santa Fe and displayed personal credentials and other documents that immediately augmented the existing turmoil.

He handed Governor Peralta a paper purporting to be a royal cedula granting all soldiers and colonists permission to return to Mexico of their own volition, if they so desired. Most of them did so desire. Peralta refused to accept the document, charging that it was a forgery, but the results of it were catastrophic. In a short time, only forty-seven lay Spaniards were left in Santa Fe.

Ordonez blustered about from mission to mission, but some of the priests refused to acknowledge his authority and denounced him as an imposter. If he was an ordained priest, he was also a first-rate scalawag. No reliable record of either his background or his true purpose has come to light, but both his actions and his attitude suggest that he was an unscrupulous soldier of fortune employed by the church to engineer a coup d'etat by which the New Mexico clergy could gain control of the civil government.

The clash between Peralta and Ordonez reached a crisis in Taos. Several soldiers arrived there to collect tribute for the governor, and the Indians were preparing to pay it when Ordonez emerged from the pueblo and ordered them to ignore the demand. The soldiers returned to Santa Fe empty-handed. Ordonez followed them. In a stormy scene, an outraged Peralta shouted that he would not be intimidated. Thereupon, Ordonez called him a heretic, a Lutheran, and a Jew, and excommunicated him.

The governor grabbed a flintlock pistol and fired. The bullet missed Ordonez but wounded two other men, one of them a friar. Ordonez promptly went before the Santa Fe town council—or what was left of it—and demanded that Peralta be arrested and removed from office. The council refused to act.

Ordonez's next move was to throw the governor's chair out of the Santa Fe church, and he issued a warning that anyone who dared to carry Peralta's reports to Mexico City also would be excommunicated and charged with treason.

Peralta, finding himself in a helpless position, decided to go to Mexico and make a personal appeal to the viceroy for relief. He started with a small escort, but got only as far as Isleta when agents of the Inquisition, obviously taking orders from Ordonez, arrested him and clapped him into a cell at Sandia Convent. He managed to escape, return to Santa Fe, and seek asylum among loyal friends. Ordonez imprisoned him again, this time on short rations.

If his purpose was to gain control of the civil government, Ordonez had succeeded; but his triumph was short-lived. In response to the reports he sent to Mexico City, in which he recounted Peralta's actions and his own difficulties, came the information that a new chief executive had been appointed and would soon be en route to Santa Fe. Both Peralta and Ordonez were removed.

At least twenty-two governors—who also held the title of captain general—would hold office in New Mexico between 1598 and 1680. The post was eagerly sought, for it proffered opportunities for profitable exploitation. Generally a man was appointed as a reward for extraordinary military or political service, but not a few were granted the plum for no more reason than that they were close friends of Mexican viceroys. If some of them deserve to be described as able administrators, it also must be said that they employed their talents to their personal advantage. And some were charlatans, unscrupulous adventurers, and plain thieves. If there was one in this eighty-two-year period—the end of which marked a major turning point in the history of New Mexico—who left the province in better condition than he found it, no evidence has been found of his achievement.

How many missionaries served in the colony during these years must remain unknown. It can be safely asserted, however, that there were no less than five times as many of them as there were governors.

New Mexico was no longer thought of as another treasure house, and, as Horgan states, "The kingdom was regarded essentially as a missionary field. The civil authority, the armed garrison, were to exist primarily to protect the friars at their hazardous work, whose object was the peaceful conversion of the Indian. But the position of the Indian under the guardianship of the encomienda was poison at the heart of the province. . . ."

There were two majesties in New Mexico—the church and the state—and neither would submit to the other.

1617

The colony of New Mexico was on the brink of complete disaster. Although they claimed to have built eleven churches and converted fourteen thousand Pueblos to Christianity, the friars saw themselves facing failure. They could only hope to survive if two conditions were met: they must gain greater, if not complete, control of colonial administrative policies, and they must receive more support in the form of military manpower over which they held jurisdiction. There remained only forty-eight Spanish soldiers and settlers in the entire province.

The churches had been built, but the number of conversions was questionable. The Pueblos were learning. Many of them obeyed the ringing of the bells calling them to mass, but the extent of their reverence was as undeterminable as their thoughts. One looking into their faces saw nothing. But the sounds of the drums and the shuffling of the dancers' feet and the singing of the choruses at least gave some indication of what was in their hearts. It was just as well, many of them believed, to submit to the demands of the padres, and thereby avoid the infliction of brutalities. Yet, in truth, the oppressiveness of the white man's religion was driving them to cling more desperately than ever to the beliefs and principles so deeply rooted in their hearts. The vaccine of Christianity forcefully injected into them was creating a slowly burning fever in their blood.

1618–1621

After Peralta had departed, a ruined man, two other governors had held short tenure in Santa Fe; but they had been weak and disinterested, and had gone their way leaving nothing behind to insure them a place in history. Presumably their disappointment had been great, for there existed in the colony almost nothing of intrinsic value, and they had not come to work at tilling the soil like peasants. Nor did they have the stomach to fight to take over the resources which the clergy had accumulated.

Juan de Eulate, however, was as curious as he was bold, as ambitious as he was irreverent. A former army officer of high rank, he had won honors on the battlefields of Flanders. If appointment to the governor's chair in Santa Fe was a reward for his service to the king, then he did not propose to overlook any opportunity for personal benefit.

In the eyes of Eulate, Indians were slaves and priests were nuisances. His scorn for both was quickly demonstrated. He expropriated *encomiendas* and increased the amount of tribute each pueblo was required to pay to him. He abused missionaries and refused to cooperate with them. Having brought a few more soldiers and sycophantic civil servants with him, he sent them about the country to force the Indians to labor under gunpoint.

Royal and viceregal decrees were ignored. New Mexico was not a missionary field. It was a private domain. Eulate issued an official edict granting permission to the Pueblos to engage in their traditional religious practices, to hold the ceremonies and the dances which the priests had struggled to suppress, to worship their own pagan gods when and as they wished. Governors were prohibited by law from engaging in trading enterprises, but Eulate acted as if he were unaware of the statute. He accumulated cattle and sheep and held them in well-guarded pastures, intending to build herds to be exported to Mexico. He sent traders with trinkets to acquire buffalo hides and other skins from Plains Indians, but barter was not always the means employed to secure them. The Navajo and the Apache had no monopoly on banditry.

The Franciscans were the chamber of commerce of the time in New Mexico. The first of them to extoll in writing the beauties and richness of the country after the founding of the colony was Fray Geronimo de Zarate Salmeron. He spent several years among the Jemez, and served at Zia, Sandia, and Acoma as well. In his eagerness to increase the number of priests in the region and to obtain larger appropriations to the church from the royal treasury, he repeatedly exaggerated the number of Indians to be saved, the number converted, and the value of the natural resources. As if he were trying to revive the dream shattered so many years earlier, he would tell in a *Relaciones* of vast treasures awaiting recovery in the mountains of the province.

Declaring that there were vast mineral veins in every part of New Mexico, Zarate Salmeron wrote: "The Spaniards that are there are too poor in capital to work the deposits, and are of less spirit: enemies to work of any sort. Well, in that country we have seen silver, copper, lead, loadstone copperas, alum, sulphur, and mines of turquoise which the Indians work in their paganism, since to them it is as diamonds and precious stones.

"At all this the Spaniards who are there laugh . . . if they have a good crop of tobacco to smoke they are very content and wish no more riches. It seems as if they had taken the vow of poverty—which is much for Spaniards, who out of greed for silver and gold would enter Hell itself to get them."

Greed was not a characteristic that had vanished—not at all—but, as Adolph Bandelier notes, tales of the existence of great metallic wealth in New Mexico were "the purest myths and fables."

Hardly more reliable was Zarate Salmeron's statement

that nearly thirty-five thousand Pueblos had been baptized, "as I have counted on the baptismal records, not counting the many that at present continue to be converted." Of this number, he alone had baptized nearly seven thousand of the Jemez people. And the few "laborers in the [New Mexican] vineyard of the Lord" had built "forty-three churches in all, large and small, at their own cost . . . thus relieving His Majesty of these expenses."

Some doubt exists as to when Governor Felipe de Zotylo took office in Santa Fe. Conflicting dates are found in the records, the earliest of which is 1621. It is probably correct, for he was in Santa Fe when New Mexico was erected into the Custodia de la Conversion de San Pablo. During Zotylo's reign, the church-state controversy subsided to some extent. Credit for the condition of comparative calmness belongs not to him, however, but to the padre who became the first *custodio* of the colony. Neither ambition nor a desire to augment his own personal fortunes were lacking in Zotylo, but in the new father custodian, Alonso de Benavides, he met a man who was his equal in every respect.

1622–1628

Fray Benavides brought with him to Santa Fe twenty-six priests. He was a missionary as practical as he was dedicated and enthusiastic. There was great work to be done, and he applied himself relentlessly to the task. He had no time for petty squabbles, and he studiously avoided administrative conflicts that would endanger the welfare and progress of the colony. He traveled extensively, was soon fully informed of the problems of each mission, and spared no effort to resolve them. A man of indomitable courage, he journeyed through the wilderness, often with no more than two or three companions and servants, until he had visited every pueblo of his vast custodia. When other priests feared to enter the country of the dangerous apostate Gila Apache in southwestern New Mexico, he assigned himself to the undertaking, and he made friends with both Apache and Navajo leaders, who had let it be known that priests entering their lands would be slain.

As a propagandist, Fray Benavides put Zarate Salmeron —indeed, all other missionaries who served in New Mexico before and after his time—in the shade. His population estimates were gross exaggerations, in some cases ridiculous,* and his reports of the eagerness of the Pueblos to be converted and of their devotion and loyalty to the church were figments of his own fancy.

Benavides possessed the faculty of seeing what he wanted to see, and he did not hesitate to use it, yet the journal he wrote—he called it a "memorial"—gave to history an incomparably valuable picture of seventeenth-century Indian life in colonial New Mexico.

Benavides's *Memorial,* published in Spain in 1630, made him famous. His readers, who included not only high church officials but the king and ministers of state, were thrilled by his dramatic accounts of his own experiences and of the miracles which occurred in the far-off land of the heathen Pueblos.

According to Benavides's report, no missionaries in the New World had been more successful than those serving in

---

*He thought there were an uncountable number of Apache, and estimated the number of Navajo to be about two hundred thousand. He was more conservative in speaking of the Pueblos, claiming that approximately thirty-five thousand had been converted, but leaving the impression that there were many thousands more to be brought into the fold.

New Mexico. The Pueblos, as a result "of the affable care which we Religious have used with them, are so well doctrinated and good Christians that when we ring the bell for Mass and the teaching of the Doctrine, they all come with the greatest cleanliness and neatness that they can, and enter the church to pray, as if they were Christians of very long standing; and the boys and girls who always come morning and evening to the Doctrine, attend with very great care and without fail; and the choristers in the chapels . . . sing every day . . . at the Morning Mass, High Mass, and Vespers, with great punctuality. And all make confession in their own tongue, and prepare themselves . . . studying out their sins and bringing them marked on knotted threads."*

The fifty churches of the pueblos, said Benavides, "sumptuous and beautiful as they are, were built solely by the women and by the boys and girls of the curacy. For among these nations it is the custom for the women to build the walls . . . and if we try to oblige some man to build wall, he runs away from it. . . ." Benavides thought that "it causes wonder to see that in less than twenty years which have passed since the baptizing began, and particularly in the last eight years, wherein the harvest of souls has been more abundant, they seem Christians of a hundred years standing. If we go passing along the roads, and they see us from their pueblos or fields, they all come forth to meet us with very great joy, saying: 'Praised be our Lord Jesus Christ! Praised be the most holy Sacrament!' "

This idyllic picture is not reflective of recorded facts. The struggle between the administrative executives and the clergy had, since the founding of the colony, kept all pueblos in a state of turmoil. The Pueblos lived in constant fear

---

*Tying knots in string was a Pueblo system for keeping track of the passage of days on a journey.

of being cruelly punished for failing to attend church services. They were no less slaves in the vineyards of the Lord than in the *encomiendas* of the governors. As to Benavides's assertion regarding the devotion of the Pueblos, the famed ethnologist and historian Frederick Webb Hodge remarks: "None of the Pueblos were ever so thoroughly converted to the teachings of the missionaries as Benavides states, for there has never been a time from the period of Coronado to the present day, that they have not held tenaciously to their primitive beliefs and practiced their ancient rites. To be sure some of the Pueblos have assumed an outward form of Christianity, but this in no wise has influenced their purely aboriginal religious ceremonies."

Control of the intertribal trade that had existed for countless centuries between the Pueblos and the more nomadic tribes had been coveted by every governor to hold office since Onate's time. Governor Zotylo was no exception, but his greed overcame his good sense. The Navajo, already implacable foes of the Spanish, refused to permit white traders to operate or priests to establish missions in their country. While missionaries had had no success among the Apache, commerce between some Plains groups of these people, notably the Lipan of eastern New Mexico, had been conducted more or less regularly for some time. Zotylo was responsible for destroying it.

Much to the delight of a padre, some members of a large band of Lipan Apache, who came to Santa Fe on a trading mission, admired a statue of the Virgin they saw in a chapel and expressed an interest in learning something of the Catholic faith. Then, as the priest would sadly relate, "the demon had recourse to one of the wiles he is accustomed to employ . . . choosing as his instrument the greed of our Spanish governor."

Pueblos who had suffered at the hands of Apache raiders

were not difficult to find, and Zotylo offered a number of these victims a chance to gain revenge, while at the same time being amply rewarded, by joining several of his soldiers in a surprise night attack on the Apache camp. An agreement was made. The assault was successful. More than a score of the friendly Apache were killed, one of them a prominent leader, and two or three times that many, among them a number of healthy young men and women, were taken prisoner. It was the governor's intention to sell them as slaves in Mexico, but priests and Pueblo leaders registered such furious protests that he was obliged to free the captives. One padre, who promised to inform the viceroy of Zotylo's barbarous act and publicly condemned him, would write that the treacherous attack "provoked a revolt throughout the entire province." It did more than that.

Peace with the Spanish, a condition the Apache of eastern New Mexico had striven to maintain in the face of repeated provocations for nearly ninety years, was no longer possible. Temporary disruptions of their commerce, swindling by traders and officials, and even the occasional confiscation of their goods were injustices which the Apache had felt they could prevent, or even endure, without recourse to extreme violence, but wanton murders could be neither forgiven nor forgotten.

For the first time, the Plains Apache sent word throughout the colony that they would henceforth wage unrelenting, all-out warfare against the conquerors of New Mexico. And it was soon raging in every sector of eastern Apacheria. Although the conflict would be marked with periods of quiet during which the Apache, for reasons best known to themselves, curtailed their aggressions, the peaceful intervals would be deceptive in their appearance. Though the fire of revenge burning in Apache blood was occasionally reduced to smoldering, it would never be extinguished.

So Felipe Zotylo gained his place in history. He would depart from Santa Fe leaving the colony in chaos, with blood spilling on every side—Navajo raiding from the west, Apache from the east and south, the Pueblos growing bolder in their defiance of both church and state, and the clergy rampaging on their ecclesiastical warpath—all of which comprised a situation that Benavides, who was re-called to Mexico at the same time, chose to ignore in his *Memorial.*

1629–1632

Sent to replace Zotylo as governor, Francisco Manuel de Silva Nieto visited numerous pueblos soon after his arrival in Santa Fe. In his travels he was guarded by a strong contingent of cavalrymen who had come north with him from Mexico. In view of the menacing aspects clearly appar-ent to him, he was thankful for the protection.

Benavides was succeeded as custodian of the colony by Fray Estevan de Perea, a missionary of wide experience. With Perea to Santa Fe came thirty priests and a dozen soldiers.

A number of new colonists, among them ex-convicts, fortune hunters, and dishonest traders, also had drifted into the provincial capital. The total number of Spanish in Santa Fe was approximately two hundred fifty, but the population was actually much larger, for the governor, his aides, civil servants, soldiers, and favored settlers owned more than seven hundred Indian slaves. Children of mixed blood were not counted in any census, of course, but reports indicate that the narrow, dirty streets swarmed with them.

Governor Nieto apparently made an effort to perform his

sworn duty to aid the missionaries in their work of gaining more converts, for he elected to accompany the priests assigned to the western pueblos. Besides the governor and his personal servants, in the column that left Santa Fe in the summer of 1629 were the father custodian, Fray Perea, the father solicitor, Tomas Manso, a man of noble birth, four other priests, and two lay religious en route to their appointed fields, thirty soldiers, and a score or more of Indian servants and camp tenders charged with responsibility for ten supply wagons and a herd of four hundred horses.

The company was apprehensive and on guard as Acoma came into view, for the padre previously stationed there had narrowly escaped martyrdom. Several years earlier, Fray Juan Ramirez, learning that the Acoma people were exceedingly hostile, had asked and had been granted permission to reduce them to Christianity. He had set out from Santa Fe alone and on foot. As he approached the *penol* on which the pueblo stood, he was greeted with a shower of arrows but was not struck. It chanced just then that a little girl of eight fell over the cliff, and landed badly shaken but not seriously injured near Ramirez. He took her up, carried her to the summit, and restored her to her people, who, being unable to see where she had fallen, believed she had been killed. After this apparent miracle, Ramirez had been favorably received. He had remained at Acoma, built a church, taught the inhabitants Spanish, baptized many of them, and induced them to construct a trail to the summit which horses could ascend.

The fact that the Keres of Acoma were usually on friendly terms with the Navajo, however, caused the governor to fear that some of those wild heathen might be lying in wait in the pueblo, and might persuade the Acomas to attack. His fears were soon dispelled, however, and Fray Perea would report that "the Indians of the Crag spontaneously proffered admission" to the missionary party. He might have added that the Acoma were not fools. Confronted by thirty heavily armed soldiers, and holding a vivid memory of the tragedy they had suffered in Onate's time, they obviously decided that discretion was the better part of valor. Another priest was welcome to stay there, if he desired, they said. They would not bother him.

The company moved on to Zuni, where they received a similar hospitable reception. The natives, said Fray Perea, "having tendered their good will and their arms, received the party with festive applause—a thing never before heard of in those regions, that so intractable and various nations with equal spirit and semblance should receive the Frailes of St. Francis as if a great while ago they had communicated with them."

Fray Francisco Letrado and Fray Martin de Arvide were appointed to minister to the Zuni. Governor Nieto issued an order that "no soldier should enter a house of the pueblos, nor transgress in aggrieving the Indians, under penalty of his life," and directed that "to give the people to understand the veneration due the priests," he and the soldiers would kiss their feet, and fall upon their knees before them. He also "cautioned the Indians that they should do the same, for this was an example of what superior men can do." The Zuni appeared to be impressed, but it would soon be demonstrated that their expressions were deceptive.

Governor Nieto was too timid to travel beyond Zuni, and, with an escort of eighteen soldiers, he turned back to Santa Fe. However, he ordered twelve soldiers to accompany Fray Francisco de Porras, Fray Andres Gutierrez, and Fray Francisco de San Buenaventura to their posts among the Hopi. The troopers also were to guard the father custodian and the father solicitor on their journey back to the capital.

Alone in the Hopi pueblo of Awatobi, where he was stationed, Fray Porras wasted no time in condemning Hopi idols, and "at this the sorcerers [medicine men] were irritated; and seeing that they were being deprived of the jurisdiction which as infernal ministers they had over those souls, they persuaded all the people that the padre and all those who accompanied him were so many liars."

This was a situation Fray Porras would not tolerate. He fell upon his knees in the pueblo plaza, crossed himself, and said a prayer. When he arose, he spat on his hands, made a mud ball, and daubed it on the eyes of a blind boy, whose sight was immediately restored.

If the incident occurred, Fray Porras made a serious mistake. The miracle did nothing to endear him to the medicine men. A short time later, he ate food that had been poisoned. He died as Fray Buenaventura was administering the last rites.

At the Zuni pueblo of Halona, Fray Letrado transformed an old crumbling house into a chapel. One Sunday, the Indians refused to respond when he summoned them to mass. An impatient man with a fiery nature, he went out into the street to gather his flock. Meeting a group of idolators, he excoriated them. Suddenly, he seemed to sense that his end had come, and he knelt down, holding in his hands a small crucifix. Arrows tore into his body, instantly killing him. His scalp was exhibited at several ceremonies.

Hearing that pagan tribes lived to the west of Zuni, Fray Arvide set out alone to carry the word of God to them. He had journeyed only a short distance when Zuni warriors murdered him. His death occurred only five days after the slaying of Fray Letrado.

Some sociologists are wont to describe the Pueblos as docile, unemotional, and peaceful, but in doing so, they overstate the case. These are generalities that demand qualification.

The Spanish learned to their sorrow that facial expressions and reactions suggesting timidity, stupidity, and lethargy were not indicative of the truly dominant qualities of the Pueblo character. If they appeared to be easily led, that was because they understood the futility of violent defiance under the muzzles of guns. In most instances, capitulation was not reflective of a lack of resolution but of plain good sense. They were possessed of inordinate patience and incomparable stoicism. As remarkable were their inherent tenacity and courage. If they bent, they seldom broke. They were not without strong feelings, indeed they were deeply emotional, but they imprisoned it in their hearts and minds, rarely permitting it to surface.

Their greatest weaknesses were not unique in the sense that they were foreign to other Indians, for the earthly courses of many red peoples were influenced, if not totally governed, by similar attributes. These were the independence so greatly valued by every Pueblo group, their pride in bloodlines, their unwillingness to join together for the purpose of fighting a common foe, their inability to organize, their deeply rooted jealousies, their universal fear of witchcraft, their constant attempts to outwit each other, and their eternal feuds based on causes more often imaginary than real. In these respects, the Pueblos were their own enemy.

Still, the Pueblos had one indestructible belief in common. It was that the day would come when they would be freed from the Spanish yoke. As surely as the sun rose, that day would come, and they never lost faith in their own ability to bring about a return to their old way of life.

The Spanish administrators made no attempt to understand the Pueblos; but, then, it would have done them no good if they had tried, for they had no capacity for such understanding. Indians were animals, as different from men as monkeys. Some priests made efforts to learn native languages, and one even wrote a *doctrina* of the Jemez tongue, but attempts to understand the Indian mind were considered a waste of time, and toleration of Indian ritual and customs was unthinkable. Besides, there was no time to consider what an Indian might have in his head. What belonged there were the teachings of Christ.

The Pueblos bided their time, enduring their sufferings, laboring in the fields and orchards and vineyards, herding the cattle and sheep, memorizing hymns and prayers and catechism, acquiring skill in silversmithing and other crafts —all with one thought, one conviction: that the day of their salvation would come, not in heaven but on earth, in their own country.

1637–1640

The church-state conflict reached a level of unprecedented savagery during the tenure of Governor Luis de Rosas, an ex-soldier who made it clear that he had come to Santa Fe for only one purpose, to get rich without undue delay, and that if the clergy attempted to thwart him, he would obliterate every missionary in the colony. If this was not an unusual attitude for a New Mexican executive, Rosas's methods of achieving his goal were extraordinarily stupid and unnecessarily cruel.

He had not been in office long before he laid the groundwork for his illegal operations by accusing the priests of attempting to gain monopolies of all Indian labor, the slave trade, and all wealth in the province. On the basis of these charges, he clapped several padres into jail. One of his next moves was to visit a number of pueblos and order the inhabitants to disobey the fathers. As a result, the Pueblos of Jemez and Taos staged celebrations that got out of control, and two priests and several Spaniards were slain.

The missionaries protested that the governor was encouraging the Pueblos to perform dances that were an invocation of the devil, but they got no satisfaction from him. The governor scoffed that Pueblo dances consisted of nothing more than "something that sounded like hu-hu-hu, and these thieving friars say it is superstitious." He laughed uproariously when he heard the story of the priest at Isleta who attempted to stop a native ceremony by parading naked through the pueblo plaza with a cross on his shoulders, a crown of thorns on his head, and a rope about his neck, beating his bare body with a clenched fist. Not so amusing was the scene at Quarai. Pueblo choristers were given fifty lashes each for singing the high mass. A warning was sent out to all pueblos that anyone who assisted in reaping the harvests of the mission fields would suffer severe punishment.

Restraint was counterbalanced by license, and the end product was complete confusion under an overhanging cloud of fear. The Franciscans charged that Rosas was encouraging the Navajo to steal horses belonging to the missions. This, of course, was ridiculous. The Navajo needed no encouragement to steal horses from whomever possessed them—horses were horses. The truth was that the Pueblos themselves were aiding the Navajo in stealing livestock of all kinds, and the Navajo were conducting raids on Spanish herds quite of their own volition. They were also attacking pueblos that ostensibly had submitted to domination by the religious.

Rosas sent no troops against the Navajo, although he

made some slave raids and caught a few of them in his net. Nor did he attempt to punish the Pueblo rebels. Instead, he sent aides to confiscate their possessions, and he took a large number of Pueblo children to be sold into slavery. He blamed the priests for all the troubles, and dispatched soldiers to drive them out of the missions at Jemez, Nambe, San Ildefonso, Santa Clara, and other towns.

Fearing for their lives, the missionaries abandoned the pueblos and gathered at Santo Domingo, where they fortified themselves. The churches were dark and deserted, the bells silent. Rosas reigned supreme, gaining a virtual monopoly of the colony's economy and forcing all Pueblos to work for him.

Reinforced by some soldiers and settlers who were opposed to Rosas's brutality and irreverence, the priests in Santo Domingo adopted Navajo tactics. They became raiders, stealing stock from the herds of the governor and the colonists loyal to him. Two missionaries murdered a close friend of the governor when they caught him off his guard.

Informed that the Plains Apache regularly went to Pecos Pueblo to trade, Rosas led a contingent of soldiers there, taking with him a large quantity of knives and other goods to be bartered for buckskins and buffalo robes. His real purpose in making the journey was to capture Apache women and children to be sold in Mexico. Not an Apache was to be found in Pecos, although several hundred had been in the vicinity only a day before his arrival. In fact, most of the Pecos inhabitants also had vanished. Seething with anger, Rosas accused a priest who happened to be in the pueblo with warning the Apache of his approach and took him to Santa Fe in chains. A missionary would write that the people of Pecos "made a great demonstration of feeling in regard to all this, because they were living peacefully with the Apaches and with them had their commerce, by means of which they clothed themselves and paid their tributes."

Hundreds of Pueblos took advantage of the opportunity to escape by fleeing to the Navajo and both the Eastern and Western Apache. The Taos abandoned their towns and found refuge among their friends, the Apache bands in the El Cuartelejo region of southeastern Colorado and western Kansas. In each place they were welcomed, not so much because they were enemies of the Spanish but because they brought with them stolen horses and guns. In El Cuartelejo, the Taos built new pueblos, and they would occupy them for a number of years before the Spanish military was able to force all of them to return to their ancient dwellings on the Rio Grande.*

1641

For more than three years, the war of attrition continued. Then Juan Flores de Sierra y Valdez arrived in Santa Fe to replace Rosas. A short time later, he died. Although Rosas was officially out of office, he had not yet left for Mexico. The colony was without a governor. Taking advantage of this situation, the missionaries stormed into the capital, forcefully took control of the government, clapped Rosas in prison, and plotted his death.

Arrangements were made with a Senora Ortiz to be dis-

---

*The changes that took place in the Navajo way of life during the latter half of the sixteenth century compose a record of acculturation that has no equal in American Indian history. Almost every Navajo custom, religious ceremonial, social system, and economic practice was blended with Pueblo culture. It was refugee Pueblos who taught the Navajos the silversmithing and weaving for which they would become noted.

covered by her spouse committing adultery with Rosas in his cell. Although Rosas was purportedly under guard, the allegedly outraged husband was permitted to enter the cell in the night and murder him.

The taste of violence seemed to create a craving for more in the ecclesiastical war party. The priests embarked on retaliatory actions against the Navajo, and for a year, supported by soldiers and colonists, conducted a relentless campaign against them in their own country. They proved to be competent military strategists, took numerous prisoners, killed several score warriors, destroyed Navajo homes, burned crops and stores of food, and recovered a large number of stolen animals. As they customarily did under the pressures of a costly offensive, the Navajo sent a delegation of old men to ask for peace. The Franciscans agreed, and halted their offensive, believing that the Navajo were decisively beaten. They had no more than returned to Santa Fe before Navajo raiders were again on the rampage throughout the land.

1642

Governor Alonso Pacheco de Heredia arrived in Santa Fe to replace the dead Sierra with secret orders to punish the persons responsible for the murder of Rosas. Feigning friendliness for all factions, he quietly gathered evidence, then struck. After stripping the priests of all civil authority, he hanged eight Spaniards who had supported their revolutionary cabildo. The Franciscans sought to discredit Pacheco by injecting a racial issue into the controversy, charging that his support came from "a Portuguese and mestizos and sambahigos, some of Indian men and Negroes and mulattos." It had no appreciable effect.

To augment his control over the Pueblos, Pacheco issued an order forbidding them to travel from one town to another without a license, and he doubled the taxes and tribute all Pueblos were required to pay to the colonial government—which meant, to him. The oppressive measures caused more Pueblos to flee to the Navajo and Apache or to go into hiding in remote mountainous country.

1644–1648

When Governor Pacheco left office, out of the one hundred and fifty pueblos occupied at the time of the founding of the colony by Onate, only forty-three now contained inhabitants.

On the other hand, the population, prosperity, and power of both the Navajo and the Apache were greatly increased. The runaway Pueblos had brought them military manpower and valuable intelligence regarding Spanish settlements, ranchos, defenses, and activities. Also, they were steadily acquiring horses and guns.

Apache and Navajo emissaries infiltrated the Pueblos, urging them to rise in unison, and offering to help them by attacking Spanish supply trains and disrupting communications between Mexico and Santa Fe. Although the seed of revolt was planted and nourished, it grew slowly among the disorganized Pueblos.

The two governors who followed Pacheco, Fernandez de Arguello and Luis de Guzman, had little time to fight friars. They had all they could do to keep the Apache and Navajo from wiping out the colony.

1649–1655

A Captain Vaca was the chief intelligence officer in the Spanish colony, and he and his aides concentrated on smelling out Pueblo plots against the government and identifying troublemakers. Governor Hernando de Ugarte y la Concha had not been long in office when Vaca got wind of a menacing situation that was developing among the Tewa, Keresans, and Jemez. These peoples purportedly were conspiring to revolt and would be aided by strong bands of Navajo. "They have already agreed with the apostates," Vaca reported to Ugarte, "to attack in all districts on the night of Holy Thursday, because the Spaniards would then be assembled"—presumably at religious services.

Quick action by the governor prevented the first organized Pueblo uprising from succeeding. Cavalry swept into Isleta, Alameda, San Felipe, Cochiti, and Jemez. Nine leaders of these pueblos were hanged without trial, and a number of others were sentenced to ten years of slavery in Santa Fe. Ugarte placed the blame for the aborted uprising on Navajo medicine men. This, of course, was reason enough for him to launch a campaign to take Navajo slaves. He sent a military force into the Navajo country for the purpose, but nothing was accomplished. Navajo had to be found before they could be captured.

Juan de Samandiego succeeded Ugarte. He carried on in the manner of his predecessor, changing no policies and making no effort to improve relations with the clergy. What his true feelings toward the church were is not known, but even if he had wished to halt the vicious feuding, he would have had little time to devote to the problem. His troops were kept busy rushing from place to place in a constant struggle to wipe out Apache and Navajo raiders.

1656–1658

The father custodian of New Mexico, Tomas Manso, demonstrated his talent as a politician. During Samandiego's regime, he bluntly told both government and ecclesiastical authorities in Mexico City that unless drastic measures were taken to halt the state-church conflict in Santa Fe, the colony was doomed. He had strong friends in both factions, was highly respected, and was regarded as an able administrator and astute wilderness diplomat. When he was asked what measures he thought would be most effective, he was ready with an answer. He made only one recommendation. It was that his brother, a highly reputable man, well known in commercial and political circles and a leading Catholic, be appointed governor. The authorities, weary of reading the venomous reports that flowed in a steady stream out of Santa Fe, found the proposal acceptable.

Governor Manso proved himself to be an extraordinary mediator. If his private feelings favored the clergy, he was able to conceal them. How much, if at all, he benefited personally during his term in office is not a matter of historical record. Obviously, however, his policies, decisions, and actions had a calming effect on the troubled waters, and for nearly four years an unprecedented peace prevailed. The only violence occurring was the constant fighting between the military and Apache and Navajo raiders.

1659–1660

Bernard Lopez de Mendizabal was named as successor to Manso, and Fray Juan Ramirez became head of the New Mexico missions. Both were hotheaded, sensitive, and stubborn. Mendizabal had a reputation as a shrewd businessman and was openly anticlerical. Ramirez was a scholar and had no patience with anyone dedicated to making a profit in commerce. They traveled north in the same supply train, argued vehemently over the question of colonial authority, and long before reaching Santa Fe had become avowed enemies. Ten new priests traveling with them, disgusted and discouraged and seeing themselves in a position to become helpless pawns in the factional conflict, turned about and went back to Mexico.

Passion soon flared with new fury in New Mexico. Mendizabal proclaimed his right to control all trade and receive the rewards of the pueblos' production. He set out at once to establish a lucrative slave trade, dispatching "squadrons of men to capture the heathen Indians and send them to reals and mines . . . to sell." At first this commerce in human captives involved mainly Apaches and other wild tribes, but he had his eyes on the Navajo. It was his contention that because the Navajo had made no overtures of peace, they could legally be enslaved as enemies of the king. He sent a force against them, but only two Navajo were captured. Fray Ramirez reported to Mexico that Mendizabal was endangering the safety of the entire colony by keeping all the soldiers on slaving expeditions, most of which turned out to be wild goose chases.

When the Franciscans increased their campaign to halt all Pueblo religious rites, Mendizabal issued an order permitting all Indians to conduct their ceremonies and dances whenever they wished. When the friars attempted to rebuild a church burned in a riot at Taos, Mendizabal named as native governor of the pueblo a Taos Indian who had stabbed and killed a priest. Fray Louis Martinez was assigned to Taos, but Mendizabal told the Taos not to obey him or work for him and charged that after raping an Indian woman, Fray Martinez had cut her throat and buried her under his house.

Unable to capture Navajo in their own country, Mendizabal watched for opportunities to seize them in other places. When he learned that a large band was expected to appear in Jemez to trade, he waylaid them, killed all the warriors and sold the women and children into slavery. Retaliation for this unconscionable act came within a few weeks. Out of the west rode Navajo raiders, striking simultaneously in several places, killing colonists and Pueblos whom they believed had submitted to conversion, burning ranches and homes, and driving off herds of livestock within a gunshot of Santa Fe. The cost to the colony for Mendizabal's barbarity was many times the profit he had made selling slaves.

The torrent of protests sent to Mexico City by Fray Ramirez and other missionaries brought a demand from the Inquisition for an investigation of Mendizabal's irreverence and his illegal and brutal activities. The investigation was begun, but Mendizabal escaped possible punishment by suddenly dying.

The depths to which the clergy were willing to descend to discredit an adversary—even a dead one—was amply demonstrated when they declared that Dona Teresa, Mendizabal's widow, was guilty of committing crimes against the church.

The following charges against her were filed with the Inquisition:

1. She bathed and changed linen on Fridays, a Jewish custom.

2. She primped on Saturdays in violation of the law of Moses, which demanded that the day be observed with religious ceremonies.

3. She and her husband had preferred to sleep in different bedrooms.

4. She read erotic books in foreign tongues and had been heard to laugh at the jokes in them. One book was identified. It was Ariosto's *Orlando Furioso*. They failed to mention, however, that Dona Teresa had been reared in Italy, spoke fluent Italian, and found delight in books published in that language.

The fathers made a mistake in taking on Dona Teresa. She sent to her persecutors a lengthy and spirited written defense of her own actions, but did not neglect to enumerate the transgressions of several score persons, some of whom held high rank and were thought to be of commendable virtue. She ruined reputations on the record, describing in detail—and noting time and place—the immoral conduct, the drunken sprees, the sacrilegious activities, the marital infidelities, and the crimes of the men and women she named. A good many residents of the colony wished that the priests had minded their own business.

1661–1663

Diego Dionysio de Penalosa Bricena y Bertugo was wanted in Peru, his native land, for the commission of a series of felonies, but influential friends in Mexico City prevented his extradition. He was a charlatan, an adventurer without scruples of any sort, a clever politician, a shrewd businessman, and an *embustero*. He was also exceedingly handsome, a lady-killer, a brilliant conversationalist, and perfectly mannered in a drawing room or the boudoir of a mistress. The same friends who saved him from prison secured for him the appointment to the governership of New Mexico.

He traveled up the Rio Grande from Mexico with a large cavalcade of servants and soldiers. From El Paso he sent word ahead that the entire colony—military, settlers, and priests—were to welcome him officially at the Piro pueblo of Senecu. Some two hundred persons were awaiting his arrival there, but many did not appear. Had Santa Fe been emptied, it would not have existed for many days. Apache and Navajo, if not Pueblos, would have burned it to the ground. Advance men arranged celebrations in his honor at every mission and pueblo on the river.

Governor and captain general were not titles enough to satisfy his ego, so he created another for himself. He became the Conde de Santa Fe, and he insisted on being addressed as such. Indians interested him only for what he could get out of them. The work of converting them to Christianity concerned him not at all, for he saw no profit in it. Every evil and illegal practice of all his predecessors was not only adopted by him but was augmented and brought greater returns than any previous chief executive had enjoyed. For nearly three years he held complete control of the colony's economy, conducted large-scale slaving raids, collected heavy tributes, and forced all Pueblos to work for him.

He countered the protests of the friars by charging them with debased cruelties. They lashed Indians for failing to attend mass on time. They cut off the hair of Indian women for minor infractions. Most of the missionaries, he declared, were ex-sailors, ex-artillerymen, ex-criminals, who took holy orders to escape punishment for their crimes or to avoid work and to live in luxury off contributions made to their order by taxpayers. The padres burned the homes of farmers to keep Pueblos from working for them. Posted on the doors of the churches were "more excommunications than bulls, and the worst thing about it is that the friars usually take action against the governors and justices. Thus the royal jurisdiction is much humbled and violated and the few inhabitants who uphold their governor, besides suffering poverty, are afflicted and snubbed by the religions with ugly and insulting words."

Penalosa was riding high, but, in the third year of his tenure, he made a fatal mistake. He gave the helpless clergy the opportunity to strike back for which they had so long been looking.

Captain Francisco Madrid, commander of the governor's cavalry, brought two Pueblo men prisoners into Santo Domingo. They slipped away from their guards and ran into the pueblo church. Madrid, hesitant to invade the sanctuary, sent a courier to Penalosa for orders. They came in the form of a squad of soldiers with directions to retake the prisoners, from under the altar, if necessary. As it was Sunday, Captain Madrid waited until after mass to perform his duty. The church door had been locked by the pastor, but Madrid took the keys from him, opened it, and dragged the two Pueblos out.

Fray Alonso de Posada, the father president of the missions, heard of the incident while at Pecos Pueblo. He immediately sent Penalosa a demand that the captives be returned to the holy sanctuary of Santo Domingo, and threatened to excommunicate the governor for violating the church.

"I recognize no judge in this country who can excommunicate me," Penalosa told Fray Posada, "neither ecclesiastic, bishop nor archbishop." And he boasted that he had been "a cleric in my own country, a padre, and I married when I was ordained as subdeacon, and I sang and intoned nicely a gloria, a credo and a prefacio." He then had the father president arrested and imprisoned him in Santa Fe.

Realizing the seriousness of the situation, Penalosa sought witnesses to justify his actions, but could find no one willing to stand behind him. As Horgan recounts, Santa Fe and the river missions "stirred with excitement. It was unheard of, to throw a prelate and a commissioner of the Inquisition into jail. Penalosa searched for a diplomatic formula that would allow him to climb down with dignity. Surely the friars would petition to free their president, whereupon he would do so with clemency. But the clergy kept an offended silence. Finally desperate, he wrote to the pastor of Isleta, asking him to call. With a show of diplomatic mediation, the incarcerated commissioner was released, and promptly made charges to the Holy Office in Mexico."

Penalosa decided that it might be wise for him to get out of New Mexico, and he resigned.*

1664–1679

Governor Fernando de Villanueva inherited from Penalosa a land not only aflame with warfare but stricken by famine.

---

*Following an inquiry, he was forced to walk through the streets of Mexico City, barefoot in a penitent's robe, carrying a lighted green candle. In addition, he was fined five hundred pesos and exiled for life from the New World.

He claimed to have discovered fabulously rich lands north of New Mexico, and he went to Spain, where he presented a plan to the court for a great new conquest that he maintained would give the Spanish king control of a vast new territory and greatly enrich the Spanish treasury. His words fell on deaf ears. Turning traitor, he tried to interest the sovereigns of England and France in financing a grand filibustering enterprise of conquest against Spain's New World dominions, but the courts in both Paris and London were unresponsive to his proposals. In France he presented the government with what he said was the narrative of an exploring expedition he had made to Quivera and other territories where great treasures awaited the taking. He had never made any expedition, of course. His report was an account of Onate's journey to the Great Plains in 1601, which he had stolen and had rewritten to suit his own purposes.

The warfare was of several kinds, and each faction had its own particular enemy or enemies, but the enduring drought was the enemy of all living things, plants, animals, and humans. If the colony was being torn asunder by factional forces, it was being destroyed by an elemental power that only nature, by its own decision, could overcome.

The conflict of the two majesties, the church and the state, was overwhelmed and weakened by the greater disaster, but the hatred and jealousy, the greed and rapacity that had created it, if relegated to dormancy, did not die. It was simply that priests, civil officials, soldiers, and colonists had to think more about finding the means of staying alive than of maligning and fighting each other.

In the first year, the winter snows were light, and after April no rain fell. The usual summer cloudbursts sweeping across the mesas like great purple brooms did not come. The grass that had started with the spring thaw was soon burnt to powder, and the ranges lay parched and bare. The little creeks were consumed by the thirsty earth, and even the Rio Grande was hardly more than a thin sheet of wetness. The leaves of trees curled and fell, and the bare limbs, gray with blowing dust, pointed upward like the naked arms of gray ghosts uplifted in appeal to the sweep of azure and the ball of merciless fire traveling across it. There were no pinon nuts, no wild herbs or roots or berries. The needles of the pines were red and fell like showers of dust at the slightest movement of the air, the trees dying shaggy and cracked like disreputable old men and women. The wild creatures were gone—where, no one knew. Dust clouds hung darkly over the plains, but the buffalo and the deer and the elk and even the wolves and coyotes had vanished. The wilderness was empty, dead.

And the second year was the same.

It was only with great effort that enough water was obtained to keep men and livestock from perishing of thirst. Little reservoirs were built to catch trickles and holes were dug to reach seepage water that was recovered with buckets or pans or cups. There were no crops, and a friar wrote that there was not a fanega of corn or wheat in the whole kingdom. People ate not only the meat of the cattle they killed but the hides as well, soaking and washing them, rolling them in cornmeal, if they had any, and cooking them with whatever herbs or roots remained unrotted in their earth cellars.

The Navajo were the best off, which was not saying much, but at least they could move into high mountains where some game, some wild foods, and some water could be found. The plains of the Apache were stricken and empty. The Pueblos were the greatest sufferers, for they were not only the victims of nature but the prey of hungry nomadic peoples. Wherever there was stored grain or livestock, both Apache and Navajo swept in and seized it, killing without mercy or even need the helpless Pueblos.

Some snows and rains fell at last, but another year or two would have to pass before the land would be fully restored and the bounties of corn and beans, game, wheat and grass, and nuts, berries, and tubers would be plentiful once more.

Hundreds of Pueblos died of starvation—450 of them in a single pueblo, said one report.

The decade marked the end of the Piro. Their pueblos along the river above Senecu and in the salines east of the Manzano Range were exposed on both sides to country inhabited by the Apache, the Gila bands to the west and the Lipan and other Plains bands to the east. One of their largest towns had been destroyed by Apache in Benavides's time, and he had found the people wandering and hiding in the hills. Thereafter, the priests had made an effort to concentrate them in bigger and stronger pueblos, but the

Apache were not to be defeated. They continued their attacks. In the drought years they delivered the final blows,
and there were not enough soldiers to combat them, no
more than five in any frontier garrison.

"The whole land is at war with the widespread nations of
the Apache Indians, who kill all the Christian Indians they
can find. No road is safe . . . ," a padre reported, and he
accused the Apache of dancing around a captive, "cutting
off parts of his body, which they cook and eat, until they
entirely consume him, cutting him to pieces alive." The
soldiers told more gruesome tales. Along the roads and
about the destroyed Piro towns they found hundreds of
Piro bodies—men, women, and children—the bones of
many stripped of flesh to gleaming white by scavaging animals and birds.

At the pueblo of Abo, the Apache tore Fray Pedro de
Ayala's garments from him, flogged him until his body was
crisscrossed with slashes, and ended his suffering by smash-
ing his skull with a stone hammer. During an Apache attack
on Senecu, Fray Alonso Gil de Avila, standing at a window
and holding aloft a crucifix, was riddled with arrows, and
the blood of some two or three hundred Indians stained to
a dark rust the walls of the ancient town.

The Piro—those who still survived—gave up the struggle. They left their pueblos with their fine big churches to
crumble in the dry winds. Some of them fled to El Paso, and
some found haven in Indian towns farther up the river. A
great many simply vanished; no one could say where, and
no one ever heard of them again.

The next calamity after the drought came in the form of
a mysterious disease that took the lives of both people and
cattle. The Spanish held special church services and prayed
long and fervently, attributing the evil to agents of the devil
lurking about them. The Indians had no monopoly on
superstition.

Death and devastation seemed to fertilize the seeds of rebellion planted in the pueblos both upriver and downriver from Santa Fe, the areas called Rio Arriba and Rio Abajo, respectively. The young plants of revolt were growing faster now, and some carried buds, signifying the fruit to come. Villanueva did what any Spanish governor would be expected to do. He tried to halt the growth with the only methods he understood. He cooperated with the priests by prohibiting Pueblo religious ceremonials and dances, and sent soldiers to arrest "as many Indian medicine doctors as possible." A good many eluded the dragnet, but forty-seven were captured. In Santa Fe they were charged with witchcraft and sorcery—crimes considered more serious than most felonies under Spanish law—and thrown into prison. All were cruelly lashed until they collapsed under the torture. Three who refused to pledge future obedience to king and church, openly defying the court, were hanged.

Then Governor Villanueva learned something that he had failed to realize before—a unity was developing among the Pueblos, under which their traditional tribal animosities, jealousies, and suspicions were being suppressed. He awakened one morning to find seventy Pueblo leaders waiting at the door of the governor's palace, a building which, incidentally, was beginning to display cracks in its walls, the result of long neglect.

After eating a leisurely breakfast, Villanueva granted them an audience. What did they want? They wanted several things. First, they wanted him to understand that they did not intend to abandon their own forms of worship. Second, they wanted to make it clear to him that without their doctors to lead them in their ceremonies, they would be without the power to overcome evil spirits, and that would be bad for the Spanish as well as for themselves. Third, they wanted him to release the medicine men at once.

It was not the custom of Spanish officials to be intimidated by Indians, said Villanueva. He could throw them all in jail by snapping his fingers. What if he refused to grant their request?

In that event, the Pueblos answered, they would abandon their homes and join the Navajo and Apache in making war on the colony. The governor could take his choice.

Villanueva could count without taking pebbles out of one box and dropping them into another, and he could keep records without tying knots in a string. All the statistics he needed were in his head. There were some twenty-five hundred colonists of both sexes and of all sizes. There were no less than sixteen thousand Pueblos. How many thousand Apache and Navajo there were he had no way of knowing, but, whatever the number, there were too many. Moreover, his munitions were in short supply, and it might be months before more arrived.

The medicine men were released. One of them, Pope, was destined for greatness. A native of San Juan pueblo, Pope possessed extraordinary talents as a leader, was revered as a man with great magical powers that permitted him to communicate with supernatural spirits, and was recognized as an outstanding military strategist.

Now, said Pope, he could look into the future, and in the vision he beheld was a great fire burning red with the blood of Spaniards.

Governor Villanueva was not displeased when he was informed that Juan de Miranda was being sent to replace him. He had pocketed the money for several score of slaves whom he had sent to Mexico. The future of the colony was not promising, and he was willing to let someone else struggle with the growing problems. At the moment, the greatest trouble came from the Navajo. There was little hope that they could be stopped without a great many more troops, an expense which the king had already stated he did not deem advisable. Moreover, the Navajo had made it clear that their raids were no longer carried out solely for the purpose of increasing their herds and taking captive women. They were determined to keep the Spanish from entering their country at all, for any reason whatsoever.

Governor Miranda learned something of the dire situation long before he had reached his post. The supply train with which he was traveling was attacked by a large band of Navajo; four of his men were killed, and all the wagon mules were stolen before the raiders could be driven off. Enough horses were saved to get him and his aides to the capital, but he was a badly shaken man. His efforts to strike back by sending out military contingents brought almost no results. A few Navajo and Apache were killed, but the burning of churches, the stealing of livestock, and the murdering of civilians and priests continued through his administration.

Pope was holding great dances and making threats. Soldiers watched him closely, but he was not arrested. To avoid being harassed, he slipped out of San Juan and went to Taos, where he kept the fires of his great vision flaming.

When he relieved Miranda, Governor Juan Francisco Trevino found himself faced with an unprecedented situation. The Pueblos were not only plotting rebellion, but openly calling for it. Trevino received reports that missionaries were being "bewitched"—probably a way of saying that they were being scared out of their wits—"with the result that half a dozen had dropped dead." He was greatly relieved when Fray Francisco de Ayeta, the father quartermaster of the colony, arrived with fifty more soldiers and a long train of supplies, including badly needed guns and powder.

A turncoat Pueblo brought word of what Pope was doing

and saying in Taos. The news was not good. Pope was claiming that he was in communication with the ancient war god Montezuma, through three underworld spirits. The spirits came each night to talk with him in the dim light of the Taos kiva, and to urge him to lead the Pueblos in revolt.

Trevino hanged three Tewas suspected of defying the faith, but he stayed away from Taos. Indeed, he seldom strayed beyond his patio until he was replaced by Antonio de Otermin. Then he scurried back to Mexico.

If he lacked experience in frontier warfare, Governor Otermin did not lack courage. He announced his intention to chastise both the rebellious Pueblos and the Navajo once and for all. His strategy called for a two-pronged campaign, using reinforcements which were expected to arrive from Nueva Vizcaya. One column would move westward from Taos and the other would start at Zia.

It was too late. The reinforcements were not sanctioned by the viceroy, who thought the fifty soldiers recently sent to Santa Fe were enough to protect the colony. A second relief train led by Fray Ayeta was still near El Paso when the fuse Pope had lighted reached the bomb he had magically constructed.

PART FIVE

Revolt:
The Summer of
Terror and
Death

1680

In the smoky kiva of Taos, Pope tied a number of knots in a cord. Outside, in the shadows of the plaza, two couriers waited beside their horses. Presently a man emerged with the cord, and one of the couriers took it and both leaped to their saddles and rode away into the night.

The cord was to be carried as rapidly as possible, in relays, to every pueblo of Rio Arriba and Rio Abajo, down the Rio Grande as far as Isleta, east to Pecos and west to Acoma. There was not enough time to take it farther west, to the Zuni and the Hopi, but messengers would tell them in due course that the time had come. Nor was it to be taken to the Piro, wherever any of them might be clinging to life along the river, for they were not to be trusted. Also, he wanted to hold the Apache as allies.

There were enough knots in the cord to compensate for the number of days required to complete the delivery circuit. When a day passed, a knot would be untied. The number remaining would indicate the number of days to elapse before the explosion was to occur. There was no question about pledges. They had been made. Everyone was ready. All that remained to be done was to set the date, and the knots did that.

For weeks Pope had talked with leaders in private. Only those of the highest rank had been told the plan, such men as Catiti of Santo Domingo, Tupatu of Picuris, Jaca of Taos, and a few others with equal authority. They were sworn to secrecy, for the element of surprise was vital to success.

When Pope became convinced—by what evidence is not known—that his son-in-law was planning to inform the Spanish of the plot, he killed him. But despite all the precautions taken, some ugly rumors were circulated. Padres and soldiers and the people on ranchos had good eyes and ears. They picked up a word here and there, and they saw unusual and unexplained movements, warning them that a storm was brewing. They sent messages telling Governor Otermin what they had heard and what they thought.

The intelligence was not very conclusive, but Otermin did not discount it. He began at once to strengthen the defenses of Santa Fe. Walls were repaired, missing gates and doors were restored, stores and fodder were collected. When the work was completed, the Villa, the governor's house, the barracks, the courtyards, stables, and corrals were in condition to accommodate more than a thousand persons, and a large number of sheep, goats, horses, and beef cattle. If there was to be an uprising, Otermin would not be caught napping.

The day Pope had chosen was August 11, but unexpected complications disrupted the schedule. Early on August 9, three leaders of the southern Tewa appeared before Otermin and told an alarming tale. Two couriers from Tesuque, named Catua and Omtua, had shown the knotted cord to them. The leaders asserted that after long deliberations they had decided not to participate in the attack, and declared that they now "regarded the Spanish as their brothers." The truth probably was that they had become convinced that the uprising, scheduled to start in two days, would be a failure. Perhaps they were jealous of the powers Pope had gained and resentful of his arrogance.

In any case, they revealed all they knew of Pope's scheme, and Otermin sprang into action, dispatching messengers to warn the soldiers, civil officials, and ranchers of

Rio Abajo, where the majority of the tiny outlying settlements were located. He also sent his *maestro de campo*, Francisco Gomez Roblado, and a squad of soldiers to Tesuque to arrest Catua and Omtua. They were brought in within a few hours. However, besides confirming the story of the knotted cord, they had little to reveal, for they had served only as couriers and had not participated in any secret councils of the plotters.

"The capture of Catua and Omtua," states Hackett, "created consternation among the other natives of Tesuque [only two leagues north of Santa Fe], and, believing that their plans were discovered, they resolved upon haste as being their only hope to successfully carry out the revolt. Accordingly, it was decided that the plans should be put into execution prematurely that night. It took time to spread the news, but practically all the northern pueblos, including San Juan and Taos, were notified to begin the revolt at about daybreak of the morning of Saturday, August 10. In the most distant pueblos, however, as Santo Domingo and Jemez, and those of Rio Abajo, the attack began later in the day, since it took the messengers from Tesuque longer to reach them."

The first blood was spilled at Tesuque, a small pueblo but for many years a center of revolutionary sentiment. On the evening of August 9, a Spaniard named Cristobal de Herrera, presumably a civil official, was killed. On the morning of August 10, Fray Juan Pio, who deliberately rode into the face of great peril to say mass and try to persuade the rebels to remain peaceful, was cut to pieces.

The underlying causes of the Pueblo revolt must certainly be obvious to anyone who has read the preceding pages of this chronicle. Yet, it is necessary to comment on the subject, for numerous works attribute the uprising chiefly to religious oppression, a conclusion with which this author disagrees.

That was only one reason out of many for its occurrence. The basis of this contention is the fact that the Spanish *did not succeed in supplanting Pueblo beliefs with the tenets of Christianity.* Indeed, they fell far short of achieving this goal. The forceful measures employed by the priests to stamp out every vestige of Pueblo rites, every element of the Pueblo faith, of course generated resentment and defiance, but they were not in themselves entirely responsible for the ultimate catastrophe.

The causes stemmed more from hunger of the belly than from spiritual craving; more from emotional traumata than from injuries caused by the suppression of ritual; more from physical suffering than from religious persecution; more from a demand for complete obedience and for undeviating compliance with social and economic systems that held the Pueblos in perpetual bondage and terrible poverty than from the burning of kachinas and the profanation of the gods they worshipped.

The fire smoldered for years before becoming an unquenchable conflagration. Small spurts of flame had risen spasmodically during this time, but the Spanish were able to extinguish them quickly because the Pueblos had no leader with the ability to unite them, to induce them to suppress, at least temporarily, the tribal jealousies and superstitions and petty grievances that created discord among them. Fate filled that void with Pope.

"Spaniards," wrote Madariaga, "always end by devouring their institutions with the acid of their corrosive individualities." That was an essential ingredient of the Spanish character, and it nurtured the debacle in New Mexico. But if it helped to weaken the beams, it was not entirely responsible for the collapse of the colonial structure. A conflict between equally destructive forces brought down the Spanish house, shattering collisions between two ways of life, two civilizations, between social, juridical, and economic systems with nothing in common, and between deeply ingrained faiths impossible to reconcile. It was not the Pueblos who were unwilling to compromise. It was the Spanish, not only in their insistence that the Pueblos submit to totalitarian rule, but in the factualism existing in their own ranks. Neither of the two majesties would give ground, and the fight could have ended in no other way but a draw ruinous to both of them.

The Spanish factions eventually did reach a provisional accord, but it came too late. In the *autos* prepared after the revolt by priests, civil officials, and military officers, no reference was made to secular or ecclesiastical oppression, to the barbarities inflicted or the heavy tributes levied on the Pueblos. The sworn testimony taken gave evidence of a general agreement to represent the uprising as founded completely on religious controversies. If the bitter differences that had prevailed for eighty years were not forgotten, they were not enumerated as causes of the calamity. In the voluminous record of the official investigation, neither state nor church partisans made charges against their Spanish opponents. All attributed the revolt to demoniac influences on a superstitious and idolatrous people. It was, of course, the safest defense for each side.

Historical documents indicate how carefully the plan of the rebellion had been prepared and how efficiently it was executed.

Early on the morning of August 10, some seventy Spaniards at Taos, and perhaps a score at Picuris, were murdered. Among the victims were a number of children and two missionaries. Two sargentos mayores, Sebastian de

Herrera and Fernando de Chavez, somehow were able to fight their way to freedom. Each left his wife and children dead in their homes. After a week of hiding by day and moving by night, they reached a height from which they could see Santa Fe. Realizing the foolhardiness of an attempt to penetrate the lines of the Pueblos encircling the Villa, they went on south and at last found safety among refugees at Isleta.

Spanish men, women, and children were slain almost simultaneously at San Ildefonso, Nambe, Pojoaque, Santa Clara, San Juan, Galisteo, Santo Domingo, Santa Ana, Puaray, Sandia, Alameda, Cochiti, and San Felipe. Scores of bodies, stripped and mutilated, lay along the roads, in the patios and buildings of haciendas and estancias. Every church was destroyed and all sacred objects and decorations burned. In time, as word that the uprising had started spread westward, Spaniards died at Acoma, Zia, Jemez, and Zuni. Four padres met their end in the Hopi towns.

The warning Governor Otermin had sent out on the eve of the revolt saved many lives. Small contingents of soldiers and armed settlers, displaying extraordinary bravery, were able to rescue not a few colonists. Groups from Los Cerrilles and La Canada were able to reach Santa Fe just before all access to the capital was cut off. Lieutenant General Alonso Garcia, with no more than six or eight troopers, prevented the slaughter of a number of persons and escorted them to Isleta.

Both Apache and Navajo joined in the onslaughts, but to what extent is not certain. Apache definitely participated in the attacks on settlers of Rio Arriba. Navajo may have aided Pueblos in the west, particularly the Jemez, with whom they were on friendly terms. Apache were raging through the southern part of New Mexico, western Texas, and northern Mexico, but their operations were more coincidental than a part of the overall Pueblo plan.

Except for the beseiged havens of Santa Fe and Isleta, the Pueblo country was devastated. "The estancias and haciendas of the Spanish settlers," writes Hackett, the outstanding authority on the revolt, "had been robbed of both household goods and of the horses and cattle in the fields, while many of the houses had been destroyed by fire. The churches, where not burned, had been stripped . . . and in every way as completely and foully desecrated as Indian sacrilege and indecency could suggest, while the sacred vestments had been made use of by the Indians as trophies in the dances and festivities celebrating their success."

Approximately four hundred Spanish men, women, and children had been killed in the first two or three days of the uprising. In addition, twenty-one priests had achieved martyrdom. A few of the most attractive young Spanish women had been taken alive and turned over to Pueblo leaders for their pleasure. Many persons were missing, and their fate would never be known.

With Governor Otermin behind the walls of the Villa were about a thousand persons, the majority of them women, children, and Mexican Indian servants. Only a hundred men were capable of bearing arms. Otermin had had an opportunity to assemble supplies and strengthen defenses, but the refugees at Isleta had no time to save any possessions or foodstuffs. They had been fortunate to escape with their lives.

With Lieutenant General Garcia at Isleta were fifteen hundred persons, not including the Pueblo inhabitants, all of whom had refused to join in the revolt. Conditions at the sanctuary were serious in the extreme. Hackett states that "owing to the great haste in which the refugees had assembled there . . . only a limited supply of provisions and munitions were taken with them, and these were rapidly diminishing . . ." Most of the hundred and twenty able-bodied men who had gained the pueblo possessed only the few rounds of ammunition they carried in their pouches.

Communication between Santa Fe and Isleta was impossible, for the entire area was infested with Pueblos hoping to waylay more Spaniards. But Indians brought messages to each place. As it would be learned later, the intelligence was fraudulent and delivered with the hope of frightening the defenders into surrendering. Otermin was informed that all the Spaniards of Rio Abajo had been killed. Garcia was informed that the governor and every person with him in Santa Fe had been slain in an assault on the Villa.

Santa Fe had been invaded first from the south. Quickly the homes and buildings in this sector, including the church of San Miguel, were sacked and burned. Spanish patrols skirmishing with the attackers reported that they were commanded by a Tewa war leader named Juan, a man Otermin knew well and with whom he had often conferred. By some means not ascertainable, the governor was able to arrange a council with him under a flag of truce.

Juan, whose Indian name is not recorded, boldly rode into the plaza to meet the waiting Otermin. He was armed with a musket, sword, dagger, and other Spanish military equipment. About his waist was a sash of red taffeta. The insignia it bore identified it as having come from the mission at Galisteo.

Otermin reminded Juan of the friendly relations they had enjoyed, and offered to pardon the Pueblos for their treasonous acts and to forgive them for the murders they had committed if they would cease the attack and return to their homes.

Juan sneered. It was, he declared, much too late for any compromise. The Spaniards had only one alternative to escape death. He had brought with him two small crosses, one red and one white. The red cross signified that the

Spaniards would continue their resistance. The white cross signified that they would abandon New Mexico. He held the crosses out to the governor and told him to make a choice.

When Otermín replied angrily that he would touch neither of them, Juan turned abruptly, mounted his horse, and rode out of the plaza. The waiting warriors, fearing that he had ridden into a trap, welcomed him with wild howls of delight.

Otermín and his officers decided that it would be to their advantage to make a sortie against the attackers, estimated to number more than five hundred, before more rebels appeared. According to Hackett, the warriors fought so furiously against the company which rushed out at them "that the governor was obliged to go in person with reinforcements for his men." The Pueblos took positions behind houses and walls, fighting with arms and munitions taken from Spaniards already killed elsewhere, "and all day long the battle raged. By evening the Indians were nearly conquered," and as darkness began to fall, having suffered many casualties, they withdrew.

During the evening, more Pueblos arrived, purportedly from Taos, Picuris, and several Tewa towns, and through the night and during the following day, other groups from Rio Grande pueblos came, setting up their camps on the outskirts of the city. Santa Fe was ringed by more than two thousand warriors. Had they launched a united attack, in all probability the Spaniards would have been overwhelmed, but for some peculiar reason, their sallies came intermittently, like small waves beating without regularity against a rocky shore. The Spaniards were able to repulse each onslaught, although on several occasions the rebels came dangerously close to breaking over the defenses of the Villa.

On the third day, the beseiged watched in horror as the water in the ditch that was their only source of supply fell to a trickle and finally stopped altogether. In the ruins of Santa Fe, the Pueblos began to celebrate with dances, to chant their songs of victory. They shouted at the people crowded into the governor's compound that the God of the Christians was dead, that their mother, Santa Maria, was dead, and that they, too, would soon be dead.

After two days and a night, with only an occasional sip of water from the small supply stored in pots, their thirst had become unbearable. The animals had had no water at all, and some of them were crazed and dropping in their agony. Whereupon, said an official report, Governor Otermin, who had sustained two severe wounds, "agreed with the experienced persons among us to engage the enemy in a pitched battle on the following morning, since it would be a better and safer step to die fighting than of hunger and thirst, shut up within the *casas reales.*"

At sunrise, Otermin and his soldiers rushed suddenly from the Villa, pouring a deadly fire at the surprised Pueblos, "and, invoking the name of the Virgin, Santa Maria, he routed and overran them, dislodging them from the streets and houses, where they were massacred with the loss of more than three hundred Indians . . ." The incredibly brave Spaniards put to flight "more than fifteen hundred Indians of the army made up of all the nations of the kingdom, and forty-seven Indians were taken prisoner. . . . These were executed."

If the official record can be believed, only five soldiers were killed in two pitched battles and several skirmishes. No list of wounded was prepared; it was merely stated that a number of men and women had been struck by arrows and bullets.

The rout of the Pueblos was not considered a decisive victory, nor was it believed for a moment that the colony had been saved. In their pleas for mercy, some of the captured warriors told Otermin that, contrary to reports given to him, not all the Spaniards of the Rio Abajo had been slain. Many had escaped to Isleta. Believing that doomed men usually blurted out truths, Otermin immediately planned to join Garcia. Perhaps if the two groups could be united, all might survive.

"Judging that they at La Isleta," he would write, "would be engaged in the same conflict as those who were at the Villa, and because of the obstacle offered by the many enemies who were found along the roads and in the pueblos of both districts, and because of being so short of animals and provisions, and of both parties being in manifest danger, and since we could not maintain ourselves in the Villa, I determined, in accordance with the opinions of all, to march out . . . on foot, and with many wounded men, to see if I could succeed in joining the body of people who were said to be in . . . La Isleta."

Even under the menacing pressures of the moment, Otermin did not neglect to comply with regulations. Throughout the evening of August 20 and the morning of August 21, state property for which he was responsible was distributed. Records were properly prepared, signed, and notarized. Colonial Secretary Francisco Xavier attested that by order of the governor he distributed "a large quantity of clothing to the Spanish soldiers, to all their families and servants, to the Mexican natives, and to all classes of people, numbering more than a thousand souls, who are in these *casas reales* in the seige which has continued for nine days . . . Of shirts, clothing, coats, shoes, and provisions I have distributed a quantity worth apparently more than eight thousand pesos; and I have also given them beasts so that they may be able to march out . . . Everyone was given what he asked for and needed free of charge . . ."

Then they all moved out on the trail that led from the

Villa over the high mesas, which were gold and dry in the hot summer sun, and on down to the Rio Grande. Santa Fe stood crumbling and blackened and deserted against the great blue background of the Sangre de Christo Mountains. They were not attacked on the retreat to Isleta. In effect, Otermin had taken the little white cross Juan had offered, and the Pueblos were satisfied.

But there were no Spaniards to welcome them at Isleta. Garcia had started south with the refugees gathered there a week before Otermin had left Santa Fe.

Couriers had reached Isleta from El Paso shortly after the revolt had begun with letters advising that a supply caravan, under the direction of Fray Francisco de Ayeta, had started north. Garcia had made several attempts to communicate with Otermin, but his messengers had failed to return, and he had concluded that Santa Fe had fallen. Even if that tragedy had not occurred, he was not in a position to send men to the relief of the Villa, for to do so would have left the women and children at Isleta defenseless. As it was, Isleta could not have held out more than a day or two against a strong assault.

Moreover, as he would state, "it was seen that many of the Indians of Isleta were going over to the enemy, because those of their own nation from the pueblos of Alameda and Sandia were in revolt . . . and those of Isleta were taking steps to do the same thing . . . and were sending ambassadors to and were receiving them from the enemy, and making other dangerous demonstrations. Thus it was feared that everyone at Isleta would perish . . ." Garcia had no way of knowing, of course, that had not the rebels been concentrating on destroying Santa Fe, an attack on Isleta would have occurred.

The Spaniards at Isleta unanimously decided "to leave as best they could for safer parts, following the route on which they would meet the wagons which were coming to these provinces from his Majesty . . . In them were being brought the supplies, and the powder and shot, which this small camp is wholly without, and it has many women and children to defend who cannot now be abandoned, and there are eight religious, sick and well."

The march down the Rio Grande from Isleta began on August 14, and "most of the Spaniards were on foot, without clothing or shoes, so that it inspires distress and horror to see them. . . . we are now so short of provisions that it is a pity. If some sheep and cattle had not escaped [the rebels], it is certain that we would have perished."

No less fearful than the Spaniards of being attacked by either the Pueblo rebels or the Apache, and perhaps by both, were the Piro still holding out in Sevilleta and Socorro, and they took advantage of the opportunity to save themselves by moving south with the Garcia company. Thus the history of the Piro as a tribal unit came to an end.

On September 4, the tiny settlement at Fray Cristobal was reached. There Garcia received dispatches from both the south and the north. From El Paso, in response to a message he had sent to the supply train, came word that Piedro de Leiva had been appointed provisional governor of New Mexico and was riding hard with an armed force and supplies up the Rio Grande to rescue him and his people. From Governor Otermin came an order to await the arrival of the Santa Fe refugees.

With six soldiers and a herd of horses, Garcia set out at once to meet Otermin. He reached him after a fast ride of two or three days near Alamillo. Otermin charged him with having deserted his post at Isleta without authority and put him under arrest. However, after hearing Garcia's account of his own actions, Otermin withdrew the charges.

Reunited, the two divisions plodded on southward, their

sufferings and fears greatly relieved by the arrival of Leiva with provisions and an escort. As the month of September ended, all the survivors were at La Salineta, near El Paso del Norte.

The colony of New Mexico had been lost, abandoned to the Indians, eighty-two years after it had been founded, and a hundred and forty years after Coronado and his army had invaded the land of the Pueblos.

1681

Knowing only too well the temper of the Pueblos, not to mention the Apache and Navajo, Otermin bluntly warned his superiors that any attempt to reconquer New Mexico would fail with the limited resources then available to him. Patriotic fervor and wounded pride, commendable reactions under the circumstances, would not accomplish the task. An expedition would require not only thoughtful planning but adequate appropriations from the royal treasury. Not a tenth of the provisions, munitions, equipment, and manpower necessary could be obtained in the dirty and impoverished settlement which had been established at El Paso. Indeed, he did not think they could be obtained in all northern Mexico.

For a year he waited for developments, struggling meanwhile with missionaries to prevent the economy of the frontier town from suffering a fatal collapse. Apache continually ravaged the surrounding territory, disrupting communications for weeks at a time. Unless they were accompanied by strong military escorts, supply caravans seldom reached their destinations without heavy losses, and sometimes they vanished as if they were consumed—wagons, mules, and drivers—by the dust clouds that swept the barren valleys and the high rocky plateaus.

At last, in September, Fray Ayeta returned to El Paso from Mexico City, where he had gone to urge the viceroy and the church to work together in organizing and financing an expedition of reconquest. The determined and daring missionary had met with considerable success. He brought with him a caravan of supplies, cartloads of munitions, a company of cavalry, and orders to Otermin to retake New Mexico with all possible dispatch. To Fray Ayeta, the instructions meant *start at once.* Otermin would have preferred to wait until early spring, but finally, although against his own judgment, he deferred to the advice of the stubborn priest.

Nevertheless, several weeks passed before preparations were completed. In the column that moved up the Rio Grande from El Paso in the first days of November were: 146 mounted soldiers; 112 "Christian Indians"; 28 personal servants of the governor and other officers; Fray Ayeta and 5 or 6 other religious; some 900 horses and mules; a train of supply wagons; and a herd of cattle.

The company traveled almost steadily for two days and two nights to get across the Jornado del Muerto, a section of the trail with few waterholes, and both men and animals suffered greatly from thirst. The first abandoned Piro pueblo was reached November 26. Raiders, presumably Apache, had done a thorough job of sacking it and destroying the church. Similar conditions were found in the ruined pueblos at Socorro, Alamillo, and Sevilleta. All estancias along the road, once occupied by Spaniards, had been burned. Smoke signals were sighted each day. The column was not attacked, but it was apparent that word of its approach was being sent ahead.

As they neared Isleta, Otermin set out in advance with

seventy picked troopers. Indian scouts reported that the pueblo was prepared to resist. Otermin divided his force into four groups and moved on Isleta from all sides early on the morning of December 6. The inhabitants capitulated without a shot's being fired.

As the soldiers entered the plaza, Isleta leaders quickly came forward to assure Otermin that it had not been their intention to fight. Searching the pueblo, the Spaniards came upon numerous sacred articles that had been taken from the destroyed church. The Indians were ordered to attend mass, and Hackett states that they were commanded to "take out of their houses . . . the idols, feathers, powders, masks, and every other thing pertaining to their idolatry and superstition. This was done, and when all such things had been collected they were piled in a heap and burned."

Otermin established his headquarters at Isleta. The commander of his cavalry, Juan Dominguez de Mendoza, was sent with seventy Spanish and some Indian troops to reconnoiter pueblos farther up the river. The weather was extremely cold and a deep blanket of snow covered the ground. Mendoza started on his mission after vespers on December 8. The governor planned to follow him two days later, but a violent storm broke on the morning of December 10, and he chose to remain by his comfortable fire.

In ten days of wandering, Mendoza accomplished nothing and learned very little of value, except that the Pueblos would not submit again to domination. Only a few sick, crippled, aged, and blind Indians were found in the pueblos of Alameda, Puaray, Sandia, San Felipe, Santo Domingo, Cochiti, Santa Ana, Zia, and Jemez. All other residents of these towns had vanished into the hills and mountains. On December 18, Mendoza and his men narrowly escaped from riding into an ambush. Indian scouts warned them of the danger in time for them to dash in retreat in the direction of Isleta.

Otermin had left Isleta on December 11. Following Mendoza's route, he burned several of the deserted pueblos. The two parties were reunited near Sandia.

1682

By the first of the year, Otermin had become convinced that reestablishing the colony and punishing the rebels could not be accomplished by his small force. Although deeply disappointed, Fray Ayeta was constrained to agree with him.

More than a hundred of the five hundred Pueblos they had found at Isleta had run away. Otermin ordered the pueblo and all the stores not needed by his command burned. Three hundred and eighty-five Isleta Indians were made prisoners. The governor announced that they would be taken to El Paso, resettled on farms, and instructed in the Catholic faith.

On January 2, the return journey down the river was begun. El Paso was reached in mid-February.

No other Spaniard would enter the land of the Pueblos for six years.

The bonds of the alliance Pope had forged steadily weakened. The rivalries, social conflicts, and suspicions that had for so many centuries made lasting unity impossible again began to surface. If something of the Pueblos' old way of life had been restored, so had their traditional divisiveness been reactivated.

Pope's success had gone to his head. The authority granted him by other leaders under the pressures of tumultuous conditions had sired delusions. He saw himself as a supreme potentate to whom all must render obeisance. He exacted tributes that were no less oppressive than those demanded by the Spanish. Moving triumphantly into the Villa, he established a *juzgado,* organized a *guardia* to enforce decrees born of willfulness, maintained a harem of attractive maidens taken by force from various pueblos, and pronounced himself the earthly emissary of the supernaturals, all of whom he claimed communicated with him in private kiva seances.

Resentment and defiance increased until neither brutality nor threats of spiritual punishment could suppress them. Fanning the flames of the chaos were the internal controversies splitting the people over whom he claimed dominion, dissensions that divided them into quarrelsome groups and often brought violence. The walls of Pope's kingdom, sustained by nothing more than a steadily deteriorating mortar of madness, crashed down upon him.

It was not Spanish apathy that gave the Pueblos a few years of relief from the yokes of the two majesties. International developments which they could not have understood even if they had been informed of them, warfare with the Apache and other tribes in northern Mexico, and the paucity of royal disbursements combined to preclude an attempt to recover the lost colony. The church strongly advocated that it be retaken, but unarmed missionaries, inspired as they were, could not perform the feat, although not a few made known their willingness to try in the face of certain death. The king was no less in favor of a reconquest, but he insisted that it must be carried out "with very little expense to the crown," a decree that placed an insuperable burden on any plan advanced.

The sovereign's reluctance to authorize the necessary expenditures, however, in reality stemmed more from cautiousness than frugality. A great deal of money was being spent in the struggle to control the Apache, and that bloody campaign was showing no signs of success. Moreover, Mexico was being threatened by outside pressures. The French were in the Gulf of Mexico. Florida and Texas might have to be defended, perhaps against the British as well as the French, and both the British and the Russians were making menacing gestures in the Pacific. The king had good reason for his conservative stand. Affluent as Spain was, its resources were not without limit.

Yet there was no thought of abandoning New Mexico. It would be reoccupied as time and circumstances permitted. That was a debt from which there could be no escape, for it was a debt owed to the Pueblos whose souls had been recaptured by Satan, therefore a debt to God, and it would be paid.

1683

Otermin was severely criticized by Mexico City authorities for failing to retake Santa Fe after reaching a point less than ten leagues from the Villa. Unacceptable as excuses for turning back were his arguments that he had been operating in bitterly cold weather with only a few men surrounded by thousands of hostile Pueblos, that Santa Fe was strongly fortified, that an attempt to retake it would be suicidal, that his officers and the religious with him had advocated a retreat, and that trustworthy Indian scouts had warned him of his peril and had reported that Pope, Catiti, Tupatu, and Jaca were again attempting to organize a force to wipe him out.

In failing health and deeply depressed by the unfair treatment, Otermin resigned.

His successor, Domingo Jironza Petris Cruzate, arrived

in El Paso late in August. The sight of the miserable little settlement might well have caused a man of less fortitude to return home. General Cruzate, however, was a veteran soldier who had won honors for his courage and ability as a field commander. If he was appalled by what he saw, he was not intimidated by the problems confronting him. The governor's residence was a mud hut. Horgan notes that Cruzate "improved his dignity, buying land from the Manso Indians at El Paso and building a new Government House of earthen brick, containing an audience hall, the secretary's office and dwelling room, a cellar vault for munitions, and another bedroom. Four other adjacent houses belonging to the Indians were purchased and provided a jail, a guardroom and eight bedrooms." Cruzate quickly demonstrated that besides being a distinguished officer, he was a capable organizer and executive.

1686

Political machinations disrupted the progress of Cruzate's administration. He was accused of committing numerous violations of colonial statutes and of refusing to coordinate his campaigns against the Indians with the operations of the governor of the adjoining state of Nueva Vizcaya. The desertion of Cruzate's *maestro de campo* was cited as giving credence to the charges.

Cruzate was suspended, and Pedro Reneros de Posada became ad interim governor. He quickly demonstrated his incapacity for fulfilling the duties of the office.

1688

An official inquiry into the accusations leveled at Cruzate had shown them to be largely without foundation. According to a contemporary account by Captain Juan Mateo Manje, one of the outstanding explorers and Indian fighters of the time, it was found that Cruzate had governed "with satisfaction, punishing the apostate enemies and defeating ten nations confederated to destroy El Paso, subjected some of these nations to obedience and established towns . . . and, after fifteen campaigns, was acclaimed by the people not so much as a governor, but as an example of charity, being more of a father to them."

Manje's statements, however, must be viewed with some suspicion, for he was Cruzate's nephew. In any case, Posada was removed for inefficiency, and Cruzate was restored to office.

Although trained in European tactics, Cruzate had been quick to realize the value of the Indian hit-and-run system of warfare, and he had soon adopted it. A series of swift surprise attacks had been successful against Apache plaguing the El Paso region. When he returned as governor of New Mexico, he gave serious thought to making a similar type of strike against the Pueblos. It was one thing, however, to campaign in a limited theater, and another to conduct an operation several hundred miles from his main supply depot. Logistics alone made such an incursion extremely difficult and hazardous, but Cruzate was a daring officer.

Early in his tenure, he had begun to organize a force of Indian auxiliaries, selecting the members with care. Most, if not all, of them belonged to tribes or groups that had suffered from Apache depredations. He had paid part of the cost of maintaining them out of his own pocket. After thorough training and testing in actual combat, neither their bravery nor their capabilities was found wanting. They were a company of well-disciplined, deadly fighters, and in numerous ways had demonstrated their loyalty to him.

Regrettably, no reliable record has been found of the size of the *Compania Volante,* or Flying Force, Cruzate led up the Rio Grande. It can be stated that the entire company was mounted, heavily armed, well supplied, and organized to travel with speed. The garrison at El Paso was normally composed of fifty to sixty Spanish soldiers, but it seems illogical to suggest that Cruzate would have taken even a majority of them with him, and thus have dangerously depleted the settlement's power to defend itself. Most probably, he had with him no more than a hundred, or possibly a hundred and twenty, troopers, but how many of them were Spanish regulars and how many were Indian auxiliaries is not known.

The Pueblos fled before him as he swept north along the river above Isleta like a small tornado, destroying towns, storehouses, crops, and irrigation works. Somewhere in the vicinity of the present Bernalillo, he struck out for Zia. What prompted him to leave the heavily populated Rio Grande Valley is not certain. Perhaps his scouts learned that a large number of Pueblos were fleeing up the Rio Jemez. If that is true, the intelligence proved to be accurate.

He found Zia strongly fortified, and within its stout walls were an estimated three thousand Indians. Cruzate wasted no time in attempting to induce them to capitulate. Immediately he attacked. Purportedly the date was August 29.

One report states that the fighting continued for a day and a night, and that fifty soldiers were wounded. Whatever the length of the battle, the reasons for its cessation are clear. More than six hundred Pueblos were slain. Zia was wreathed in flames. Besides those killed in combat, several hundred men, women, and children were burned to death. Ninety persons were shot attempting to escape, but a number had gained their freedom under cover of darkness.

With seventy prisoners, Cruzate promptly started back to El Paso. He had accomplished his objective, which was to deliver a crushing blow to the Pueblos.

1689–1691

The slowness of communications and Apache warfare prevented Cruzate from restoring New Mexico to the crown. Word of his victory over the Pueblos did not reach Carlos II until the summer of 1690. Before that time, Cruzate had completed plans to reoccupy Santa Fe, but he had been obliged to postpone the campaign to fight the Suma Apache. When he was again in a position to give his attention to reducing the Pueblos, he was informed that the sovereign had awarded both that task and the governorship of New Mexico to Diego de Vargas Lujan Ponce de Leon.

Apparently the king began to fear that he might have acted in too much haste and had selected the wrong man for the reconquest. He adroitly sought to amend his decision in a cedula that reached Mexico City in June 1691. The viceroy, Conde de Galve, was instructed to thank Cruzate in the name of His Majesty and to advise him that he had been rewarded "with the Robe of three military orders." Perhaps, thought the king, Galve would find that Vargas "had not ruled with equality." If such a situation should develop, it would please His Majesty to have Cruzate returned to the governorship a third time, and Vargas could be given some other high post.

But the contingency did not arise.

If the king had some qualms about Vargas's ability to fulfill the rigorous demands of the dangerous northern office, none existed in Galve. Numerous competent field commanders were available, but it would have been difficult to find one whose record was more illustrious and who was also extremely wealthy and a scion of a great family whose members for generations had won renown in serving both the state and the church.

Diego de Vargas had demonstrated his competency as an officer on European battlefields. He might have devoted himself to managing the vast estates that were his heritage, living the life of a gentleman with palaces in Madrid and Granada and enjoying the glamorous festivities of the Spanish Court. Instead, a strong desire for adventure had moved him to request an overseas appointment, and in 1672 he had been sent to New Spain in a relatively minor diplomatic capcity. He had risen rapidly in the provincial government, displaying unusual talent as a foreign service official, and becoming a respected advisor and a confidant of several viceroys. The weight of his official responsibilities, however, had not prevented him from making good use of his inherent capabilities as a businessman, and he had acquired extensive holdings in Mexico which brought him a fortune. Deeply religious, almost to the point of fanaticism, he had vigorously supported the position of the church that, if for no other reason, New Mexico should be recovered to save the souls of the Pueblos who had reverted to idolatry after the revolt.

But that could hardly have been the only reason that Vargas, as intimately acquainted with affairs as he was, advocated the reconquest. There was a rumor—how it got started no one seemed to know, but it was widely accepted as fact—that some fabulously rich quicksilver mines existed in a New Mexico mountain range called the Sierra Azul.

Then there were reasons involving political, economic, and jurisdictional questions. The boundaries of New Mexico remained officially undefined. Indeed, it was still unknown how far the continent extended to the north. Under such circumstances, Spain's claims were open to dispute. Moreover, with the Indians in control of New Mexico, Mexico was without an adequate buffer zone on the north to protect it from an invasion by some other European power. There was still another reason, and it would have weighed on a man of Vargas's character. It had to do with pride. For the first and only time in the New World, a horde of savages not only had successfully defied the military strength of Spain but had continued to profane for years the only true faith.

Whatever may have been the force or forces motivating Vargas, he sought and won appointment to the governorship of New Mexico. It is not improbable that the decision to name him was greatly influenced by his offer to contribute a substantial sum to help defray the expenses of the reconquest or, if necessary, even to underwrite the entire cost of an expedition.

He had taken command in El Paso and was engaged in fighting Apache before the king's quibbling cedula had been digested in Mexico City. Viceroy Galve, knowing him to be a capable soldier, a skilled diplomat, uncompromisingly devout, a man of vigor and good health at the age of forty-eight, and very rich, saw no reason to remove him. He dismissed the king's suggestion from his mind and settled the question by appointing Cruzate governor of the state of Sonora.

PART SIX

Reconquest: The End of an Age

1692

The Apache were far from being defeated, but the campaign to retake New Mexico could be delayed no longer. The French had gained control of the Mississippi Valley and were reported to be pushing westward across both the southern and northern Great Plains.

Vargas received word that fifty well-equipped soldiers were being sent from Parral to serve under him in the reconquest, but he did not wait for them. Leaving orders for them to follow, he left El Paso in the terrible heat of late August for the Pueblo country. He had with him less than two hundred armed men—some reports say a hundred and sixty—three padres, a herd of livestock, and a supply train. Except for the thirty or forty regular troopers, the force was composed of Indian auxiliaries and volunteer colonists, but all were experienced frontier fighters. In not a few of the Spaniards, emotions ran deep, for they were setting out for the land in which, twelve years earlier, they had left the butchered bodies of their wives and children.

Shortly after passing the ruined Piro pueblos of Senecu and Socorro, Vargas left most of the supply train with guards at the site of a destroyed hacienda. They were to await the reinforcements from Parral and then all were to rejoin him.

Unencumbered by the slow-moving wagons and animals, he advanced at a fast pace up the Rio Grande.

All the pueblos passed on each side of the river were deserted. Scouts reported seeing smoke signals in the vicinity of Cochiti, and Vargas set out for it. But not even a dog was to be found there. He moved on to Santo Domingo. It, too, was empty.

Once more scouts came in with reports. They had seen Indians moving toward Santa Fe, and, following them, they had seen smoke rising above the former capital. Wondering if he were to be disappointed again, Vargas climbed La Bajada Mesa and made camp for the night. The scouts were right this time, for reconnoitering the rolling plain ahead, they had seen the light of campfires.

It was an hour before dawn on the morning of September 13 when Vargas led his men across the fields before Santa Fe. Five times they shouted in unison: "Glory be to the blessed Sacrament of the altar!" He had ordered that no shots were to be fired without a signal from him. If possible, the recapture of Santa Fe was to be a diplomatic triumph, not a victory of warfare.

Pueblos crowded along the tops of walls and on the roof of the governor's house, accompanying their derisive taunts and words of defiance with howls and yaps and barks. In the dawn light Vargas and the priests and interpreters rode forward. A trumpet sounded. Vargas held aloft a banner. On one side of it was the royal crest of Spain; on the other, the image of the Blessed Virgin. He rose in his saddle and displayed a rosary and a cross.

He told them that he wanted to avoid bloodshed, but that he was prepared to fight. He had come to restore New Mexico to the crown. If they surrendered in peace, the priests with him would absolve them of their sins against the king and the Heavenly Father. If they fought him, they would die.

A Pueblo with a dignified bearing stepped to the edge of a roof and silenced the others with a wave of his arm. He was known as Bolsa (Pouches) because of his heavy jowls.

The Pueblos would not surrender, he said, because if they did, they would be forced to rebuild the churches, and they would be whipped and starved and forced to labor in *encomiendas* as slaves and to pay tributes that impoverished them. Wouldn't they?

Vargas's answer was evasive. The men who had inflicted cruelties and injustices on them in the past were not with him, and they would never return, he told Bolsa. The Pueblos would be required to pledge their allegiance to the king and to become Christians, as they once had been, to be Catholics and disavow their paganism. Then he turned away with a warning that they would have only one hour to make their decision.

As he waited, he tightened the ring of arms and trained two small cannon, brought up in carts, on the entrance to the governor's palace, which had been closed with heavy timbers and stones. Soldiers moved forward to place powder mines against the walls. The acequia which carried water into the Villa was dammed and the flow wasted into a field.

The Pueblos were quiet as several unarmed leaders emerged and asked for a council. They would surrender, they told Vargas, if he would withdraw his troops and remove his cannon beyond range, and would enter the governor's house himself to receive their pledges of obedience. Vargas agreed and embraced each of the emissaries.

In reality, the cutting of the water supply and the preparations he had made for an attack had brought him a military victory, but he chose to construe it as an accord reflecting his proficiency as a negotiator. Not a man to ignore protocol under any circumstances, even when dealing with savages, he put aside his armor and field clothes and donned a silk and linen court costume. But he qualified propriety to the extent of carrying a gun.

An opening had been made for him in a wall, and he passed through it, a tall, handsome ambassador striding gracefully, his expression denoting the gravity and importance with which he regarded the occasion. In the plaza before the dilapidated government buildings, Pueblos— men, women, and children—swarmed about him, kneeling as they swore their allegiance to him, while "I stood there dismounted, embracing them, shaking hands with them, and speaking to them with tender and loving words."

To the wild cheers of "Long Live the King," the emblem of Spain was raised over Santa Fe, and the padres intoned the Te Deum Laudamus. On the following day, a special mass was sung, after which all Pueblo children born since the revolt were baptized.

In the course of the next few days, governors from several pueblos came to pay their respects to Vargas and to assure him of their loyalty. They appeared one at a time, but the similarity of their statements suggested that they might have reached an agreement in conference on a course of action and a policy to be followed. The most prominent visitor was the influential Tupatu of Picuris, a leader of the rebellion. He arrived on horseback, his saddle adorned with Spanish trappings. His garb was representative of both races, consisting of a threadbare soldier's uniform, animal skins, military insignia, shells, and turquoise ornaments. He bowed and knelt down with great solemnity, and Vargas, extending the courtesies due a ranking officer, shook his hand and invited him into his tent for biscuits and chocolate.

From Tupatu, Vargas learned that Pope and the other two chief lieutenants of the great medicine man—Catiti of Santo Domingo and Jaca of Taos—were dead. As for himself, Tupatu no longer harbored evil thoughts about the Spaniards. He had come to proffer his cooperation in restoring order and peace. Most of the northern pueblos would submit quietly to the Spanish and obey the new governor. However, Vargas might expect trouble from Taos, Jemez, Acoma, and Pecos. Indeed, the people of Taos and Pecos already had fled to the mountains. If Vargas intended to visit these places, he would willingly accompany him and aid him to the best of his ability.

Vargas accepted the offer, and announced that he would go to Pecos first. He was en route there when the reinforcements from Parral joined him. The great pueblo of Pecos was deserted, but several Indians were captured in the adjacent country. They were released unharmed and told to inform their people that the Spaniards sought no revenge and that all would be absolved for their crimes of taking up arms against God and the king. Vargas waited five days in Pecos for the inhabitants to return, but none of them appeared, and he started back to Santa Fe. Some of his men thought the pueblo should be destroyed but he refused. He left it as he had found it, the contents of the houses and the stored supplies intact.

Next he made a rapid journey up the Rio Grande, meeting no resistance. A new pueblo had been built by the Keres a short distance from the ruins of Zia, where Cruzate had slaughtered and burned to death so many of them. They bowed to Vargas's demands. The oath of obedience also was taken by the Pueblos of Santa Ana, Jemez, Sandia, San Felipe, Santo Domingo, Cochiti, San Ildefonso, Pojoaque, San Juan—all the others. If the leaders of Taos had made plans to defy him, they had changed their minds. He was received hospitably, and the Taos acknowledged him as their ruler.

In several pueblos, Vargas had found survivors of the revolt, among them three (or possibly four) Spanish women who had given birth to children. The other captives were

Mexican Indians and half-breeds who had been servants of colonists and officials. He ordered that they be restored to their relatives and homes in Mexico.

Back once more in Santa Fe, Vargas wrote a lengthy report to the viceroy. The reconquest, he declared with justifiable pride, had been conducted without violence, indeed without a shot's being fired. He had, he told Galve, "conquered for the human and divine majesties" all the pueblos for thirty-six leagues up and down the Rio Grande, and the priests had baptized a thousand pagan children who had been born since the revolt. There was no doubt that the colony could be held by a hundred soldiers. He thought that at least fifty families should be recruited as colonists to be sent north in the coming year, and he recommended the sending of a number of experienced convict craftsmen from Mexican prisons to train others and to work as miners.*

In Taos, Vargas had been told by Pueblo traders who had recently arrived there from the west that the Zuni were attempting to organize a strong war party to attack the Spaniards. After another trip to Pecos, where he found the people again in their homes and readily willing to submit, he started on the long journey to the western pueblos.

Although the valley of the Rio Grande was warmed with late fall sunshine, snow had already capped the mountains, and night winds carried the chill of rapidly approaching winter. Vargas started the wagons, the rescued colonists, and some of his soldiers on the river trail back to El Paso. He took with him a troop of cavalry, two or three priests, a number of servants, and camp tenders, eighty-nine persons in all, and a pack train. Some of his officers thought that

---

*Vargas's dispatch reached Mexico City late in November, and the viceroy ordered that his victory be celebrated with special church services and the illuminating of the cathedral.

the long western campaign should be postponed until spring, for Indians had warned that blizzards might be encountered in the high country ahead, but Vargas was determined to complete his march to all pueblos. If the western Pueblos were plotting to engage him, he thought it necessary to convince them of the futility of such an undertaking.

On the last day of October, they put the ruins of Isleta behind them. Acoma was reached November 3. The people of the Rock were prepared to defend themselves. They were unwilling to accept Vargas's pronouncement that they would be pardoned for their offenses, and they asked him to pass on to Zuni and give them more time to deliberate on the matter. Vargas persisted in his demand that they capitulate, and at last was able to persuade them that he came to grant them amnesty. He, the priests, and a squad of soldiers were permitted to climb the narrow trail to the *penol* summit. Ceremonies of submission were conducted in the pueblo plaza, and nearly a hundred children were baptized.

Moving on toward Zuni, Vargas made no attempt to open negotiations with the Navajo, accepting the advice of some Pueblos traveling with him that an entrada into Navajo country could only result in warfare that might be disastrous to him. The Navajo, however, were observing him; they did not attack, although one night they stole several of the company's horses.

The report that the Zuni were belligerent was accurate. They had prepared strong defenses, but not a stone was thrown nor an arrow fired at the Spaniards. After a tense hour, Vargas was able to calm their fears, and they agreed to resume their former status as subjects of the king. Some three hundred children were baptized. The priests were overjoyed to find that, although the church had been destroyed, all the sacred objects and the property of the martyred missionaries had been preserved. A Zuni led Vargas into a small room where the governor was astonished to see several candles burning on a crude altar. Not the slightest indication of respect for the Catholic faith had been shown in any other pueblo. The only explanation that the Zuni gave for the unusual occurrence was a shrugging of shoulders.

The weather turned bitterly cold and the mesas were blanketed with snow as Vargas doggedly went on to the Hopi towns, which were reached on November 19. The Navajo had been there a few days previously, spreading the false report that the Spaniards were wantonly murdering people as they passed through the country. More than eight hundred Hopi warriors took battle stations on the first mesa as the troops approached. Signaling that he came in peace, Vargas requested a conference and retired to await their decision. On the next day, a delegation headed by a leader identified only as Miguel emerged from the battle line to meet him. All the Hopi people, said Miguel, incited by the Navajo, were prepared for hostilities. Once more, in the convincing manner that he had employed with such great success in every pueblo between Taos and Zuni, Vargas stated the purpose of his mission. He had only one demand to make: that the Hopi accept the Spanish king and the Christian God as their masters. That done, he would leave as he had come—in peace.

Vargas and Miguel shook hands and embraced. During the next three days, Vargas and his men were ceremoniously welcomed in each Hopi pueblo. In the course of their tour, they observed some small pots of a vermillion metallic substance. How was it used? It was a paint employed in dances and other rituals. Vargas and others examined it and, rubbing it on their hands, found that it left a purplish luster and was greasy. Quicksilver! The quicksilver for which they had been looking. Trying to conceal their excitement, they asked from whence it came. From a canyon to the west, was the reply. The Hopi would be glad to show them the place, but the journey to it was long and difficult. No, samples would be sufficient now, and they would pay for them with whatever articles the Hopi desired: buttons, ironware, clothing, knives, swords—anything. Quickly leather pouches were stuffed with the strange substance, and the barter was completed. Besides being a paint, said the Hopi, it was also medicinal. It removed blemishes, such as smallpox scars, and preserved the condition of the face, and squaws thought it enhanced their beauty. There was a great demand for it from women all the way from the river of the west [the Colorado] to the buffalo plains on the east, and traders sold it by the spoonful, asking a very high price.

With his precious cargo, Vargas returned to Zuni. From there, at the end of November, he set out toward the southeast, breaking a new trail to the Rio Grande. Socorro was passed on December 10. He rode on down the river road with his soldiers, a gratified and proud man. Without a drop of blood being shed, he had reconquered New Mexico, but he had left no doubts among the Pueblos that he would soon return to resettle the colony, and that he would expect all to obey Spanish laws and accept Catholicism. He had, he felt certain, made them understand that no defiance would be tolerated.

The peacefulness that had marked the campaign was abruptly shattered, however, when the dreaded part of the road known as the Jornada del Muerte, below Cristobal, was reached. There the Apache were waiting for him. A running battle of several days' duration followed, but the casualties were light. One officer was killed and a trooper was wounded. Several Apache were thought to have been slain, and one was captured.

Under questioning accompanied by a beating, the captured Apache admitted that he had participated in raids on Spanish settlements. Vargas ordered him shot, but the execution was delayed long enough to let a priest baptize him and christen him Augustin. ". . . This having been done," wrote Vargas, "I ordered the lieutenant of cavalry to have four soldiers take the said Indian off to one side and shoot him forthwith, giving him a good death."

The company rode into El Paso on December 20 with banners waving, and there were wild cheering, a blowing of trumpets, and a rolling of drums.

1693

Vargas's requests for soldiers, colonists, priests, and supplies were approved, but his plan to start up the Rio Grande no later than early summer was overruled. Viceroy Galve directed him to join Captain Francisco Ramirez in Casas Grande and launch a campaign against the Apache. Vargas protested that the delay would give recalcitrant Pueblos more time to organize resistance and make more difficult the work of rebuilding the ruined churches and restoring apostates to the faith. Converting any Indians without sufficient troops to support the missionaries, he declared, was an impossibility. Diversion of the military he commanded to another field would leave the colonists and priests helpless and idle in the vitiating atmosphere of El Paso, and they might well lose interest and desert.

If Galve was impressed by Vargas's contentions, he viewed the Apache reign of terror as a more urgent problem, and he announced his intention to stand, at least temporarily, with the military and civil officials of the northern

Mexican states, who were vehemently objecting to the proposal to send a strong column to Santa Fe when soldiers were so badly needed to protect the people of their jurisdictions. If Vargas did not wish to obey orders, his only alternative was to resign.

Vargas chose to remain. He and Captain Ramirez merged their forces and carried on a campaign for several months which took them through much of northern Mexico and northward as far as the Gila River, presumably at some point in far western New Mexico. The results were negligible; one officer maintained that the only achievement of the strike was to drive various Apache bands into a "formidable union."

Meanwhile, more colonists and soldiers had been arriving in El Paso, and loyal aides of Vargas, complying with his orders, had managed to hold the expedition together and continue preparations for the march. At last, probably in the early fall, Vargas received backing that no colonial authority could ignore. The king commanded that the resettlement of New Mexico be undertaken at once. Couriers sped to El Paso with the royal order.

In the long column that crawled with painful slowness along the dusty river road above El Paso during the early days of October were: a hundred professional soldiers, many with wives and children; eighteen padres; about four score families of settlers; a large contingent of Indian allies; an extraordinary conglomeration of adventurers, convicted thieves, swindlers, and degenerates freed to begin a new life in the remote colony; a few men and women of high birth; several licensed lawyers; some hopeful shopkeepers; and a few masons and carpenters. Numbering more than eight hundred persons in all, they were followed by a snaking line of eighteen supply wagons and carts, three of which carried small cannons, a thousand mules, two thousand horses, nine hundred cattle, and bands of sheep and goats.

It was a poor time of year to be starting north. The upper Rio Grande region would be locked in winter before they reached it. The foodstuffs carried were not sufficient for the long journey. Most of the animals were bony and weak, having been driven long distances across the northern Mexico deserts to El Paso. Vargas had been advised that more supplies were on the way to him, but he had refused to wait for them.

Nor did he dwell in disappointment on the report he had received regarding the vermillion metallic substance he had sent to the viceroy. It said that an assay of the samples had been made and that they contained no quicksilver. The mines would be found, he declared, still unwilling to believe that they did not exist. But finding treasure was merely one purpose of the reconquest. There were greater glories to be gained by serving God and the king.

Troubles and tragedies came in rapid succession. The terrible ordeals of the Jornada del Muerto and a strange intestinal sickness took the lives of thirty women and children. The trail was marked with the carcasses of animals that had died of weakness, hunger, and thirst. Several soldiers and convicts deserted and vanished against the endless backdrop of barren mesas to a fate unknown. The Apache watched, and smoke signals were seen, necessitating continual scouting by day and the posting of a strong guard by night. For reasons best known to themselves, the Apache did not attack, but they sent word to the Pueblos that the Spaniards were returning.

From Socorro, Vargas went ahead with a cavalry escort to reconnoiter. Information he obtained was distressing. Pecos leaders, who had kept their promise made to him the previous year to remain peaceful, told him he could count on the friendliness of the people of San Felipe, Santa Ana, and those who had survived Cruzate's slaughter at Zia, but most of the other river pueblos were hostile. In his absence, the governor's house and adjoining buildings on the north side of the Santa Fe plaza had been newly fortified by several Tanoan groups. In the west, the Keres of Acoma, the Zuni, and the Hopi, had girded to resist him.

Vargas returned to the main caravan. Patrols sent out were able to obtain substantial quantities of corn, although it was given grudgingly and they were obliged to take it by force in some pueblos. It was a welcome supplement to the sparse rations of hard bread and meat distributed each day. The marchers now were suffering more from cold than from hunger.

On December 16, a vanguard of soldiers and priests came up to the outskirts of Santa Fe. Pushing through deep snow, the padres entered the plaza singing hymns. Vargas dismounted and followed them. Before the heavily barricaded governor's compound, he stopped and gazed up at several hundred Pueblos spread along the roofs and walls.

He had returned as he had said he would, he told them through an interpreter. He had returned to bring Christ to them. He wanted nothing but their friendship and confidence and their loyalty to God and the king of Spain, to live in peace with them. They would be treated with justice, and the soldiers would protect them from their enemies.

There was no reply. The Pueblos stood motionless and silent, only their cold faces speaking their distrust and their defiance.

Vargas spoke again in a conciliatory voice. The property they occupied belonged to the crown and the church. He had made plain to them before his desire to avoid bloodshed. Now he would make another demonstration of his sincerity. He would retire and allow them all the time they required to evacuate the Villa. He would establish his camp at the edge of the town, and his troops would interfere not at all with them as they departed.

"Go back to your homes in peace," he said, and then he turned and strode out of the plaza without looking back, the padres struggling along behind him in their icy robes.

Day after day a smoke haze rose from the Pueblos' stronghold, and night after night their fires burned caverns in the purple sky, until eleven days and eleven nights had passed without an emissary emerging to negotiate with Vargas. In the camp of the Spaniards, twenty-one persons had succumbed to the extreme cold and the mysterious affliction of the bowels, and their stiffened bodies awaited burial in frozen ground that would not yield to a spade.

Vargas seemed unable to comprehend—or, at least, he was unwilling to believe—that, to the Pueblos, his diplomatic overtures and his patience indicated cowardice and fear. He went again to the plaza on December 28 and delivered what he pronounced as a final plea to them to leave. This time he was answered with blasphemy and insults. The old man Bolsa, his jowls bigger than ever, was there. Go back to your fraudulent God and Maria, he shouted with a stream of curses. If the Spaniards stayed, they would all be killed. Vargas returned to his tent and summoned his officers to a *junta de guerra.*

On the brittle morning of December 29, the soldiers knelt in new snow as prayers were said. The flag bearing the image of the Virgin was raised. Shouting praises to the Santo Sacramento, they moved forward in two columns, and spanned out into uneven lines. Guns cracked and acrid fumes soiled the clean air; Pueblos disappeared with screams from the parapets, but others rose up—men, women, and young people—to shower arrows and stones and pour boiling water on troopers who came up under the walls, driving them back. If the defenders had guns, they had no powder for them.

Files of Indians began to trickle down from the surrounding heights, and the soldiers were obliged to concentrate their fire on them to keep them from gaining the compound. There was hand-to-hand fighting at times, and both Spanish and Pueblo blood marked the sites. The reinforcements were scattered and driven away.

The little short-range brass cannon did much to turn the tide of battle when, at last, with heroic efforts, the gunners were able to drag them far enough forward through the snow-covered rocks to fire them point blank at the main gate. The timbers and mud shattered. Then sappers, covered by a heavy fire, dashed in to set powder mines. Flames of the explosions ate at the debris.

The main gate and the adjoining walls had been opened, but Vargas decided to postpone the attempt to break into the compound. The mountains were already wrapped in the twilight of the short winter afternoon. He felt the assault could be delayed with safety until the next day.

With his exhausted, bleeding men, he withdrew to the comfort of campfires, and all ravenously gulped the hot chunks of meat and the corn gruel which the Mexican Indian cooks had prepared.

The night brought no alarms from sentries. Now and then wailing and moaning floated up from the compound, death chants, and faded into the engulfing blackness. At last an eerie stillness settled, a stillness so intense that it troubled sleep, making people listen for some reassuring sound.

In the early sun, after gulping their mutton soup and biscuits, the soldiers, aching with the cold and lingering weariness, knelt again in the snow and responded to prayers and crossed themselves. Then they moved forward, some of them so painfully crippled and bruised that they were un steady.

No attempt had been made during the night to repair the breached wall. No shouts came out from the buildings. No arrows were shot. As the soldiers closed, some warriors suddenly appeared on the roof of the governor's house. The signals they gave were clear. The Pueblos had surrendered.

In the patios and gardens where for nearly a century governors had taken their siestas, bodies lay in grotesque positions. Women and children were huddled together, trembling with fear, their obsidian eyes appealing for mercy. Men lifted their arms and bowed and fell upon their knees and made the sign of the cross, crying out their pleas for amnesty.

Patience no longer lived in Vargas, and if mercy ever had been a quality of his nature, it, too, had died. Seventy men, among them Bolsa and other leaders, were herded by his order into the plaza and shot to death, the screams of the squaws and children and the spared warriors rising to a crescendo of terror at every volley from the muskets of the executioners. Then, as if his revenge had been sated, Vargas commanded that the survivors—more than four hundred men, women, and children—be distributed as slaves among the soldiers and colonists.

He brought his entire company into the warmth and safety of the compound. He slept that night between clean linens and under downy quilts in his own shabby, dirty chamber in the governor's house. His pallet stood not far from the statues of Christ and La Conquistadora, the expedition's patroness, that had been carted in altar cloths and batting all the way from Mexico.

Santa Fe was once more a Spanish colonial capital.

There would be more serious troubles with the Pueblos in the last years of the seventeenth century, but not all of them would be caused by Spanish despotism and religious oppression.

The traditional divisiveness of the Pueblos, too deeply ingrained in them to be more than partially subdued on rare occasions by the forces of their own reasoning, increased in these years until it had become a scourge inflicting suffering and death. In the great valley and on the high western plateaus, throughout all the immense land, pueblo fought pueblo for causes that had no roots in reality. Yet all of them wanted one thing more than anything else, and that was to be free from Spanish oppression, to live in their own individual way, in their own individual isolation. But that was a hope beyond the realm of possibility, a dream forever shattered.

Ironically, it was the Spaniards who put an end to the intertribal fighting. They forced Christianity and civil obedience on the Pueblos with guns, and with the same weapons they forced them to live in peace with each other.

Never again after the days of Diego de Vargas were the two majesties driven out. Their guises and their attitudes and their ways have changed, but they are still there. Tires hum on the freeways, and church bells peal, and legislators enact laws and police or soldiers enforce them, and engines exhale hoarsely in the turquoise sky, and masses are intoned.

But there are answering sounds. There are the rhythmic beating of drums, the soft shuffling of dancers' feet, the clicking of medicine sticks, the chanting of choruses in the sunny ancient plazas, answering sounds blended in a paean to the spirits of the underworlds and the heavens, to the supernaturals of all living things, indestructible in their realms, a paean that all the powers of men and machines, in combined awesomeness, have never silenced.

EPILOGUE

Burros with funereal faces stand between battered, muddy, rust-eaten pickups and cars. Electric wires dangle over cracked walls. Squaws bend to sewing machines beside age-worn hand looms. There are coin-operated washers and dryers in the trading posts, but clothes scrubbed at stream side and in galvanized tubs still flap colorfully on lines stretched along terraces. Half-gallon tins of peaches and plastic-wrapped bread loaves sit on tables between pottery bowls of homemade chili con carne and the eternal corn and beans.

As this is written, there are an estimated 32,800 Pueblos, 23,900 in their traditional homelands and 8,900 in other localities, some near the reservations and some far distant from them. They come and go, struggling to survive in two worlds.

All recent enumerations show that they are steadily increasing, in some tribes at a rate far greater than that of the nation as a whole. The population figures which follow have been rounded to the next highest hundred in each case.

TANOAN LINGUISTIC FAMILY—TOWA DIVISION

Jemez	1,100
Off reservation	500
Total	1,600

TANOAN LINGUISTIC FAMILY—TEWA DIVISION

Nambe	200
Pojoaque	100
San Ildefonso	300
San Juan	700
Santa Clara	600
Tesuque	200
Off reservations	1,700
Total	3,800

TANOAN LINGUISTIC FAMILY—TIWA DIVISION

Isleta	2,000
Picuris	100
Sandia	200
Taos	900
Off reservations	1,200
Total	4,400
Total Tanoan	9,300

SHOSHONIAN LINGUISTIC FAMILY—HOPI

First Mesa	1,300
Second Mesa	1,000
Third Mesa	1,200
Moenkopi	800
Off reservation	900
Total	5,100

ZUNI LINGUISTIC FAMILY

Main pueblo and four adjacent villages	4,200
Off reservation	1,000
Total	5,200

KERESAN LINGUISTIC FAMILY

Acoma	1,700
Cochiti	400
Laguna	3,000
San Felipe	1,100
Santa Ana	400
Santo Domingo	2,000
Zia	400
Off reservations	3,600
Total	12,600

Only twenty-seven Pueblos can remember the years of the Great Conquest. Small children still play in the sunny plazas; in the whitewashed rooms squeezed together by heavy, wrinkled walls, women still busy themselves at cooking and weaving and mending; in the shadows of low, crooked doorways, ancient ones doze and dream; people young and old hoe in little fields down in the washes and herd goats and sheep on the tilted flats; and everyone still watches the white thunderheads mounting the distant mesas, making a silent prayer to the gods.

Only twenty-seven very old Pueblos, still alive, still bearing their burdens of time with bent shoulders, still refusing to give up—twenty-seven left out of more than a hundred and fifty that were there when the Spaniards came.

SELECTED
BIBLIOGRAPHY

Aberle, S. D. *The Pueblo Indians of New Mexico: Their Land, Economy and Civil Organization.* American Anthropological Association, Menasha, Wisc., 1948.

Alvarado, Hernando de, and Padilla, Juan de. "Account of Journey from Cibola to the Rio Grande Pueblos in 1540." In George Parker Winship, trans., *The Narrative of the Expedition of Coronado by Castaneda.*

Amsden, Charles Avery. *Prehistoric Southwesterners from Basketmaker to Pueblo.* Southwest Museum, Los Angeles, 1949.

Bahti, Tom. *Southwestern Indian Tribes.* Flagstaff, 1968.

_____. *Southwestern Indian Arts and Crafts.* Flagstaff, 1970.

_____. *Southwestern Indian Ceremonials.* Flagstaff, 1971.

Bancroft, Hubert Howe. *Native Races.* 5 vols. San Francisco, 1886–1890.

_____. *History of Arizona and New Mexico, 1540–1888.* San Francisco, 1889.

Bandelier, Adolph F. A. *Historical Introduction to Studies Among the Indians of New Mexico.* Cambridge, 1881.

_____. *The Delight Makers.* New York, 1890.

_____. *Final Report of Investigations among the Indians of the Southwestern United States.* Cambridge, 1890.

_____. *Contributions to the History of the Southwestern United States.* Cambridge, 1890.

_____. *Documentary History of the Zuni Tribe.* Boston, 1892.

_____. *The Gilded Man.* New York, 1893.

Bandelier, Fanny. *The Journey of Alvar Nunez Cabeza de Vaca and His Companions from Florida to the Pacific, 1528–1536.* Translated from the 1542 edition of Cabeza de Vaca's *Relacion.* New York, 1905.

Bannister, Bryant, Dean, Jeffry S. and Gell, Elizabeth A. M. *Tree Ring Dates from Arizona—E.* University of Arizona, Tucson, 1966.

Bartlett, K. *Prehistoric Mining in the Southwest.* Museum of Northern Arizona, Flagstaff, 1935.

Beck, Warren A. *New Mexico, a History of Four Centuries,* Norman, Okla., 1969.

Benavides, Alonso de. *Memorial of 1630.* Translated by Mrs. Edward E. Ayers. Chicago, 1916.

Benedict, Ruth. *Patterns of Culture.* New York, 1934.

Billington, Ray Allen. *Westward Expansion.* New York, 1949.

Bishop, Morris. *The Odyssey of Cabeza de Vaca.* New York, 1933.

Bloom, Lansing B. "Was Fray Marcos a Liar?" *New Mexico Historical Review,* April 1941.

———. "Who Discovered New Mexico?" *New Mexico Historical Review,* April 1940.

Boas, Franz. *Race, Language and Culture,* New York, 1949.

Bolton, Herbert Eugene. *Spanish Exploration in the Southwest.* New York, 1916.

———. *The Spanish Borderlands.* New Haven, Conn. 1921.

———. *Coronado.* New York, 1949.

Brand, Donald. "Prehistoric Trade in the Southwest." *New Mexico Business Review,* Vol. 4, 1935.

———. "Aboriginal Trade Routes for Sea Shells in the Southwest." *Association of Pacific Coast Geographers Yearbook,* Cheney, Wash., 1938.

Bryan, Bruce. *The Manufacture of Stone Mortars.* Southwest Museum, Los Angeles, 1970.

Castenedo, Pedro de. *"Narrative of the Expedition of Coronado."* In George Parker Winship, trans., *The Narrative of the Expedition of Coronado by Castaneda* (q.v.).

Chard, C. S. *New World Migration Routes.* College, Alaska, 1958.

Colton, Harold S. "Prehistoric Trade in the Southwest," *Scientific Monthly,* April 1941.

Colton, Harold S., and Hargrave, L. L. *Pueblo II in the San Francisco Mountains.* Museum of Northern Arizona, Flagstaff, 1933.

Coon, Calton S. *The Story of Man.* New York, 1962.

Coronado, Francisco Vasquez de. "Letter to Viceroy Mendoza, August 3, 1540." In George Parker Winship, trans., *The Narrative of the Expedition of Coronado by Castaneda* (q.v.).

————. "Letter to the King of Spain, October 20, 1540." In George Parker Winship, trans., *The Narrative of the Expedition of Coronado by Castaneda.*

————. "Relacio Postrera de Sibola." In George Parker Winship, trans., *The Narrative of the Expedition of Coronado by Castaneda* (q.v.).

————. *Relacio Del Suceso.* In George Parker Winship, trans., *The Narrative of the Expedition of Coronado by Castaneda* (q.v.).

Crane, H. R. "Antiquity of Sandia Culture: Carbon 14 Measurements." *Science Magazine,* June 1955.

Cummings, Byron. *Kinishba.* University of Arizona, Tucson, 1940.

Curtin, L. S. M. *Preparation of Sacred Corn Meal in the Rio Grande Pueblos.* Southwest Museum, Los Angeles, 1968.

Cushing, Frank Hamilton. *Zuni Fetishes.* Bureau of American Ethnology, Second Annual Report, Washington, 1883.

————. *Outlines of Zuni Creation Myths.* Bureau of American Ethnology, Thirteenth Annual Report, Washington, 1896.

Dale, Edward E. *The Indians of the Southwest.* Norman, Okla., 1949.

Davis, W. H. H. *The Spanish Conquest of New Mexico.* New York, 1869.

Densmore, Frances. *The American Indians and Their Music.* New York, 1926.

Dittert, Alfred E., Jr., and Eddy, Frank W. *Pueblo Period Sites in the Piedra River Section.* Museum of New Mexico, Santa Fe, 1963.

Douglas, A. E. "Dating Pueblo Bonito and Other Ruins in the Southwest." *National Geographic Magazine,* June 1935.

Dozier, Edward P. *The Pueblo Indians of the Southwest.* American Anthropological Association, Menasha, Wisc., 1964.

———. *The Pueblo Indians of North America.* New York, 1970.

Driver, Harold E. *Indians of North America.* Chicago, 1961.

Eggan, Fred. *Social Organization of the Western Pueblos.* Chicago, 1950.

Ellsworth, Clarence. *Bows and Arrows.* Southwest Museum, Los Angeles, n.d.

Fergusson, Erna. *Dancing Gods.* University of New Mexico, Albuquerque, 1931.

Fewkes, J. W. *Two Summers' Work in Pueblo Ruins.* Bureau of American Ethnology, Twenty-second Annual Report, Washington, 1904.

———. *Ancestor Worship of the Hopi Indians.* Smithsonian Institution, Washington, 1921.

Forbes, Jack D. *Apache, Navajo and Spaniard.* Norman, Okla., 1960.

Gladwin, Harold S., Henry, E. W., Sayles, E. B., and Gladwin, Nora. *Excavation of Snaketown: Material Culture.* Gila Pueblo Papers, No. 25, Globe, Ariz., 1937.

Goddard, Pliny E. *Indians of the Southwest.* New York, 1913.

Hack, J. T. *The Changing Physical Environment of the Hopi Indians.* Peabody Museum, Cambridge, 1941.

Hackett, Charles Wilson. *Historical Documents Relating to New Mexico, Nueva Vizcaya, and Approaches Thereto, to 1773.* Washington, 1923.

_____. *The Revolt of the Pueblo Indians of New Mexico and Otermin's Attempted Reconquest, 1680–1682.* University of New Mexico, Albuquerque, 1942.

Hallenbeck, Cleve. *Journey and Route of Cabeza de Vaca.* Glendale, Calif., 1940.

Halseth, Odd S. *Prehistory of the Southwest.* Phoenix, 1949.

Hammond, George P. *Coronado's Seven Cities.* Albuquerque, 1940.

Hammond, George P., and Rey, Agapito. *The Narratives of the Coronado Expedition.* Albuquerque, 1940.

_____. *Don Juan de Onate, Colonizer of New Mexico, 1595–1628.* University of New Mexico, Albuquerque, 1953.

_____. *The Rediscovery of New Mexico.* University of New Mexico, Albuquerque, 1966.

Hargrave, L. L. *Pueblo II Houses in the San Francisco Mountains, Arizona.* Museum of Northern Arizona, Flagstaff, 1933.

Harris, Arthur H., Schoenwetter, James, and Warren, A. H. *Archaeological Survey of the Chuska Valley.* Museum of New Mexico, Santa Fe, 1967.

Haury, E. W. *The Canyon Creek Ruin and Cliff Dwellings of the Sierra Ancha,* Gila Pueblo Papers, No. 14, Globe, Ariz., 1934.

_____. *The Stratigraphy and Archaeology of Ventana Cave.* Albuquerque, 1950.

Haury, E. W., Sayles, E. B., and Wasley, William W. "Lehner Mammoth Site, Arizona." *American Antiquity,* Vol. 25, No. 1, 1959.

Hays, Alden. "The Missing Convento of San Isidro." *El Palacio,* Vol. 75, No. 4, 1968.

Hendron, J. W. *Prehistory of El Rito de los Frijoles, Bandelier National Monument.* Coolidge, Ariz., 1940.

Hibben, Frank C. "Association of Man with Pleistocene Mammals in the Sandia Mountains." *American Antiquity,* Vol. XI, 1937.

_____. *Evidence of Early Occupation in Sandia Cave, New Mexico.* Smithsonian Institution, Washington, 1941.

Hodge, Frederick W. *Spanish Explorers in the Southern United States.* New York, 1907.

_____. *Handbook of American Indians North of Mexico.* Bureau of American Ethnology, Washington, 1907.

_____. *History of Hawikuh.* Southwest Museum, Los Angeles, 1937.

_____. *The Excavation of Hawikuh.* Museum of the American Indian, New York, 1966.

Hooton, E. A. *Indians of Pecos Pueblo.* Phillips Academy, New Haven, Conn., 1930.

Hopkins, David M., ed. *The Bering Land Bridge.* Stanford University, Stanford, Calif., 1967.

Horgan, Paul. *Great River: The Rio Grande in North American History.* New York, 1954.

Hull, Dorothy. *Castano de Sosa's Expedition to New Mexico.* Santa Fe, 1916.

Hunt, W. Ben. *Kachina Dolls.* Milwaukee Public Museum, 1958.

Jaramillo, Juan. "Account Given by Captain Juan Jaramillo of the Journey Which He Made to the New Country, on Which Francisco Vasquez Coronado Was the General." In George Parker Winship, trans., *The Narrative of the Expedition of Coronado by Castaneda* (q.v.).

Jeancon, J. A. *Excavations in Chama Valley.* Bureau of American Ethnology, Washington, 1923.

Josephy, Alvin, M., Jr. *The Indian Heritage of America.* New York, 1968.

Keeler, W. W., et al. *Report to the Secretary of the Interior by the Task Force on Indian Affairs.* Washington, 1961.

Keleher, William A. *Turmoil in New Mexico.* Santa Fe, 1952.

Kelly, William H. *Indians of the Southwest.* University of Arizona, Tucson, 1953.

Kidder, Alfred Vincent. *An Introduction to the Study of Southwestern Archaeology.* New Haven, Conn., 1962.

Kreiger, A. D. *Earliest Cultures in the Western United States.* New York, 1962.

Lambert, Marjorie F. *Paa-Ko, Archaeological Chronicle of an Indian Village in North Central New Mexico.* Laboratory of Anthropology, Santa Fe, 1954.

Lange, Charles H. *Cochiti, a New Mexico Pueblo.* Southern Illinois University, Carbondale, 1959.

Libby, Willard J. *Radiocarbon Dating.* University of Chicago, 1955.

Lowie, Robert H. *Primitive Society.* New York, 1961.

Lummis, Charles F. *The Spanish Pioneers.* Chicago, 1893.

―――. "Fray Zarate Salmeron's Relation." *Land of Sunshine Magazine,* Vols. XI and XII, 1897–1898.

―――. *The Land of Poco Tiempo.* New York, 1906.

McGowen, Kenneth. *Early Man in the New World.* New York, 1950.

McGregor, John C., *Southwestern Archaeology.* New York, 1941.

Madariago, Salvador de. *Rise of the Spanish American Empire.* London, 1947.

Mangelsdorf, P. C., and Reeves, R. G. *The Origin of Indian Corn and Its Relatives.* Texas A & M University, College Station, 1939.

―――. *The Origin of Corn,* Botanical Museum, Cambridge, 1959.

Mangelsdorf, P. C., and Smith, C. Earle. *New Archaeological Evidence in Maize.* Cambridge, 1949.

Manje, Juan Mateo. *Luz de Tierra Incognita.* Translated by Harry J. Karns. Tucson, 1954.

Martin, Paul S., Quimby, George I. and Collier, Donald. *Indians Before Columbus.* Chicago University, 1947.

Mendoza, Antonio de. "Letter to the King of Spain, April 17, 1540." In George Parker Winship, trans., *The Narrative of the Expedition of Coronado by Castaneda.*

Mera, H. P. *The Rain Bird: A Study in Pueblo Design.* Laboratory of Anthropology, Santa Fe, 1937.

Mooney, James. *The Aboriginal Population of America North of Mexico.* Washington, 1928.

Morris, Earl H. *Archaeology Studies in the La Plata District, Colorado.* Carnegie Institute, Washington, 1939.

Nequatewa, Edmund. *Truth of a Hopi and Other Clan Stories of Shungopovi.* Museum of Northern Arizona, Flagstaff, 1936.

Nunez Cabeza de Vaca, Alvar. *Relacion.* See Fanny Bandelier, *The Journey of Alvar Nunez Cabeza de Vaca and His Companions from Florida to the Pacific, 1528–1536;* Cleve Hallenbeck, *Journey and Route of Cabeza de Vaca;* Frederick W. Hodge, *Spanish Explorers in the Southern United States;* Buckingham Smith, trans., *Relacion de Alvar Nunez Cabeza de Vaca;* John Upton Terrell, *Journey into Darkness;* George Parker Winship, trans., *The Narrative of the Expedition of Coronado by Castaneda.*

Nusbaum, Jesse L., Kidder, A. V. and Guernsey, S. J. *A Basket-maker Cave in Kane County, Utah.* Museum of the American Indian, New York, 1922.

O'Kane, Walter Collins. *The Hopis.* Norman, Okla., 1953.

Ortiz, Alfonso. *The Tewa World.* University of Chicago, 1969.

————. *New Perspectives on the Pueblos.* Albuquerque, 1972.

Parsons, Elsie Clews. *The Pueblo of Jemez.* Phillips Academy, Andover, Mass., 1925.

————. *Isleta, New Mexico.* Bureau of American Ethnology, Forty-seventh Annual Report, Washington, 1929.

_____. *Taos Pueblo.* American Anthropological Association, Menasha, Wisc., 1936.

_____. *Pueblo Indian Religion.* University of Chicago, 1939.

Peckham, Stewart. *Prehistoric Weapons in the Southwest.* Museum of New Mexico, Santa Fe, 1965.

Pepper, G. H. *Pueblo Bonito.* American Museum of Natural History, New York, 1920.

Powell, John Wesley. *Indian Linguistic Families North of Mexico.* Bureau of American Ethnology, Seventh Annual Report, Washington, 1891.

Quebbeman, Frances E. *Medicine in Territorial Arizona.* Arizona Historical Foundation, Phoenix, 1966.

Roberts, F. H. H., Jr., *Shabik'eschee Village: A Late Basketmaker Site in the Chaco Canyon, New Mexico.* Bureau of American Ethnology, Bulletin 92, Washington, 1929.

_____. *Early Pueblo Ruins in the Piedra District, Southwestern Colorado.* Bureau of American Ethnology, Bulletin 96, Washington, 1930.

_____. *The Ruins at Kiatuthlanna, Eastern Arizona.* Bureau of American Ethnology, Bulletin 100, Washington, 1931.

_____. *The Village of the Great Kivas on the Zuni Reservation, New Mexico.* Bureau of American Ethnology, Bulletin 111, Washington, 1932.

Roe, Frank Gilbert. *The Indian and the Horse.* Norman, Okla., 1955.

Sayles, E. B. *An Archaeological Survey of Chihuahua, Mexico.* Gila Pueblo Papers, No. 22, Globe, Ariz., 1936.

Sayles, E. B., and Antevs, Ernst. *The Cochise Culture.* Gila Pueblo Papers, No. 24, Globe, Ariz., 1941.

Scholes, France V. "The Supply Service of the New Mexico Missions in the Seventeenth Century." *New Mexico Histori cal Review,* Vol. 5, 1930.

————. "Civil Government and Society in New Mexico in the Seventeenth Scentury." *New Mexico Historical Review,* Vol. X, 1935.

————. "Church and State in New Mexico." *New Mexico Historical Review,* Vol. XI, 1936, Vol. XII, 1937.

Simpson, Ruth De Ette. *The Hopi Indians.* Southwest Museum, Los Angeles, 1953.

Smith, Anne M. *New Mexico Indians.* Museum of New Mexico, Santa Fe, 1966.

Smith, Buckingham, trans. *Relacion of Alvar Nunez Cabeza de Vaca.* Washington, 1851.

Spicer, Edward H., ed. *Perspectives in American Indian Culture Change.* University of Chicago, 1961.

————, ed. *Cycles of Conquest.* University of Arizona, Tucson, 1962.

Sterling, M. W. *Origin Myth of Acoma and Other Records.* Bureau of American Ethnology, Washington, 1942.

Stubbs, Stanley A. *Bird's-eye View of the Pueblos.* Norman, Okla., 1950.

Swanton, John R. *The Indian Tribes of North America.* Bureau of American Ethnology, Bulletin 145, Washington, 1952.

Terrell, John Upton. *Journey into Darkness.* New York, 1962.

————. *Traders of the Western Morning: Aboriginal Commerce in Pre-Columbian America.* Southwest Museum, Los Angeles, 1967.

————. *Estevanico the Black.* Los Angeles, 1968.

————. *The Navajo.* New York, 1970.

————. *American Indian Almanac.* New York, 1971.

————. *Apache Chronicle.* New York, 1972.

Thomas, Alfred Barnaby. *After Coronado.* Norman, Okla., 1935.

Titiev, Mischa. *Old Oraibe: A Study of the Hopi Indians of the Third Mesa.* Peabody Museum, Cambridge, 1944.

Twitchell, Ralph E. *Leading Facts of New Mexico History.* Cedar Rapids, Iowa, 1914.

———. *The Spanish Archives of New Mexico.* Cedar Rapids, Iowa, 1914.

Underhill, Ruth. *The Red Man's Religion.* University of Chicago, 1965.

Villagra, Gaspar Perez de. *History of New Mexico.* Translated by Gilberto Espinosa. Los Angeles, 1933.

Walker, Edwin F. *World Crops Derived from the Indians.* Southwest Museum, Los Angeles, 1967.

Watkins, Frances E. *Hopi Toys.* Southwest Museum, Los Angeles, n.d.

White, Leslie A. *The Acome Indians.* Bureau of American Ethnology, Washington, 1932.

———. *Pueblo of San Felipe.* American Anthropological Association, Menasha, Wisc., 1932.

———. *Pueblo of Santo Domingo.* American Anthropological Association, Menasha, Wisc., 1935.

———. *Pueblo of Santa Ana.* American Anthropological Association, Menasha, Wisc., 1942.

———. *Pueblo of Zia.* Bureau of American Ethnology, Washington, 1962.

Whitman, William. *The Pueblo Indians of San Ildefonso.* Columbia University, New York, 1947.

Winship, George Parker, trans. *The Narrative of the Expedition of Coronado by Castaneda.* Bureau of American Ethnology, Fourteenth Annual Report, Washington, 1896.

Wormington, H. M. *Prehistoric Indians of the Southwest.* Denver Museum of Natural History, 1947.

———. *Ancient Man in North America.* Denver Museum of Natural History, 1957.

Wormington, H. M., and Neal, Arminta. *The Story of Pueblo Pottery.* Denver Museum of Natural History, 1951.

Wright, Barton, and Roat, Evelyn. *This Is a Hopi Kachina.* Museum of Northern Arizona, Flagstaff, 1965 (pamphlet).

Zarate Salmeron, Geronimo de. *Relaciones.* Translated in *Land of Sunshine Magazine,* November 1899 to February 1900.

INDEX

DATE DUE

DEC 2 '77

DATE		ISSUED TO
		FREISIG
	MCDONALD CATHY	